A YEAR
OF MUD
and **GOLD**

A YEAR
OF MUD
and **GOLD**

SAN FRANCISCO
IN

*Letters and Diaries,
1849–1850*

Edited by
WILLIAM
BENEMANN

University of
Nebraska Press
LINCOLN &
LONDON

Illustrations on pages xxiv and 16 appear courtesy
of The Bancroft Library, University of California, Berkeley

© 1999 by the University of Nebraska Press
All rights reserved
Manufactured in the United States of America

(∞)

Library of Congress Cataloging-in-Publication Data
A year of mud and gold : San Francisco in letters and diaries,
1849–1850 / edited by William Benemann.
    p.   cm.
Includes bibliographical references and index.
ISBN 0-8032-1293-3 (cl.: alk. paper)
    1. San Francisco (Calif.)—Biography. 2. San Francisco
(Calif.)—History—19th century—Sources. 3. San Francisco
(Calif.)—Social life and customs—19th century—Sources.
4. San Francisco (Calif.)—Social conditions—19th century—
Sources. 5. California—Gold discoveries—Sources. 6. Pio-
neers—California—San Francisco—Diaries. 7. Pioneers—
California—San Francisco—Correspondence. I. Benemann,
William, 1949-   .
F869.S353A28   1999
979.4'6104'0922—dc21   98-55444
                                                  CIP

TO THE MEMORY OF MY PARENTS

Joseph Robert Benemann
Laura Luella Sperry Benemann

Contents

Preface

The California gold rush presents us with a unique window into nineteenth-century America. One of the most striking features of this historical event is that it attracted a large number of literate—even well-educated—participants who were eager to record their experiences in the form of letters, journals, and contributed newspaper columns. Unlike so many other aspects of American history, in which the voices of an elite few speak for the experiences of the whole, there exist eyewitness reports from thousands of individuals describing a wide range of personal experiences from this time.

Whether they took the long ocean route or the shorter but more arduous overland journey to California, these Argonauts were very conscious of the fact that they were embarking on a fantastic adventure, perhaps the one great adventure of their lives. For this reason many kept diaries or travel journals, and sent home letters that are crammed with observations about sweeping social events and small but fascinating daily occurrences. This writing was not merely social intercourse; there is a strong note of intentional record-making that weaves its way through their prose, as though they were writing not only to their loved ones but also to their own returned selves. These are the notes that would later serve as the basis for a lifetime of stories told around the family hearth.

Thousands of such letters and diaries survive. It is an indication of the immense volume of gold rush correspondence that all of the writings excerpted in this volume come from one source: The Bancroft Library of the University of California, Berkeley. This body of manuscripts gives a detailed view of life in gold rush San Francisco, but unfortunately for modern readers that view is incomplete. Many voices remain unheard. Little survives of the writings of the Mexican and Indian inhabitants of San Francisco during this crucial year, though their appearance in these letters—defiant and proud in the foreground, or silent and apprehensive in the shadows—speaks eloquently of what their lives must have been like under the invasion of foreigners. Some of the newcomers were illiterate or were able to write little more than brief, halting notes. Others came from regions that lacked a reliable postal service, and thus the task of writing long letters to loved ones would have been considered an act of futility. Still others succumbed to disease or accident before they could put pen to paper, and some were overcome with the shame of failure and lapsed into silence. In the 150 years since the gold rush many manuscripts have been lost or destroyed. The letters and journals in this collection—writings from a total of forty-nine different correspondents—represent the efforts of generations of family members, collectors, and archivists who have preserved the stories of ordinary people caught up in an extraordinary event.

The letters and journals that do survive present something of a challenge for an editor. To the usual problems of deciphering nineteenth-century penmanship is added the fact that many letters were written under awkward circumstances: on a small board balanced on the knee or on a barrel top, by the light of an oil lamp in a small tent with rain turning the floor to muck, in a crowded rooming house with bedmates drinking and playing cards. The distractions resulted frequently in the omission of some words and the unnecessary repetition of others ("the the"). Rather than pepper the text with [sic]s, I have supplied the missing words in brackets and deleted the repetitions.

Some of the writers used very little in the way of punctuation, depending instead on the appearance of a capital letter or a line break to indicate the beginning of a new sentence. This makes for difficult reading in the originals, a difficulty that is only compounded by a literal transcription into printed text. I have supplied periods where it was clear that a sentence was meant to terminate, and I have inserted commas when necessary to make the meaning clear. As noted earlier, many of these correspondents were well educated, and their literacy is certainly demonstrated in the quality of their writing. A few contributors, however, display only a meager grasp of spelling and grammar, and these letters I have transcribed as literally as possible, retaining the errors as an indication of educational level. For the others I have corrected an occasional minor spelling error but transcribed the grammar exactly as it appears. Ampersands have been transcribed as "and," but "&c" has been retained as written; whenever a reader encounters "et cetera" it represents an exact transcription of the written words in the letter or journal. Scholars of nineteenth-century orthography should, of course, always refer to the original manuscripts.

These letters as a group include much repetition, as might be expected from writers describing the occurrences of one year in one city. Few correspondents can resist giving a grocery list of the exorbitant price of beef, pork, flour, eggs, etc. These lists are charming the first and second time they are encountered, but they quickly become somewhat tedious to read. I have retained a few as examples and edited out the rest. On a few occasions several writers describe the same event; these I have retained despite some redundancy as they provide interesting information about differing viewpoints.

I have grouped these excerpts into eight chapters, each focusing on a different aspect of the gold rush experience. As a whole I believe they provide a unique view of one year in the life of San Francisco, the raucous year during which it grew from a village to a city. The story is told in the voices of ordinary people who surface in these letters, alive and vivid, and then disappear into the dull data of U.S. census records. These are not the movers and shakers of California history, but their stories give, I believe, a much more accurate view of the way it really was at the birth of a truly remarkable city.

Acknowledgments

In many ways this volume is a tribute to the women and men who have labored (almost from the days of the gold rush) to build the library collections of the University of California, Berkeley. They have created a cultural resource for the state of California that is second to none. From the first time that I wandered into the Doe Library as a callow nineteen-year-old, Berkeley's libraries have played a central role in my development as a scholar and as a person. It has been my privilege during the ensuing years to know personally many of the librarians, library assistants, and students whose legacy of dedication and professionalism in the face of enormous (and growing) challenges has made it possible for me to gather the resources presented in this collection. I thank them all for that great gift.

One of the brightest jewels in the crown of the Berkeley campus is certainly The Bancroft Library, and it is from its riches that I have drawn these letters and diaries to present an eyewitness account of the birth of gold rush San Francisco. I would like in particular to thank Bonnie Hardwick, former Curator of the Bancroft Collection, for her continued support of this project. At a time when circumstances had led me to put the work on hold, it was a nudge from her that gave me the motivation I needed to bring the manuscript to completion. I am grateful also to Jack Von Euw, Curator of the Pictorial Collection, for making special arrangements for me to draw from the library's extensive collection of gold rush images.

A group of my former colleagues at The Bancroft Library merits a special acknowledgment: Bonnie Bearden, Alyson Belcher, Marilyn Bolak, Terry Boom, James Eason, Franz Enciso, Jean Gibson-Ordoñez, Barbara Hoddy, Rebecca Jabbour, David Kessler, Richard Ogar, Annegret Ogden, Kelly Penhall-Wilson, Merrilee Proffitt, David Rez, Teri Rinne, Kenneth Sanderson, Wayne Silka, Mark Takaro, Geoff Wexler, Paula White, and Xiuzhi Zhou. Their high personal integrity and amazing courage under fire have not been forgotten.

In writing the chapter introductions I have drawn on the scholarship of many historians who have written about gold rush San Francisco from many different angles. Two works were of particular help: Jesse L. Coburn's *Letters of Gold: California Postal History through 1869* and Roger W. Lotchin's *San Francisco 1846–1856: From Hamlet to City*. Mine has truly been a case of a dwarf standing on the shoulders of giants, and I thank them for the much-needed boost.

Finally, and always, I thank Kevin Jewell, whose faith sustains me and whose love turns all my mud to gold.

Introduction

On 24 January 1848, at around ten o'clock in the morning an earthquake that nobody felt shook the village of San Francisco to its very foundations. Everything changed profoundly, and yet no one suspected what had just occurred, nor what would unfold during the ensuing year. San Francisco would serve as the host for one of the largest migrations in American history, and its population of barely a thousand would by the close of 1849 swell to more than thirty thousand determined, restless souls from five continents, all come to profit from the small glitter of gold that James Marshall lifted from the tailrace of Sutter's Mill.

The men (and women and children) who poured into California during the first year of the gold rush came with little knowledge of what they would find there. Some came armed against a potential Indian attack, unaware that California's indigenous population had long been reduced to a few powerless bands. Most expected to find themselves in an environment that was vaguely "Spanish," though they were unsure of what exactly that term meant. Few had any knowledge of the long, rich, complex history of the territory they were about to grab.

When the Spanish first sailed north from Mexico there were an estimated three hundred thousand Native Americans living in California, eighty thousand of them along what would become "the mission strip," a fertile, temperate narrow band of land that stretched from San Diego in the south to San Francisco in the north. In the 1700s this region represented the highest population of Indians in North America.[1] The California Indians were divided into more than one hundred distinct tribes, each with its own language and customs, the San Francisco Bay Area being home to the Miwoks, Wappo, Costanoan (or Ohlone), and Yokuts.[2]

Though they depended almost entirely for subsistence on hunting, fishing, and the gathering of wild plant foods, the Indians of the San Francisco Bay Area developed a much more complex culture than most hunter-gatherer communities. They were for the most part conservative and politically stable, and they developed elaborate systems of economic exchange with neighboring tribes, keeping conflict at a minimum. Contact with the outside world was limited to sightings of the sails of foreign trading ships on the horizon and the occasional salvage of Asian manufactured goods whose crates washed ashore after shipwrecks. The Indians of the coastal area north of the Golden Gate were perhaps the first Californians to dine off of blue and white Chinese export dinnerware.

In the sixteenth century, Spain became the dominant power in the Pacific by combining the regions explored by Columbus and Magellan. The Spanish king established a colonial empire that was administered from Mexico City (the capital of New Spain) and linked somewhat tentatively by a small fleet of galleons. From 1565 to 1815 a single annual ship was dispatched from Acapulco to the Philippines carrying a year's worth of correspondence, supplies, and payroll. The galleon usually left Mexico in June and sailed south until it caught the prevailing easterly trade winds that would speed it to Manila, usually in less than sixty days. This ship would be loaded with Peruvian and Mexican silver to be traded for Asian wares, particularly Chinese silks, porcelain, and jewelry.

Because of the strong clockwise winds and ocean currents, the galleon was usually unable to retrace its route home to Acapulco. Instead, it would sail north until it caught the Kuroshiro current, which would carry it across the Pacific to the coast of North America. During this leg of the voyage it was not uncommon for the ship to be out of sight of land for as long as six months. Fresh food would eventually run out and the crew often developed beri beri or scurvy. The long trip down the coast of the Californias would find half the crew incapacitated by illness, and on one occasion an entire crew died—the galleon was found drifting off Acapulco filled with "silk and cadavers."[3]

In 1602, hoping to find a harbor somewhere in Alta California where the ships could land to take on fresh food and water, the government of New Spain sent Sebastian Vizcaino to reconnoiter the coastline. Sailing north against the prevailing currents he discovered what he termed "the best port that could be desired," and diplomatically named it after his superior, the Viceroy of New Spain, the Conde de Monterey.[4] To Vizcaino's chagrin not even flattery sufficed to assure the establishment of a colony at Monterey Bay. The bureaucracy in Mexico City became distracted with other concerns, and for the next 160 years the Manila galleons continued to sail past the fertile California coast, their crews suffering and dying from want of fresh supplies.

It was the emerging threat from Russia and Great Britain that finally forced a reappraisal of the Spanish presence in Alta California. In 1769, under the command of Gaspar de Portolá a Spanish expeditionary force pushed northward. They reached Monterey Bay and discovered that Vizcaino's "best port that could be desired" was actually little more than a rocky cove, but they returned with the exciting news of the discovery of a huge inland bay entered through a narrow passage that would be easily defensible against Spain's enemies. They named the bay after St. Francis.

Displaying a level of ossification that would eventually lead to their demise, the bureaucrats in Mexico City insisted that the long-discussed plan for a port and colony at Monterey be followed despite new information about a better alternative. The provincial capital was established at Vizcaino's site and designated as a refuge for the galleons. The port found little favor with the galleon captains, though, who preferred to stay out at sea rather than risk the dangers of the shallow, rocky harbor. Between 1769 and 1815 only around a half-dozen Manila galleons stopped in Monterey on their journey homeward.[5]

Meanwhile, under the leadership of Fray Junípero Serra the Franciscans began establishing a chain of missions in an area that stretched from San Diego to San Francisco, each roughly one day's ride from the next. Though the influence of Spain's other missions in North America was waning, the missions in California were soon at the very heart of the social order there, supported by their own ranchos that boasted four hundred thousand head of cattle, sixty thousand horses, and three hundred thousand sheep and goats.[6]

Nearly the entire coastal population of California Indians between San Francisco and San Diego was gathered into the missions, with as many as fifty-four thousand baptisms performed. The missionaries, while sincerely motivated to bring the word of God to people they viewed as unenlightened savages, instead brought disease, poverty, suffering, and death. Once gathered into the missions the California Indians were exposed to new diseases whose virulence was aggravated by generally poor living conditions. The number of Indians living along the mission strip plummeted from eighty thousand to eighteen thousand in only a few years, and the Indian way of life was virtually eradicated.[7]

On the far northern edge of the province, at the site of what would become the city of San Francisco, the Spanish founded a presidio, or fort, in 1776, and the accompanying Franciscans established a church, the Mission San Francisco de Asis (Mission Dolores). The location was bleak and windswept, and the government in Mexico came to view the fort somewhat as a minor penal colony, posting recalcitrant soldiers there as punishment.[8] The pueblo that grew up along the cove, between the presidio and the mission, was optimistically named Yerba Buena, after the wild mint that grew in profusion on the treeless hills.

In 1821, after struggling for ten years to throw off the yoke of colonialism, Mexico gained its independence from Spain, and California became part of the new Mexican Republic. The California Missions, already discredited because of their treatment of the Indians in their care, lost further favor with both the Mexicans and Californios by siding with the King of Spain in the struggle, and in 1833 the missions were secularized. Though the buildings were supposed to be converted to ordinary parishes, most of the Spanish priests returned to Spain and few Mexican priests were attracted to the harsh life of the stripped missions. By 1846 only five priests remained in California.[9] The confiscated church property was redistributed in a series of more than eight hundred land grants totaling thirteen million acres, 42 percent of which went to non-Hispanics (mostly Americans who had become naturalized Mexican citizens).[10]

It should not be surprising that so many residents of California were not Spanish or Mexican by birth, for the province was far from isolated. Beginning in the eighteenth century the trading ships of England, France, Holland, Russia, Portugal, and the United States linked the California coast with Asia, the East Indies, Australia, and Polynesia. The California colonial economy was based on the hide and tallow trade, and the Californios raised and slaughtered over a million head of cattle, selling the by-products for manufactured goods.[11] Yankee merchants recognized the wisdom of having an agent in place to represent their interests on the Pacific coast and soon a class of wealthy, shrewd businessmen arose in the California ports. To the east, trappers working for the American Fur Company and the Rocky Mountain Fur Company discovered passes through the Sierra Nevada into California's fertile Central Valley. They then returned to the Mississippi frontier with stories of rich farmland, and many trappers in turn became guides, leading parties of American immigrants into the territory. By 1845 more than six hundred American settlers had made the overland journey to California.[12]

The province of Alta California grew slowly but steadily, welcoming nearly anyone willing to set down roots in the sparsely populated territory. But in Washington DC a different future was being mapped out. Manifest Destiny called for the United States to extend from the Atlantic to the Pacific, and President James Polk began behind-the-scenes maneuvering to make sure that the inevitable happened. Polk issued secret orders through Secretary of State James Buchanan to the American consul at Monterey, Thomas O. Larkin. Larkin was to encourage the Americans living in California to mount an insurrection against Mexico. The aid and protection of the United States government was promised—though it was understood that the government would not openly sponsor the secessionist movement until Mexico initiated hostilities.[13]

Mexico in turn was embroiled in a bitter struggle over Texas. Having never recognized Texas's independence in the first place, the Mexican government was outraged when the region proclaimed that its southern boundary was the Rio Grande, not the Nueces River. President Polk dispatched John Slidell to Mexico City, both to negotiate the dispute over Texas and to offer forty million dollars for the purchase of Alta California and New Mexico. When the Mexican president refused even to receive Slidell, Polk ordered General Zachary Taylor to cross the Nueces and occupy the disputed territory. The Mexicans resisted the invasion, several Americans were killed, and Polk had the excuse he needed to ask Congress for a declaration of war. On 13 May 1846 the United States officially proclaimed itself at war with Mexico.

When the word of war reached the Pacific coast the reaction was swift. On 14 June a group of thirty American settlers descended on Sonoma. They imprisoned General Mariano Vallejo, proclaimed California an independent republic, and hoisted a flag emblazoned with a red star and the image of a grizzly bear. The Bear Flag Republic was dissolved three weeks later when Commodore John D. Sloat sailed the Pacific Squadron into Monterey Bay and, having raised the American flag over the Custom House, claimed California as a possession of the United States of America.

Further up the coast the conquest of San Francisco was being played out as if scripted by Gilbert and Sullivan. On 1 July, John C. Frémont and twenty of his men waded ashore and slipped into the nearly abandoned Castillo de San Joaquin, the Mexican fortification built to protect the narrow entrance to San Francisco Bay. They found a fort in ruins, its round shot ammunition coated with rust and its gun carriages rendered inoperable by decay. Undetected, they spiked the ten cannon they found there, including three ancient Spanish pieces cast in 1623, 1628, and 1693. A week later Captain John Montgomery sailed the U.S. ship *Portsmouth* through the Golden Gate and trained its guns on the small village that hugged the cove. The very model of a modern naval officer, Montgomery scribbled out a note to William A. Leidesdorff, the American vice-consul stationed in what was nominally a Mexican town. It warned that on the morrow, 9 July, he would land "a considerable body of men under arms." They would invade the town and "hoist the Flag of the U States under a salute of twenty one guns from the Portsmouth, afterwhich, the Proclamation of the Commander in Cheif Commodore Sloat will be read in both languages for the enformation of all classes."[14]

The next day a landing party of seventy men—the sailors resplendent in white frocks and black hats, the marines in dress uniform—came ashore at Clark's Point. The only resistance they encountered was an expanse of mud flats that caused them to abandon their boats and slog ashore through ankle-deep bay sludge. After a short stumble through sandy "streets" to the Plaza, they raised the American flag on the pole in front of the Custom House (to the accompaniment of one fife and one drum), fired the guns, and read the proclamation in English and in Spanish. Three huzzahs went up from the conquerors, and the small crowd of vanquished San Franciscans, "principally foreign residents, seemed cordially to join."[15]

The major California conflict of the Mexican-American War occurred in southern California the following January, when the combined forces of General Stephen W. Kearny's soldiers, John C. Frémont's riflemen, and Commodore Robert F. Stockton's naval troops defeated the Mexican forces at the final battle of Cahuenga Pass. In

Mexico the American army under the command of General Winfield Scott achieved a more decisive victory at the battle of Chapultepec. Under the resulting Treaty of Guadalupe Hidalgo, signed on 2 February 1848, most of what would become New Mexico, Arizona, Nevada, and California was ceded to the United States.

A substantial American presence in California already existed at the time it was relinquished by Mexico. In the summer of 1846 Jonathan Stevenson recruited a regiment of 250 New Yorkers to aid in the conquest of California. Taking the long route around Cape Horn they arrived in San Francisco on 6 March 1847, after hostilities had already ceased. Most of the regiment elected to remain in California. The previous summer 136 Mormon men, women, and children had arrived on the ship *Brooklyn,* under the leadership of a printer named Sam Brannan. Their hope was to find a haven from the religious persecution they had experienced in the United States. Brannan was a man of considerable business acumen and his personal resources were augmented substantially by the tithes paid by the Mormons under his leadership (monies that came under his direct control). When Brigham Young demanded that the tithes be forwarded to Salt Lake City, Brannan is said to have replied, "I'll give up the Lord's money when Young sends me a receipt signed by the Lord, and no sooner."[16] The combination of his personal money and the collected tithes soon made Brannan one of the leading businessmen in San Francisco.

One of the chief figures in California prior to the gold rush was the German Swiss adventurer, rancher, and autocrat John Augustus Sutter. Hounded by creditors and unhappy with his straight-laced wife and four demanding children, Sutter escaped to America in 1834. After various adventures while traveling with fur traders throughout the West, Sutter sailed to the Sandwich Islands for a four-month visit. In 1839 he returned to the North American mainland by way of San Francisco Bay, but was turned away since Yerba Buena (then the name of San Francisco) was not a valid port of entry for foreigners. Sutter continued on to Monterey where he struck up a friendship with Governor Juan Alvarado. When, on a whim, Sutter asked Alvarado for a grant of land, the governor invited him to travel up the Sacramento River and choose any spot he wanted. Alvarado hoped that Sutter's new settlement would check the growing power of his political rival, Mariano Vallejo.

In August 1839, Sutter and eight Kanakas (Hawaiians), a Belgian, a German, and an Irishman established a camp near the juncture of the

Sacramento and the American Rivers. They first built Hawaiian-style grass huts, but soon replaced them with more substantial adobe structures. Sutter established his own fiefdom in the wilderness and called it Nueva Helvetia (New Switzerland). The camp was eventually to extend for thirty-three square miles, or about forty-nine thousand acres. The compound quickly prospered and by 1840 Sutter had six hundred men working in his wheat fields and boasted twelve thousand head of cattle, two thousand horses, and fifteen thousand sheep.[17]

Nueva Helvetia, though legally part of the Mexican Republic, was in reality a world apart, a little kingdom run according to Sutter's rules. Sutter affected a gold-braided Mexican uniform, printed passports for his "citizens," and exercised something of a *droit du seigneur*, particularly with the Indian inhabitants. As one of Sutter's employees later wrote, "Everyone knew that Sutter was a typical Don Juan with women. In addition to the large number of Indian girls and women in his harem, there was also in the fort many Indian loafers who rarely worked, but were fed and nicely clothed because their wives received special consideration from the master of the fort."[18]

Sutter, though his sympathies lay with the Mexican government, managed to weather the change from Mexican to American control of the territory. In 1848, as American and Mexican representatives gathered in Mexico to sign the Treaty of Guadalupe Hidalgo (ceding California to the United States), Sutter was the supreme authority in his compound on the Sacramento River. It is not surprising, then, that he greeted the news of the discovery of gold with mixed emotions when James Marshall came to him, mud-spattered from riding through a soaking rain, and showed him a white cotton cloth filled with gold dust and pea-sized nuggets. Sutter was already a wealthy, powerful man, and while he welcomed greater wealth he knew what this gold rush would mean: the disintegration of his tightly controlled domain.

His fears were well founded. When gold was displayed in San Francisco in May, the population dropped from around one thousand to less than one hundred in a matter of days as gold fever spread through the small community. A visiting U.S. naval captain wrote that "nothing but the introduction of lunatic asylums can effect a cure."[19]

News of the discovery spread slowly but inexorably. Gold seekers arrived from San Francisco and Sonoma in May, from Monterey and San Jose in May and June, from Mexico in July and August. It took longer for word to reach the United States. American newspapers first reported the finds in August and September 1848, but the news aroused little interest. It was not until mid-September, when Lieut. Edward F. Beale arrived in Washington DC bearing official dispatches and a vial of gold, that a cautious buzz began along the East Coast. The subsequent written report of Richard Mason, California territory's first governor, was even more persuasive. Mason's detailed, sober evaluation of the situation in California was delivered to the War Department; it was leaked to the newspapers and eventually made its way into the December State of the Union address of President Polk.

And the rush was on.

The decision to take part in the gold rush was not an easy one. While many felt the prickle of gold fever under their skin, the journey was usually preceded by weeks or even months of indecision. Few of the adventurers could simply walk away from their family obligations, whether they be sons, husbands, or fathers. As will be seen in the letters that follow it was not a wild dream of fantastic riches that motivated the migration west, but frequently "stern, iron necessity." Certainly bonanzas danced in most men's dreams, but what drew them was the more attainable goal of making enough to get ahead. A few months in the gold fields could give them the resources to pay off debts, to buy a piece of land, or to open a small business—achievements that could otherwise take years of hard work and sacrifice.

For those with dependents, one of the major decisions that had to be made was whether or not the entire family would emigrate. Since the transfer to California was viewed as temporary, most men left their wives and families at home. The few women who chose to brave the hardships of the journey and the uncertainties of the new country were usually unwilling to expose their children to such dangers; small children were often left behind in the care of relatives.

Once they had made the difficult decision to leave home, the Argonauts were faced with the first of many new decisions: how to get from where they were to where they wanted to be. Should they take the slow ocean route, or the shorter but more arduous overland trail? If traveling by sea, should they make the long voyage around Cape Horn or the disease-ridden portage through the jungles of Central America? Whichever route was chosen, the long journey and the bewildering arrival would be the subjects of their first letters home.

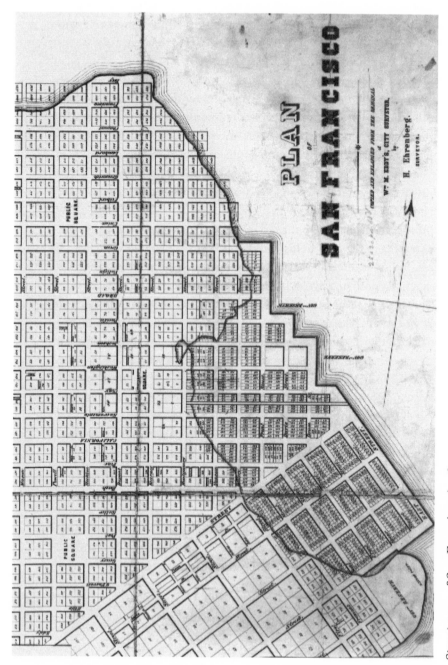

Street map of San Francisco in 1850.

A YEAR
OF MUD
and GOLD

Chapter 1

First Impressions

For American Argonauts seeking their fortunes in gold or commerce, three main routes existed from the United States to California: due West overland by foot, horse, or wagon; around Cape Horn and up the Pacific coast by schooner; or by ship (sailing or steam) to the Isthmus of Panama, by portage overland to the Pacific, and then by water again, hugging the coastline all the way to San Francisco. Each method had its advantages and its rigors.

The overland route could be the hardest journey of all. It required months of trudging across prairies that seemed to be always powder-dry with dust or axle-deep with mud, through burning alkali deserts, and up steep, barely passable mountain trails that too soon clogged with winter snow. The journey took two to three months by horseback, three to five months by wagon. Though it was a severe challenge it was also the most popular choice.

For those Argonauts living on the frontier of the Mississippi Valley their starting place was already a third of the way to the goal; it would have made little sense to backtrack to the East Coast to board a ship when the gold lay westward. Standard farm equipment such as horses and wagons could easily be physically converted to a proper trail outfit, and the overland trail, while difficult, was comparatively well known. The Oregon Trail was so firmly established by the time of the gold rush that it was possible to find one's way simply by following the litter that marked the route. By the fall of 1850 nearly all intervening rivers and creeks had either been spanned by bridges or were served by commercial ferries.[1] Far from stepping off into an unknown wilderness, wagoneers were likely to find themselves backed up in a traffic jam at ferry crossings, waiting two or three days to pass over to the other side. Some entrepreneurs even offered "express" wagon trains that promised a rapid trip to California with all the necessities supplied. These package tours rarely proved financially successful either for the organizers or their customers, however, and they soon disappeared.[2]

One of the most colorful chroniclers of the California migration was the historian Hubert Howe Bancroft, whose research collection—which was purchased by the University of California—became the nucleus of The Bancroft Library. Bancroft came to California in 1852 to open a bookstore, and was soon enthralled with the rough and tumble adventure that surrounded him. He became an obsessive collector of books, documents, and personal recollections, and eventually wrote (or, more accurately, edited) the classic *History of the Pacific States of North America,* thirty-four volumes of effusive, anecdotal history.

In Bancroft's telling, the overland journey was perilous but not without its charm. "Yet, after all, it was not always hard or horrible. There was much that was enjoyable, particularly to persons of health—bright skies, exhilarating air, and high anticipations."[3] That qualifier—"particularly to persons of health"—is an important one. In the winter of 1848 cholera broke out in both New York City and New Orleans, and by the summer of 1849 had spread to St. Louis and the jumping-off cities of St. Joseph and Independence, Missouri. Particularly for those setting out in late 1849, the route west was marked by shallow graves scraped out hastily by survivors eager to flee the dreaded disease. Too often victims were poorly buried; wolves and coyotes easily dug the bodies up and left grisly signposts for those who followed. "So great was the terror inspired," Bancroft wrote, "that the victims were often left to perish on the roadside by their panic-stricken companions. On the other hand, there were many instances of heroic devotion, of men remaining along with a comrade while the rest of the company rushed on to escape contagion, and nursing him to his recovery, to be in turn stricken down and nursed by him whose life had been saved."[4]

Weighing cost against comfort and safety against speed, more than twice as many of the early Argonauts chose the overland route instead of the sea passages. During the first wave of migration approximately fifty thousand adventurers made the overland journey; nearly ten percent of them died along the way.[5] These travelers usually went directly to the gold fields, and traveled on to San Francisco only later when the weather made panning impossible or when the lure of the big city drew them to spend some of the precious dust they had accumulated.

The second most popular choice of travel in 1849 was to sail from an Atlantic port (or New Orleans), pass around Cape Horn or through the Straits of Magellan, and continue on up the Pacific coast, a trip of seventeen to eighteen thousand nautical miles that took four to six months to complete. Like the overland trail, this was a well-known route. By the time of the gold rush, trans-Horn merchant shipping operations were routine and most vessels, even if they were not outfitted as passenger ships, were willing to take on anyone willing to pay his or her way. As the demand for carriers increased, sleek clipper ships were fitted out with elegant staterooms in which wealthy Argonauts could travel in style. Even when the accommodations were more spartan, well-heeled passengers frequently brought special food and drink for themselves and their friends. Most ships were soon divided into cliques and factions which, as the monotony of shipboard life took hold, found themselves at odds and rancor sometimes degenerated into open violence.

During the early years of the gold rush men frequently organized into commercial companies, usually among neighbors or at least inhabitants of a common region who banded together to lease or buy a ship to take them to California. Ignorant of the California terrain and economy, they sometimes assumed they could sail their vessels all the way to the gold fields, or planned to sell their ships in San Francisco to recoup their costs (not realizing that the harbor was already filled with drifting, crewless vessels). Most companies disbanded soon after arriving in California, as mining in the early years did not readily lend itself to group effort.

The Cape Horn route was the most disease-free way to travel, but it did sometimes take a severe mental toll. Many suffered under the strain of six months of enforced inactivity during which they had little to do but miss their families and worry about whether they had made the right decision in dropping everything to go west. Whereas those on the overland journey were presented with daily challenges that took skill and grit and muscle to overcome, those aboard ship could do little to affect the success or failure of their voyage. As Bancroft described it, "Storms and other dangers brought little inspiration or reliance to counteract oppressive fear. Man lay here a passive toy for the elements."[6]

The least popular of the gold rush routes involved sea travel to the ports of Chagres or Colón on the Atlantic side of the Isthmus of Panama, a transfer to transportation by land across the isthmus to the Pacific, and then passage by steamship north to San Francisco. The land route had been used by the Spanish for more than two centuries, and with the inauguration of the U.S. Mail Steamship Company on the Atlantic and the Pacific Mail Steamship Company on the Pacific, the infrastructure was in place to offer a relatively rapid journey: from New York to San Francisco in five to eight weeks.[7]

Unfortunately the isthmus route was also the most disease ridden. Yellow fever, black water fever, cholera, amoebic dysentery, and malaria were common scourges. In addition, from May to December the voyagers could encounter as much as 126 inches of rain, a deluge that soaked baggage and rotted clothing.

Moreover, a ticket covered only passage from a U.S. port to the east coast of the isthmus and from the western coast of the isthmus to San Francisco; the land portion of the trip was entirely the responsibility of the passenger. Travelers were dumped, usually at Chagres, where they were at the mercy of unscrupulous boatmen and baggage handlers in their efforts to make their own arrangements to go by dugout boat to Gorgona or Cruces. Having traveled upriver they then needed to bargain for pack animals to take them over a narrow, muddy, winding seventy-mile trail through the jungle to the city of Panama. Once they reached the Pacific (if they hadn't succumbed to disease along the way) they discovered that while they held a ticket that promised passage on a steamer to San Francisco, that ticket did not guarantee them a place on any *particular* steamer. Huge crowds of would-be gold seekers filled the docks at each departure. When the steamer *Panama* arrived on 18 May 1849 to pick up its load of 209 passengers, over two thousand angry Argonauts were on the docks struggling to get on board.[8]

Desperate to get out of Central America, weak with disease, running out of money, and nearly prostrate with the frustration of being so close to a dream that seemed to recede with every stage of the journey, some Argonauts decided to forego the steamer and simply booked passage on the next sailing vessel leaving port. Because sailing ships relied on the prevailing winds and currents rather than on steam power, they often had to sail far out to sea. It was not unusual for a traveler to find himself visiting Hawaii before reaching San Francisco; his promised "quick trip" could actually take up to five months.

It is no wonder, then, that the first expressions of the new arrivals are relief that a difficult journey had ended, gratefulness for health and safety, and amazement at the bizarre metropolis that rose suddenly out of the fog.

Anonymous

Journal of a voyage from New Bedford to San Francisco
21 September 1849

This morning thick and foggy. 2 p.m. stood in for the shore. At 4 p.m. made Point Reyes. . . . Last evening before retiring, I went on deck and found the wind had increased to a gale. Orders had been given at seven o'clock to stand out towards the Faralone Islands. . . . As the wind had increased after the orders were given for the night, and finding them implicitly obeyed regardless of the increase of the wind, caused me to be fearful of some disaster before morning if some counter orders had not been given, or discretionary power [given] to the mates. It appears this had not been done. Consequently, feeling somewhat anxious, I remained up to see her wear round at ten o'clock.

I felt safe then for the two hours to come, tho' the wind increased. I went below and "turned in," reasoned and addressed myself to sleep. I awoke second time wearing round, and near the third, by the healing of the ship, I could tell without getting up or making inquiry. At eight bells (4 o'clock) just as the third mate was descending [the] companion-way from his watch, I inquired if the watch was up, and the ship had gone round. He answered she had at that moment.

I again turned myself over and "addressed myself to sleep." In less than an hour from that time I heard a great noise and confusion on deck, and the same instant the second mate thrust his head down the companion-way and shouted as loud as he could bawl, "Call Captain Seabury! We are close aboard of rocks or a sail!"

I took hold where he left off and passed the word along to the top of my voice, and such leaping from rooms and such "getting up stairs" never was before seen in our ship, some in their night caps some with shirt and trowsers, some as near nude as one could imagine, others with trowsers on "hind side before," some frightened out of their senses and many lost their voices. Some thought their journey of life was to end on this, the last day of their voyage, and thought nothing of it.

But as quick as our captain has always been in cases of emergency, he was not quick enough this time. Orders were given spontaneously throughout the ship to "Up the helm!" "Hard up!" "Hard a'starboard!" &c &c. A perfect Bedlam prevailed for some time on the decks. It is needless to say more than that when we past it, the receding wave from the rock washed up the ships side, and were but half of a ship's length from it! *Heavens!* Many striking remarks in consequence of what might have happened this a.m. First mate Hathaway said, "You can eat your breakfast now, but if the old ship had struck, you'd have had to eat rockweed for your breakfast before now."

Run from 7 till 12 m., where breakers were heard leeward which warned us to wear again. They were but a short distance from us when we got about. Still foggy. A fine fellow, a Lascan [an Alaskan?] sailor, said this morning that the fog would light up and clear off this afternoon. Another man, Mr. Macomber, formerly a mate, said at one o'clock, "In less than a half an hour our top gallant sails would be set." In a few moments after, sure enough, the fog began to open, wind breezed, sun came out, and in a few moments land was visible nearly all around us, and our people instantly became as "Merry as a marriage bell."

On we went towards the "Golden Gate" all in high glee. The passage through from the ocean is about seven miles in length and from two to four in width, with nearly perpendicular mountain bluffs on either side. Ships can run close in shore without the least danger. In fact, a ship might run her bowsprit into one of these banks or cliffs and still be afloat. A ship close in looks as small comparatively speaking as Tige would lying down beside University Building. It blows a strong breeze through this passage throughout the year.

As we rounded to on entering the harbour I could think of no other place than New York, so thick and dense was the forest of masts and spars presented to the view for miles in extent. Vessels of all nations are here, from the Oregon, and north coast, down through "Spanish Main" S.A., United States to Pasmaquaddy; from all parts of Europe, and some from China. All styles of nautical architecture may be seen too, from the "Gundalor" to the "long low rakish looking dark schooner," up to the magnificent ocean steamer, and from the Chinese junk to the almost perfect symmetry and proportions of some of our men-of-war, here.

It is an enlivening sight at any time to look upon so many vessels all at anchor in one port, and particularly so to one unaccustomed as

I am to such sights, and so long at sea as I have been to, renders the view more particularly interesting and agreeable. There being no wharves here, every vessel lies at anchor, hence, a better opportunity presents itself to observe the different models of vessels, style of rig, and to compare one with the other &c &c.

5 P.M. We have just dropped our anchor in the far famed Port or Bay of San Francisco! Be it for health, wealth, or otherwise—here we are, at the end of our journey after a successful voyage of one hundred and seventy four days—or nearly six months—at the *"El Dorado!"* The town from our ship looks small and meagre, though it is impossible to describe it on account of the forest of ship masts between us and the shore. Two ships entered the port with us—twenty seven came in in one day just before we arrived, and on the preceding day sixteen. There are also hundreds of vessels up the various rivers leading out of this bay, and hundreds more are on their way here.

8 P.M. Captain Seabury has just returned from the town and brought me the most gratifying intelligence of having seen my brother-in-law and the assurance of his good health, and is very anxious to see me. This is the best news of any I have heard. None of the vessels at Colon when we were there [are] here, though many sailed before us. This is just as I predicted when there. Our ship and our Captain are both first rate sailors.

Anne Willson Booth

Journal of a voyage from Baltimore to
San Francisco California on ship Andalusia
21 September 1849

We had a strong wind all night, making some 10 or 12 knots an hour. A heavy fog this morning prevented an observation being made. The Capt. knew, however, we were very near the Land, so stood off a little. At 1 o'clock, the mist and fog began to disperse. In the course of a very few minutes, we were gratified by seeing the land only about 1/2 mile distant. I cannot tell my first emotions at this moment, so mingled were they—joy at having safely arrived certainly was one feeling, but the predominant feeling is that of a sad realization of my distance from home.

The breeze sprang up and carried us in beautifully. The entrance into Sacramento [i.e., San Francisco] Bay is very pretty and the scenery of the boldest character. Just at the entrance there stand the remains of an old Spanish Fort which reminded me of castellated ruins I have often read of. There is an old Mission station near the entrance also. Just in the middle of the entrance between the two points, called "the Gate," there is a small Island, on either side of which is a channel deep enough to admit vessels of the largest class.

As we rounded the point, we began to see the masts of the vessels in the harbour. Such a fleet I never saw before, and it was with difficulty our ship was guided to her berth. We became entangled with several, but were soon extricated, [and] by 7 o'clock we were safely moored about 200 yards from the shore, and in the midst of vessels so close, as to enable us to converse with ease. All along the hill sides, tents were pitched near which fires were burning. In the twilight we could just discern persons moving about. On the whole, it was the most picturesque scene I ever beheld.

And now that we have arrived, our first enquiry is for news and letters from home. Some of the gentlemen went ashore immediately and returned about 9 o'clock. Among them Mr. Cardwell, one of our most intelligent passengers. He came into the cabin and imparted all the information he had gleaned during his short stay, to which we listened with breathless interest. In the first place, our previous fears of the Cholera being in the States was confirmed, the report being that it was raging with much violence there. Oh, *God! spare us the horror of hearing the death of any of our beloved ones.* The post office being closed, we cannot get our letters until tomorrow.

The news from the mines is, the gold is inexhaustible, but sickness very prevalent. . . . Mr. Price brought his brother on board, who came out in the *Greyhound.* He has been up to the mines and contracted the bilious. He is preparing to return to the United States, having become wearied already of California.

Caroline Stoddard

Journal
28 November 1850

About five in the afternoon yesterday judged the ship was within a few miles of land. So dense a fog had set in, the ship was hove to until early this morning. At nine the fog has practically cleared off, and in the distance distinctly to be seen are the Farollones, three small islands, at the mouth or entrance of San Francisco bay, a large ship just to the leeward of us. Thousands of teel and wild geese are in flocks, to appearance quarter of a mile in length, around us. Such excitement, such hallooing and exclamations among our passengers can hardly be imagined. We have only *four*, what could it have been, where they stood crowded upon deck as many ships have gone? About 6 in the evening of the 28th our Pilot came on board, rejoiced were we to see him. Although we were all so anxious to get in, we felt quite contented even to hear the order given to let go the anchor. Pilot brought us two or three California papers. Before I retired for the night went on deck for a peep and to appearance the land was over our ship's deck we were anchored so close to it. It is at least 6 or 800 feet high, frightful looking enough a mass of barren rock on the side of the Island which is called Virgin Id. Once in the night we were not more than the length of the ship from it. Pilot acknowledged in the morning we came near going on shore, they got the boat out twice to tow her off. At seven got fairly started again, and from that time till four in the afternoon we were drifting up the harbour. Passed a curious rock with an arch in it, and on it, and around it, were hundreds of pelicans, it is called "Arch rock" [probably Alcatraz, which means "pelican"]. Had the pleasure of spying at a lady on board ship *Howard* of Boston as we passed her, the first one I had seen for more than four months. I could see her laugh as I took the glass to look at her.

Robert Beck

Journal
7 July 1849

At 9 o'clock AM—made the Land. Ran in until quite close to shore When our Capt, supposing he had made a mistake in his observation, tacked and again ran out to sea. Fortunately other vessels were in sight which kept on towards the shore and disappeared from our sight. It being evident there was a "hole in the wall," we followed and entered the "Golden Gate" where we found an "Inland Sea" dotted with Islands containing numerous vessels that had already arrived from different ports.

At 9 o'clock PM dropped anchor in front of the Canvass City of San Francisco.

William Graves

Journal
26 May 1850

This Morning at 8 oclock we once more made Land o'wrd Bow and Towrde the harber onse more. At 11 oclock we made the Harber And Contray to all the derection our Capten Stood off derect for it Where he shood have keep Clost to the North of the Channel And owin to this Wiffull Blunder We soon found our selves under the opesit shore out of the way of the current of Wind and a Courrent Setting us fast upon the Sea Shore on a Large ledge of Rock & we shoold have sertently gon to peasies if we had not come to Anchor jest as we did. This caused a grat meny Curses to be heep upon the Capt. By the Company an also the Mat[e]s. Thus we Layed untill 4 oclock when the a Pilot came on Board and we Tryed to get under way again By standing out to Sea onse more But this we did not suceed in dooing on the count of the Cournet And we had to come to Anchor once more And layed untill about Sone Set when agood Breese sprang up And we weigh Anchor and we was soon making good Progress [toward] the harber at which place we arived at 9 in the Evening and came to Anchor in full Sight of the City of San Francisco. We found layin at Anchor something lik 5 to 6 hundred Sailes of vessels of diffrent kinds and sizes From all parts of the World. The Popperlation of the City is astimated at about 20,000 of Inhabertency Made up of Californians Mexicans Americans Spaniards Chinees Portergees Englishmen & Some Indians. The City is Situated upon the South West side of the harbar Neer the entrence As the ground riseses upon the outer age of the City It overlooks one of the most plended Harbar of the know World one that is estimated to be large enough to be capeable of holding the hole Navy of the known World.

Robert Smith Lammot

Letter to his father
15 December 1849

Here we are at last arrived at our destination after a passage of 127 days from the Capes of Delaware. We made the land on the 12th about noon, but in consequence of bad weather, we were obliged to lay off and on until the following day, when we ran in to the harbor with a fair wind, and anchored in the bay in the afternoon, but too late to go on shore. Yesterday morning we went on shore, but I will first give you an idea of the bay. The entrance is about a mile wide, each side rising in a rocky bluff two or three hundred feet high covered with green moss, with a fine depth of water ranging from eight to ten fathoms. About a mile from the entrance, on one of the southern bluffs, stands the old Spanish fort, which is now in ruins.

After passing the fort the bay begins to open on the right, with the most magnificent view I ever saw. At least four hundred vessels lay at anchor there, some of them run ashore and converted into boarding houses. On the hills around were scattered numberless tents of every description while frame buildings of every kind were being erected. The rainy season commenced about a fortnight since, and it has rained almost without intermission ever since, so you may suppose the unpaved streets (that is to say, every street) were in a most aweful condition: mudholes of a kind that would rival some of Delaware County's worst roads are abundant, and though the town is laid out (or rather pitched together) on a succession of hills, the roads are almost impassible, for the water don't seem to run off. But oh! *such* houses! Little frames, such as not the meanest hand or laborer about you would live in, are bringing $800 to $2000 per month, as stores.

William Robert Prince

Letter to his wife and children
17 June 1849

At last I write to you direct from this famed City, where we arrived early in the morning of the 13th and had supposed before arrival that 24 hours would suffice for arrangements here, but the *Florence* not having arrived, I have had to purchase an outfit complete—and we leave here tomorrow for Stockton on the St Joaquin (pronounced St Workeen). I will now say in short what is important, having but little time, and after this don't expect letters oftener than once a month, and if the private hand from the mines should delay, it may be the 2nd month before it goes by the monthly Steamers. . . .

In this town the state of things is so peculiar that I can scarcely explain to you on paper. Board is $21 per week, and the lowest in mere canvass houses $2.75 per day or $14 per week. In the latter you find your own bedding, and in the former beds are on tables, floors and on a mat or blanket, or any thing. In every street there are houses and stores of canvass and probably 1/2 of the stores are so. Houses and stores rent from $3000 to $10,000 that would not cost over 15 cents on the dollar to build them in Flushing, these renting for more than 6 times the gross amount of the cost of similar buildings at Flushing or New York. . . .

The forenoons here are delightful, but the afters and nights the wind blows quite severely and the air is cold and austere and piercing and very disagreeable, and fires needed in the evening. They say it is warmer in winter than summer here. I would not live here, but a few miles back the climate is entirely different. I have had many bathings in the Pacific at the different ports and onboard the Steamer. I have let my whiskers and hair beneath my chin grow to save time in shaving. Fanton shaves the rest twice a week so far.

There are 80 to 100 ships at anchor in the harbor, which presents a most imposing appearance. There are more than 200 tents of Americans at the south side of the town where our tent is located. The miners now in the City buying provisions &c and tell all sorts of tales. It appears that the collectors of dust and lumps vary from $5 to $30 per day, and in extraordinary cases by accident or luck, more. I believe if a man averages $20 a day it is doing fairly. We are here in good season, and it is but lately that the most favorable season commenced on the St Joaquin branches—although there have been numbers working all winter in all directions.

One India rubber bag of our clothes was lost by the Steamer, but I hope to be repaid. The cost about $50. I feel always anxious to know that you are enjoying yourselves, and hope all will go on pleasantly and happily and on my part I shall do the best possible, but there is good luck needed as well as good management.

Love to all—Charty, Phiny, Willie and Le Baron.

Charles H. Randall

Letter to his parents
12 September 1849

Our ship arrived here last Sunday the 9th inst, all well after a passage of sixty days from Valparaiso. You cannot imagine the pleasure we all felt at seeing a voyage of 171 days from New York ended, let what would be our fate in this country. As we came into the harbour it was a sad sight to see so many fine ships lying at anchor from which they probably will never be released except by decay. Ship owners and agents are offering seamen $150 per month; some offer $1500 from this port to New York or the states, but no sailors can be induced to go [even] at these extravagant prices.

The city here does not exactly fill the imagination I had formed. There are very few wooden buildings, nearly all are rude light frames covered with common cotton cloth. The site is very uneven. The climate is very different from my anticipations: in the morning it is thick and muggy until about 10 o'clock, when from that until two it is quite warm. At the later time a breeze springs up daily that is cold and blows the dust here so bad that all comfort is blown away with it. I have worn my overcoat all the time since my arrival and have found it comfortable for keeping the wind off. Of all the places I have ever seen, this is the meanest climate, most disagreeable temperatures and I verily believe the dirtiest place in the world. I learn that it is much pleasanter up the river, where the sea has no influence, although quite hot, it is even in temperature.

Soon after landing I met Uncle Robert. He has been here four weeks. He was well and gave me considerable information which has already been of much advantage to me. During the time he has been here he has cleared $400. He had one of the most aristocratic houses to live in that this city can boast of, being the main hatch house of the *John G. Coster*. He sold it Sunday for more than double what he gave for it, but today he leaves here for the gold mines, from which we hear every kind of story—good, bad and indifferent. But very nearly all the miners that come down here return again in a few days.

By this time you must have a general description of almost everything appertaining to this part of the world, which would render it useless for me to enter into the minutia of everything. Of one thing you may be certain: that there is gold here and plenty of it but to get [it] a man must work and work hard, and I advise any one that wished to come here not to do so unless they are willing to throw away all the luxuries and nearly all of the comforts of life and to use themselves at the hardest kind of labour, whether they do it at the mines or any other place in California. None but labouring men are needed, and they are the kind that will realize the most from their efforts. As far as I can judge, many that never did do anything at home are here, and they will not forsake their second nature and exert themselves with work even to obtain a fortune. Do not believe any stories that say a man cannot make money and make it fast in this Territory. So far as I have seen, I am perfectly satisfied that I shall get what I come for.

I have written this letter to let you know of my safe arrival and health and what I intend doing. By Saturday next I shall be on my way to the mines in company with E. M. Young of Providence, and C. M. Van Schaick of Easton, NY. We three have formed ourselves into a company for the purpose of digging gold, taking care of each other if sick, with mutual interest in whatever any of us may obtain. Mr. Young is from home and I am satisfied that we shall do well, all feeling the necessity of doing and doing quickly. Mr. Y. has a friend (perhaps lover) at home, Miss Caroline C. Simmons, to whom he has written in such a manner that his letter will serve for an introduction with my family and vice versa. This will do for the same purpose on the other hand, which may be a source of pleasure to you while I am in this country with Mr. Y., and you probably may be able to hear from us through each other oftener than you would were you to remain strangers. . . .

If I attempt to write the state of things here it would be an endless job, and nothing new to you, for it would be hard work to represent things in too large a way. I will mention a melancholy circumstance I fear that took place on our ship while at sea: nine men left our ship in a small boat when we were a hundred miles from Monterey in a calm, with two days provisions. The next day it blew strong and they have not been heard from since, and undoubtedly have been lost and nine men met a watery grave. Do not fear I shall expose myself, for I will not hazard my life or health even for gold.

As regards trouble or safety, give yourselves no uneasiness. A man here is hung for stealing. Everything in the streets or at the mines is perfectly safe left out doors. Good order prevails. The worst thing I have seen is the amount of gambling, which is immense. More money gambled every day in this territory than there is in Wall Street. Every opportunity that I get you shall hear from me. . . .

I wrote you from Valparaiso, which I suppose you will receive before this, as this will not leave until the first of next month, at which time I shall be up to my eyes in dirt. I have brought too much luggage and shall have to store it here. I shall probably spend the winter at the mines, unless some other speculation offers by which I can make more money.

William Smith Jewett

Letter to his family
23 December 1849

Here we are at last, in that wonderful land we have heard so many stories of, stories of every character, length and interest. I have been ashore and am not able to contradict one of them. I should think, by the appearance of things, that all you hear in the papers is quite true. They have, however, got through their riots and now perfect order reigns, strict laws, and every man seems to mind his own business and to let his neighbours alone. Such perfect harmony you would look for in vain in a[nother] place so densely populated. This is very important to well-disposed people, and I think they by far out number any other class, natives, foreigners and all of the rowdy sort. There is scarcely a crime and rarely a theft.

We arrived here on the 17th, making one of the quickest voyages from the States—just five months sailing time, and every man of us in perfect health. This town is composed of the greatest conglomeration of trapsticks for the protection of humanity from the elements that the world ever knew. It is about the size of Pokeepsie: houses, tents, hen-coops, dog-kennels and all. Your first impression is that there has been a great earthquake, shaking up a city, houses, men (I would say women and children, but there's none to shake), but every thing that is here looks as though it has been shaken into a complete jelly, for the rainy season is now at its height, and the mud is on the average three foot deep, and the few houses and many tents yet holding up their heads are as yet in part undissolved particles of matter which, if there is much more water added, certainly [will] decompose.

The first thing we done after casting anchor was to jump for the shore—we must see those big lumps and Californy. We had long pre-viously prepared ourselves in the morning by brushing our shoes and shaving our faces (for we have always shaved on making port), putting on white shirts, best coats and pants, and stood wistfully look-ing for the town with our spyglasses as we floated slowly into the har-bour with the tide. It was a calm, beautiful day with the thermometer at 50° and "Oh!" we constantly exclaimed, "what a lovely winter's cli-mate!" And gradually as the beautiful bay opened to our view, the town appeared. The vessels first—ships, ships beyond ships stretch-ing away to the southeastward until shut out by the hills the city is to be built upon. There are about three hundred sail here, and as many more up the Sacramento—*and gold enough for all!*

as many more up the sacramento — and gold enough for all:

This is as it appeared to us on entering harbour the city being behind the central hill and tents whitening them in all directions — vess.

This is as it appeared to us on entering harbour, the city being behind the central hill and tents whitening them in all directions. Vessels sunk and rotting down around the bay and all nearly deserted. We came to anchor and cast off one boat for the shore. On landing, it was quite dark by this time and the lights of the town were shining forth in every part, which seemed all alive with people. We started up from the wharf. It's true there was a little mud, but it must, thought we, be drier farther in the town! Not yet, we must pick our way! Pick, jump, stride and totter and we got somewhat into something that no doubt looks very like a street on a map but it was not recognizable in its natural form, although they call it "Broadway." It proved so to us, for some got across and some got half way across and some tried to get across. But they all succeeded in getting *stuck*. Stuck fast in the mud, blacked boots, *best* pantaloons and all.

"Oh, help me out!" cried one. "I can't get out myself!" says the other. "Oh dear," says a third, "I've lost my boot." "Shocking! What shall we do?" say we all. "Go on board again and wait for daylight." And all coming to the conclusion that we never found such heavy mud anywhere at home, concluded that it must be caused by the gold in it, [and] thought it best to comply with the recommendation, so with much ado we got back on board our comfortable vessel, where we scraped and washed as well as we could.

The next morning at breakfast time the port captain by his example when he came on board taught us how to dress. He said it wasn't so bad now as last week—now the boots [were] only required to be four feet long. So we put on our *four footed* boots, coarse clothes and went ashore the second time.

Take the poorest parts of your village, knock down all the houses, build them up again, cover their roofs with straw beds ticks, sprinkle over the whole a good-sized Methodist camp meeting and you have a

San Franciscan compound—*above the mud.* The New York influence here is very strong, and by way of keeping up its good old customs, they had a fire here yesterday among all this rubbish. With you it would not cost ten thousand to rebuild the houses, yet here the paper of today makes a literal statement of each individual house and it amounts to over a million, and two days ago it would have brought it in cash. The world's age never knew such an era as this. No sagacity could have predicted it; no human intellect can foretell its result. It is difficult to say which predominates here: mud, men or gold.

Issac W. Baker

Journal
12 January 1850

San Francisco. "A beautiful country, romantic scenery, excellent harbor, a fine climate and plenty of game. This is the place for *me* in the winter season," thinks I as I came on deck and looked around on the morning after we anchored.

* * * * "It's the most degraded, immoral, uncivilized and dirty place that can be imagined, and the sooner we are away from *here* the better for us," were my after thoughts five minutes after being landed on shore!

'Twas the latter part of the rainy season. After a long pull from the vessel against a very strong tide, and passing vessels of all descriptions and of every nation—English, French, Hamburg, Danes, Swedes, Norwegians and Russians as well as Yankees—some ashore, aground, sunk or capsized, some hauled up, stripped, and with notices attached, such as "Storage," "Lumber for sale" [or] "Boarding & Lodging" &c in large capitals continually staring us in the face from all sides, as we approach the landing. And that landing was a curious place too. After having forced our boat through a fleet of others which lay alongside a sort of pier (at the end of which was a hulk for the double accommodation of storage and boarding house), we mounted a flight of steps and found ourselves in the interior of a hotel (hot hell if you choose), a wooden building perhaps thirty to forty feet square, boarded and whitewashed outside, and inside ceiled with cotton cloth, and, excepting overhead, papered with fancy hangings; a door at each end, and a complete thoroughfare. On one side was a bar with the "choicest liquors"—on the other, a table, a man, a pack of cards, and a heap of dollars and doubloons! The latter of which lay invitingly "piled up" and offering a grand chance of making a splendid fortune in a few minutes, for *somebody else* than yourself, if you had plenty of money to hazard. The fact is—I was in a gambling house and grogshop as soon as I touched the shore, but as I had not a particle of money, I was safe enough, and passed independently through, merely "taking an observation"!

Upon getting through this saloon we emerged into a—bed of mud, any where from ankle deep to "off soundings." Uphill too at that. I looked, found 'twas no use, put my trowsers inside my boots, and started. Got along bravely, but as I was for sight seeing, soon halted to recconnoitre. Attracted by music, entered another building with "Exchange Office" over the door. More drinking, more gold and more gambling. Roulette tables, cards, dice with every chance to exchange your gold and silver for—nothing! Came out on the piazza and looked around. Plenty of business on a small scale, sundry peddlers of knives, trinkets and clothing, with their arms filled with their different wares and their feet deep in the mud, and alternately attending to one and the other.

I was much amused at the sight of a "Restorator" opposite, with its attracting signs: "Hot coffee, cakes, &c." It consisted of a two-wheeled old fashioned covered wagon, backed to the verge of a hill and there stuck in the mud. Between the shafts stood a man, with his bed, bedding, W. T. Goods and all his little wares behind him, in the wagon, and outside or in front, a table formed by the shafts placed on a couple boxes, with boards across on which were his attracting viands: bread and butter, buns, cakes &c. He had a fluent tongue, and considerable custom.

Directly alongside was another specimen of humanity, in the shape of an "Old Tar," snugly ensconced in a little tent of "twilled cotton" which covered perhaps ten square feet of—mud! In front of him was his chest, answering for a table, on which were a set of knives and forks and cups and saucers, a few loaves, pies cakes and buns, and alongside a tea kettle of hot coffee sizzling over an iron furnace. Presently along came a couple of customers. Jack politely introduced them into his *saloon,* and as they sat on his *beds* (a heap of straw), served them with the "fixins" with the grace and skill of an accomplished waiter!

Crossing the narrow street, I looked into another of these "respectable" dens, a bar room, well furnished with mahogany chairs sofas and tables, and covered of course with no small quantity of mud (the floors being *shovel'd* instead of swept). Behind this bar was a lady(?)—the first I had yet seen—dispensing the liquor to various customers, and taking in the "quarters" "fist over hand."

Farther up in the city, things are pretty much the same, but on rather a larger scale: larger buildings, houses and stores of various kinds, larger streets with larger *fields* of mud, large and more splendid gambling shops, a pretty large square with a liberty pole in the centre, around which, and underneath the American revenue flag which was flying at the top, are gathered a crowd of people of all nations bidding for houselots, horses or any other articles offered by the Auctioner, who, encased in long boots, is talking the "soft sawder" into the surrounding speculators.

The city is laid out in squares, and from the highest hills, makes a splendid appearance, as not only are there many fine looking buildings, which shew well at a distance, but also hundreds of tents of all sizes and descriptions, and of various colors, squads of which scattered around on the hill sides, fill up the valleys, and shew to great advantage. A beautiful view of the bay and surrounding scenery may here be taken, the entrance to the harbor at the westward, and that of the Bay of San Pablo at the northward, while directly beneath lay crowds of shipping shewing flags of all nations—a miniature forest—boats pulling here and there, discharging cargo, steamers running to and fro, and all the peculiar business-like appearance of any large Atlantic or European city. Such is San Francisco *now*. What it formerly has been, what it was only one year since, we all know, and (as with every other new country) what it eventually will be still remains to be proved.

Robert Smith Lammot

Letter to his father
30 December 1849

We have been ashore now 15 days and until today I have not had one moment to write before. The first week it rained incessantly, and in consequence the streets are almost impassable. Mr. Graham, Palmer, myself and two others engaged board and lodging at one of the hotels(?) for a week at $22, which was considered remarkably low. The eating was good enough—but the sleeping—six berths fixed in a stall like a box in an oyster cellar about six feet square—three on each side with just room enough between the berths for one man to stand.

These stalls are framed with wood and covered with colored cambric, open at the top, so that no one can speak without being heard over the whole room. And as there are twenty of them in one room of about 50 by 25—or as they say here "fine accommodations" for 120 sleepers, not counting about 50 who sleep on the floor—you can form some idea of the comforts of those who lodge there. To add to the list, the fleas are innumerable. . . .

Please send me out by some vessel two pairs of long boots, the legs may be continued almost indefinitely, as you cannot cross a street, scarcely, without getting knee deep in mud. Let them come six inches above the knee, and get one of the boys to give them a good coat of dubbing. Those that Hawes made us are very good but will not keep the feet dry, especially when the soft mud comes in over the tops. Please send us also a dozen *blue twilled* flannel shirts, such as are worn by sailors. They are much better than red, let them be washed before sending, as the color comes off at first and washing is an expensive luxury here.

Lucius Anson Booth

Letter to Newton Booth
16 July 1849

Would you rather have a short and unsatisfactory letter or none at all? If the former—here goes. I came here a week ago (9 days) on the Schooner *Swallow* from San Blas and Mazatlan—(31 days from Mazla. from S. B.) I wrote you last from Guadalaharo—previously Mexico V. Cruz &c—from G. had a good time to S. B. Had a *long* passage and not very pleasant of 31 days on the Schooner. I should like not to cut things so short, but give you some particulars but my time from now till tomorrow, when I expect to leave here for the mines is more valuable to me than I dare tell you, and I have been gaining necessary information and waiting for the Steamer to arrive, hoping to get letters from you and then answer in full, but have concluded to go up the river sooner than I had expected. The Steamer *California* came up last night, but her mail will not be open till tomorrow morning, so that I will barely have time to get my letters before starting—but I will try to answer them from Sacramento City in time for this Steamer's return—and if I get time in California I will write you many things which I would like to, but can not now—but I will candidly say I doubt if I ever get the time here. I must write very few letters and short ones—or rather to but few persons and they must tell my other friends. There is no regular mail above this place [San Francisco], hence another difficulty but *as I can* you shall hear from me. But *you* and all my other friends who will, write to me and *the oftener the better* (postage is the only thing cheap here) I *will remember* and treasure.

I have to cook my share and wash my own clothes—I can't yet afford to pay $6.00 per dozen for washing, and I must sleep enough, wash up &c on Sundays, when business stops or I shall "run down" like a watch—even though I could earn $30 per day and I expect to bring it up very near that as quick as I can communicate with Mort and perhaps before. Mort, Ten Kate, Denis, Blackman, Mel. and Wallace are up the river (Sacramento) but I can't tell till I go up what they are making. Others up there are getting about an ounce per day. Capt. Stewart went up the San Joachinn. I have seen none of the boys since they left N[ew] O[rleans], but have seen one who traveled with them to this place. They left here some four weeks ago, *all in good health.*

The prospects here are better than I expected in many respects. Gold is plentier, and if we keep our health I shall ask no farther guaranter of as large a fortune as my moderate acquisitiveness desires, in a very short time. Still lest you should read this to some friend, let me say that I advise no one to come to California. I give no *advice* on the subject. Those who *do* come, make the journey, and live to get their fortunes and carry them home, *will have earned them.* But I am glad that I am here and sorry that some of my friends I could name (who thought of it) did not come *when* and *how* I did. The same route could be taken by the proper [illegible] but this is not so good a time of year on account of sickness in Vera Cruz, &c. It is now sickly at Panama— the cholera is there and *very hot.*

It almost bewilders one to look around and see so many things in which one could make an immense fortune at a dash as it were. For instance—and if I give you one I shall never know when to stop— there is not a dray here, but there are a few carts and they are worth $600.00 apiece—with harness (Sacramento City, Stockton, &c &c above are in the same condition). There are now and will be this year 300 ships to discharge, store cargo &c. There is employment in San Francisco today for 50 drays besides the carts. Cartage per load is $2.00 the *shortest* distance—3 if any distance. One man who owns a cart told me his driver with whom he divides equally earned the day before $41.00. Hand carts light and strong and wheelbarrows could be sold here to the extent of some *thousands,* and these articles there is no reason to believe are on the way out from U.S., nearer than which they can not be procured. The town is on the side of the hills, hence the great want of wheelbarrows.

A small schooner with some heavy things I could name for ballast might leave N.Y. at once and sell out here (next February) at a profit of 500 to 1000 per cent. But first let me tell you, lest you think this is but temporary, that the *gold is here* and people will pour in here for *years* to come. I should like to send to N.Y. for many things, and thought of asking you to sacrifice my little interest in Terre Haute and take 50¢ to the $ for it and invest in the *right* things on which I could make 1000 per cent—and should do so, if I did not think I could make all I want any how.

I'll give you some of the prices going here: labor per day $8.00, carpentry $14, blacksmith 20 to 30, clerk $10, a lawyer charges $200 for making out a deed, a druggist $1.00 per ounce for salts, magnesia, c[od liver] oil &c &c, a Dr. $16 for a prescription. Saleratus is $10.00 *per. lb.* (scarce now), butter is $1.50 lb., cheese 50¢, salt 20¢ lb., coffee 18, sugar 18, molasses 75, lard 50, flour 12 1/2 (by the barrel $14.00), a pie costs 50¢, glass of liquor 25¢, cup of coffee 25, loaf of bread 25, bottle of ale $2.00, tin pan for washer $5.00 &c. Shaving is $1.00, hair cutting $2.00. Dry goods of any kind by the yard there is no sale, for there is nobody to make them up. Ready made clothing is cheap. The above are retail prices, but at auction many things are selling very low and often below cost. Heavy shippers will loose on many articles. Clothing can be bought at auction at N.Y. prices or less. Everything retails at round prices without much *if any* regard to cost.

I went for some candles last night and asking how many I could have for a dollar, was told three (they were eight to the [illegible] short [illegible]). I told him I ought to have four as I had had before. "Very well," says he, "I only wanted to ask enough." At the same time he was weighing out some "country produce" (i.e., gold, in small specks and lumps) for a chap just down from the mines who was paying a debt he owed for one pair [of] pistols which he had bought of the merchant three or four weeks before on a credit. There was some 2 lbs and 1/3, amounting however to just $450.00. This *I saw. . . .*

I have told you almost nothing that I should like to. To all the family I have much love to send, and while at present I can not address you separately, I shall take it as a kindness if you, dear Lu, and Lizzie as well as all the rest will write to me here. . . . Tell anyone who writes to *particularize.* One of my friends (Hays) who came with me from N[ew] O[rleans] is writing for the N.O. *Cresent.* Read his letters—what happened to him did to me.

Alfred DeWitt

Letter to his brother George
28 August 1849

I intended to write to you while at Panama, but concluded while there to postpone it until we arrived at this place, with the intention of then giving you a full account of our trip to this new but I hope temporary home. I hope that you will not entertain the idea that I have lost the natural affection of a Brother, for from my not writing as promised I fear you might think that I had become careless and indifferent, and I feel that I ought to have redeemed my promise long before this. Though I have not written to you, yourself and family often share my thoughts and your letter received here during my absence has been read by us frequently and with a desire to receive more from you, and that our correspondence will be more frequent. . . .

We kept in sight of the coast nearly all the way, and several times I took my wife on deck to see the whales sporting around the vessel. We arrived here 4 June. I landed early in the morning and took Harrison [his business partner] by surprise. He had heard of my detention at Valparaiso and did not expect me back in a month, and when I told him that I had a wife on board he laughed and took it as a joke and continued thinking so until he had read a part of Uncle John's letter which mentioned the fact. He went with me immediately to secure quarters, and after looking around and finding nothing but miserable shantees which they asked $200 [to] $300 per month for, we concluded to purchase a neat little cottage near the store in joint account. We were given possession of it the next day and I brought my wife ashore and we have since lived as comfortable as we could wish, and have a pleasant family. We number five: Mr. Harrison, Mr. West (our bookkeeper), Henry [his brother] and ourselves. We have enjoyed good health with the exception of a few days my wife and self took turns with an attack of dysentary. Henry is now unwell with an attack of fever and we have kept him at the house; we expect he will be at his duties again in a day or so.

I have been so much engaged since I returned that I hardly know what is going on, except as regards our own business. We have had a large emigration pouring in here from all parts of the world, drawn by the stories of gold mines to make their fortunes in this El Dorado, as it is called in the east. Some are fortunate and by industry, energy, etc. do pretty well, but from what I see, the majority are not pleased with the country and climate, are not as fortunate in finding such vast amounts of gold as they expected, and become disappointed, discouraged, some go home. Others would go if they had the means. This sudden influx of a large population has caused a great deal of suffering, many who come here are not suited to the hardships and want of comforts they have to undergo. They try their luck at the mines and after finding it requires more than they can endure, endeavor to procure places as clerks in stores, or other situations to which they are better adapted. The effect of it is that a great many are idle, and in this country where board and labor is so high, they can get out of money and become disheartened. . . .

Many economize by putting up a light frame and covering it with canvass. Our winter commences the latter part of November, I expect to see then a great scattering of the rag houses. The town has a most singular appearance, houses from the States, from China, England, sheet-iron houses, canvass houses, and tents are all mixed up helter skelter. If a fire should take place in one end of the town nothing could save the whole from conflagration. We are in some measure secure, being somewhat removed from the main collection.

Since we have been here my wife has connected herself with the congregation of the Rev. Mr. Williams. We have church in a large tent. I have written home for a church frame to be sent out—very few are willing to give anything towards such objects and the expense falls heavily on them, but we think if we get a good church up the attendance will be better, and have a beneficial effect on the character of the people.

It is now 11 1/2 O'c P.M. and I have written quite a long letter which I hope will be acceptable to you, though I have deferred writing much longer than I anticipated. Business must be my excuse. I hope that you will favor me with many more letters, and if you wish to know any thing more particular about the country that I have not described, you must ask me the questions and it will give me the greatest pleasure to [illegible] what I can pick up in my intercourse with the trading. I must say though that I am not yet versed in Castilian parlance, and in fact we are now so Americanized that there is not much use for it.

Macondray & Co. Records

Letter to J. M. Forbes, Esq.
1 September 1849

We arrived here on the 18th prepared to find an extraordinary state of things, and confess the reality exceeds our expectations. A speculation is going on here in real estate wilder than anything that we have known. Lots of land which sold for $1500 six months since have been sold lately for $15,000 [to] $20,000, and the mania is not confined to this place alone. The old game of paper cities is playing through this whole place. Lots in Sacramento City 80 x 80 bring $15,000, and titles here are all worthless. Quit claims are the only transfer of property, and such a thing as a warranted deed is unknown, except a swindling warranted, which warrants and defends against one's self their heirs and executors.

It is all based upon credit, a small per centage only being paid down. We see nothing to warrant such a state of things except the enormous rates of rents. In some instances a man can pay these enormous rates, erect a building, and let rooms enough to pay the whole rent in one year. Gamblers infest the place, and by the enormous rates which they are able to pay—$1800 a month in some instances—establish the rents. Almost the entire population is involved in this mania, so that money is very scarce and brings enormous rates. . . . How long it may continue you can tell as well as we can, but it seems to us that there must be a wind up before long.

This state of things has embarrassed us somewhat in getting a place suitable to do our business in, but we have refused to purchase real estate, preferring to pay high rates for short leases believing that these prices must come down. The market is generally overstocked. . . . Of course there is no such thing as insurance here, and if a fire should take place during the high winds which prevail daily, the whole place would be swept.

We find a much better population than we expected. There is better security for property here than in N.Y. The streets in the evening or Sunday are as quiet as a New England village. Doors are left unlocked at night and large amounts of gold are left unguarded in counting rooms remote from dwellings, and goods unwatched on the beach. Immense quantities of good[s] are suffering for want of storage and must be ruined when the rainy season comes on, as it will be impossible to get storage for them, and we fear our friends will receive some Flemish[?] accounts.

The receipts from the mines continue undiminished and new deposits are continually discovered. We can say to you what we would not to anyone else, that we believe the largest houses here are very much embarrassed and we should feel no confidence in consigning to them, and further, that business is generally conducted in a careless manner and with great unfaithfulness to the interests of the principals. This may seem to you presumptious, after so short a residence here, but we cannot resist the evidences which come to our notice. It is perfectly idle for us to quote prices for anything and we refuse to do so, for the greatest irregularities exist in the market. No quotations can be relied on as a basis for future transactions. Everything must depend upon the amount of goods coming here.

We regret that we have not been able to do anything for you in Gold dust for this Steamer. She takes a large amount of specie no doubt, but shippers generally prefer sending the dust under insurance, and so much money is locked up here in real estate that merchants do not seem ready to make prompt remittances. Then we have been here but a short time and we have actually found some difficulty in drawing the whole amount placed in Appleton's hands. . . . There is no demand here for Exchange or London, we have not had one application, which is also the case with an agent of the Rothschild's who came out with us. We think we shall be able to do something for you by the next Steamer. We think a decided advantage might be gained if you would authorize us to draw at 60 ds. sight when we cannot ship the dust by the same steamer which takes the Bills, as they refuse freight for 24 hours before sailing day, and people often put off buying Exchange to the last moment. If we could draw up to the closing of the *mails,* we might often, we think, do so at an advanced rate and you could by a subsequent steamer get the dust nearly if not in time to meet the Bills. Sixty day Bills are the custom here.

The *Memnon* arrived on the 28th and is consigned to us. She is our first ship. Most of her cargo is well adapted to the market and we hope we shall be able to send her owners a good account of her. The labor scheme has been generally a failure. They break up almost without an exception immediately on arrival. We shall use what influence we have to prevent this [from taking] place when those in which you are interested arrive.

William F. Reed

Journal
9 September 1849

Since arriving here I have continued to live on board the *Magnolia* as have the most of the crew and passengers, as they had the privilege of stopping on board for the space of a fortnight, and the most were glad to avail themselves of this chance until they were prepared to start for the "diggins," for board on shore is $12 to $16 per week and no vegetables at that. Labor and other things are in like proportion, as truckmen will not go with the smallest load the shortest distance less than one dollar. Boatmen get one dollar for each passenger they take from ship to shore or from shore to ship. The clink of money is heard every where. A man gets as much for one day's work here as he does at home for a weeks'. Gaming houses carry on a great stroke of business, the betters losing and winning thousands as cool as a cucumber. The town is full of emigrants and they are constantly arriving. Hundreds of tents cover the hills around occupied by those getting ready to go up to the mines. Store houses can not be built fast enough to receive the goods that are continually arriving, and the streets are lined with merchandize of all descriptions, much of it spoiling. The most of articles such as tools, fire arms, thin clothing can be obtained as cheap as at home, and we are sorry that we brought our provisions or clothing of any kind, any more than we required for the passage or a few weeks more, for if we leave our chests in store while gone to the mines (and we cannot carry them with us, freight is so high) the storage will amount to as much as they are worth in the first place.

William F. Reed

Journal
14 September 1849

For the last four days have been living on shore in our tent, which by the way is a fine one as there is in all California. Our company is diminished to eight, three having sold their shares to the remainder the day after we arrived; it seems to be a difficult matter for these companies to hold together and our company is not alone in dividing. Our situation is a very pleasant one, being in a valley amid a little village of tents something like a half mile from the city(!) of San Francisco and a few rods from the beach, behind us on lofty hills covered with a species of live oak which only grows in a kind of scraggly bush, the soil for miles around is a dry sand and does not seem capable of producing anything, but it is said that during the rainy season the grass grows luxuriantly. At present there is no signs of rain. I was much disappointed in the climate which is anything but agreeable; the nights are cold foggy and unwholesome and the middle of the day hot dusty and sultry.

Anne Willson Booth

Journal
23 September 1849

Being Sunday, we resolved upon going ashore and attending church. Accordingly, set off in the boat for the shore. On ascending the beach, the whole town burst upon our views. Tents and houses, alternately arranged as to location. We walked pretty much all over the city. I should suppose there are about 2400 houses, some of them quite tastefully built, all pretty much in the cottage style. We saw some miserably squalid looking creatures, living in tents and in the midst of dirt and wretchedness. There are a great many Chinesemen here. They have a very singular appearance, and are easily distinguished from the Spaniards.

We attended the Baptist chapel. Mr. Taylor preached, having received an invitation to do so from the pastor, Mr. Wheeler, who reminded me very much of Mr. Morris in manners and appearance. There was a large congregation, very respectable, about one dozen Ladies, all of whom were perfectly genteel in appearance, and dressed quite fashionably. After church, we were passing out the door, a Lady and Gentleman were standing, having a little boy by the hand, very nearly the size of our dear little George and not at all unlike him. We stopped involuntarily to look at him, when the Lady and Gentleman inquired if we were not strangers. Telling them we were, they gave us a very kind invitation to walk into their dwelling, which was a few yards from the church.

We did so, and were delighted at finding any thing so perfectly beautiful in California. The house is but one story, surrounded by a balcony, entrance in the middle, with large rooms on either side. The rooms are 14 in number and open into each other by large folding doors. The walls and partitions are covered with a white canvass, which appears to be whitened and seamed with black, giving it somewhat the appearance of column paper. The rooms are handsomely furnished, and had an air of comfort and elegance we were not prepared to see in San Francisco. Mr. and Mrs. Ross are from New York, they informed us. There were very few ladies here, but what little society there is might be called very good. They gave us a very kind invitation to visit them frequently, and told us they would call on board to see us. Remaining about an hour, we left much pleased with our visit.

We then took another stroll through the town. Every thing was very quiet and orderly, although there does not appear to be a general suspension of business [on Sundays]. Gambling houses are numerous, are kept open all the time, day and night. We saw large piles of gold and silver, heaped up on the tables, and were told there is more gambling here than in New Orleans. At 1 o'clock we returned to the ship very much fatigued and covered with dust. I forgot to mention that Capt. Codman took breakfast with us this morning—we were all pleased to hear him converse, he is very conversant and made himself very agreeable.

Ephraim Garter

Letter to his Parent
13 January 1850

I was eight months and two days on my journey from Medina to this place and during all the way I had my health admirably, till about four days after my arrival here when I was taken quite sick and remained so for about 3 weeks, after which I began to mend and am now nearly well again. . . .

[I] arrived here on the 13th of Dec. I was lucky to find Gibson, Smith and Bartlett here. They are carrying on the Banking Business and they also keep a lodging room in the same establishment. They kindly invited me to take up lodging with them which I readily accepted and they have done what they could for me under the circumstances. Young Bucker of Thourdeville also did me good service by giving me physics, tonics, etc. I am now recovering very fast and expect to be entirely well in a few days. I had but a little over a hundred dollars when I arrived here and a considerable part of that is gone already. Money is nothing here so far as spending it for living is concerned. Everything is high beyond imagination. Board for instance is from $15 to $45 per week and other things in proportion. I of course have paid no such prices, for I have got along with the kindness of my friends in another way. But I don't despair—I shall get into some business or employment till the dry season begins which will probably be by the first of March, when I shall go to the mines and try what I can do there in the way of digging gold. . . .

One word as to California. It is not worth a pin for farming purposes. Then there are a few scattering valleys of excellent land, but not one acre of it in a thousand can possibly ever be tilled. It is very mountainous and the few narrow valleys must be irrigated before they will produce in this climate and there is not one in ten of them that has sufficient water to do that. The country is almost wholly destitute of timber for fires and building and one of the northwestern states is worth 100 such counties of this to live in.

Anonymous

Journal of Voyage from New Bedford to San Francisco
23 September 1849

Lodged last night with Edward at bachelors hall. Mr. Palmer and partner from Nantucket owned by them, large enough to lodge 6 or 8. Headquarters for all people from that Island. Welcomed me and invited me to make it my home &c. I met Mr. Summerhays and some half a dozen others who had seen me when I visited their "good old Nantucket" as they call her.

A gentleman from the mines put into my hands a specimen piece of gold he dug weighing 19 ounces. It had a very fine feel, valued it at 500. Some fine singing, plenty of wine, cigars &c. Visited Happy Valley. This name is a great "misnomer" by the way, for [a] more squalid unhealthy place I never saw. Hundreds of tents in and about it with vast numbers of sick lying in them on the ground and about them in all directions. Poor fellows, many of them must die from the melone-kolly fact of having no one to do or take the least interest in them. If one is without friends or money and becomes sick, he has little or no chance of ever being better.

Persons of most all vocations live in these tents: dry goods, hardware, eating places, liquor establishments, boarding, lodging—some are occupied by families, some with a large number of children—gambling hells [*sic*]—private tents of associated mechanics, laborers, &c—tents for killing cattle, selling clothes, boots, shoes, hats, caps—

for washing—for buying and selling gold—keeping school and holding religious meetings in &c &c &c. And such quantities of good[s]. Cost of clothing, boots, shoes, hats, caps, cravats, shirts &c is astonishing to behold. Washing being from six to eight dollars per dozen, won't pay to get them washed. Are worn till they are as dirty as they can be endured, then a new suit is bought and sometimes taken to the shore. The individual then washes himself, casts away his old and puts on his new rigout, wearing it as the other, buying new &c as before. Great numbers of the most respectable purchase shirts by the dozen, wearing them as long as they can with decency, put on a clean one and toss the soiled out of their windows. Hose in same manner—in fact their whole wardrobe comes under the same head. I saw a copy of an advertisement: "Prof. Williams will continue his school for the present in the Presbyterian Church (Large Tent) on Dupont Street."

James S. Barnes

Letter
28 February 1850

We arived here a week ago to day and the steamer sails to morrow i cant give much acount of the country every thing is very high board is from 14$ 30$ a week carpenters wages is from 10 to 16$ a day i got work the first day i came here i found anthany Moubry the first day i came ashore he was to work putting a † on a roman Catholic Church he was not dead as was reported he will rite your a few lines and put it in this letter Anthany and thomas Collins and myself and 4 other young men live together we keep bachelers hall it costs us about 8$ a week to live we live first rate we have one cook and baker we have good Orang County butter and potatoes and beef stake and every thing els that is good i have not eat butter 3 times since i left the States butter is worth 85 cts a pound potatoes 15 cts a pound ever thing els in proportion i went to church last sunday and heard a good serman it was the first serman i have heard since i left the States there is 5 Churches here i would advise all young men who are in good buisness to stay where they are all though iam satisfied that i have come the worst undertaking is to get here i pased from cold to hot wether and from hot to cold it is very pleasant here at presance the tops of the mountains are covered with snow the middle of Jan where i was the thermometer stood at 90 deg in the shade i have not seen nor herd from Calvin sloat i have forgotton where his folks told me to inquire for him i wish you would ask them and let me know in your next letter i have not got your papers yet rite me a long letter for the postage is high it is 40 cts i am in good health and good spirrits rite rite often

Anne Willson Booth

Journal
24 September 1849

All hands up bright and early this morning, making ready to move ashore. . . . During the passage, the Capt. sold the house over the main hatchway to one of the passengers for the sum of $60—it cost about $25 in Baltimore. He has refused an offer of $500 for it since we arrived. I would be ashamed to write all the different incidents illustrating the plenty of money in this country that have come under my observation, so incredible they appear. Dr. Buckner remarked this morning, he should not attempt to give his friends a description of the place and its condition—but would refer them to the miraculous stories in the Arabian Nights, as he thought we were about to realize things equally as wonderful. . . . The weather is damp and raw, with a heavy fog, every morning until about 10 o'clock—the breeze then sets in from the sea, and it clears away again. There has been no rain here for six months—the rainy season will soon begin.

J. K. Osgood

Letter to George Strang
20 August 1849

I am in an odd humor but in San Francisco one has an undoubted right to be, it is an odd place: unlike any other place in creation, and so it should be; for it is not created in the ordinary way, but hatched like chickens by artificial heat. The climate is the most disagreeable that Nature in her most fitful mood, ever formed for man to respire under.

The mornings are generally quite warm until 11-12 o'clock, and then owing to the rarefaction of the air by the large body of water forming the bay, and the heat of the high land surrounding it, a strong breeze sets in from the sea and blows very fresh, frequently a very moderate gale, until evening. Consequently the latter are quite cool and comfortable for over coats, but the worst and decidedly the most disagreeable is the dust which owing to the sandy soil is very plentiful and which is hurled about in clouds in the most unmerciful manner, much to the injury of one's eyes, and very much in opposition to their comfort. Such a thing as cleanliness is unheard of, for half an hour's exposure in the streets turns one's shirt collar a complete brown, but not only is the dirt manifest to a person's sight, but most uncomfortably so to his feelings. The sand perforates every pore; in every movement one feels its grating. It gets into boots, into hats, into pockets, into one's hair into his mouth, and into every place where there is a crevice to lodge it. To retail grocers it may be profitable, but to us poor devils who are obliged to pay $6 a dozen for washing, it is the reverse: it is all together wrong and a great mistake in Natural Economy to furnish abundance of dirt and no washer women.

Our costume is not yet decided upon, the disposition to ape foreign customs leading some to adopt the Mexican poncho or blanket, a very graceful garment when concealing a commanding figure. Some of them are of very fine texture and high cost. Most of us staid and sober citizens adopt the New York dress, barring the cleanliness and taste which characterise the Gotham-ites. Cloaks are worn by those fortunate enough to own them. Not being one of the lucky number, I luxuriate in a Monkey Jacket which, disdaining all ornament, prides itself upon its utility and is a valuable garment withal, a garment of good parts. Moreover I have an affection for it, it having shared with me the voyage round the stormy cape, received the seas which old Neptune in moments of ill humor would shower upon me, and in various occasions it has furnished undoubted proofs of its fidelity, so I cannot discard it. Straps are not worn nor polished boots. If pantaloons are long, we turn up the bottoms to keep them out of the dust.

The cost of living varies according to the comforts that one desires (by comforts I mean California comforts). Boarding cost at the restaurants from $14–$21 per week, and 3–5 dollars per day by single meals. Lodging with a comfortable room—that is, with a chair and wash stand and fixtures in it—costs $15–$24 per week; full board and lodging $30–$40 per week. Nearly half of the population resides in tents and considerable business is transacted under the same covering.

Merchandise of all descriptions is very low, especially heavy goods and all articles of ship's use. In retailing however, sellers manage to obtain high prices; they would soon break if they did not, for their store expenses are enormous. Real estate is extravagantly high; lots in not very eligible situations 24 x 60 feet commanding $11,000, others in the vicinity of and on the Plaza occupied by gamblers have sold much higher. A building recently built by Steinburger of 2 stories about 18 x 60, rents for $4500 to gamblers.

These prices you can see are beyond all reason and are only supported by the extensive immigration. The gold, although abundant, does not furnish basis for any thing like the height to which they are extended. There is no commerce, nor no exports except the gold, which furnishes basis for less trade than any article which the earth produces because it does not require the corresponding labor, (which after all is the true wealth of a State) and then the money does not remain here. The gold leaves us as fast as it is accumulated, and consequently we must continually create new capital. Yet in spite of these things, I have no doubt that prices will be sustained for some time owing to the immigration, which will continue to flow hither so long as gold continues to be found in any abundance. . . .

Coin of all kinds is very scarce, it being extremely difficult to obtain enough to pay the duties on foreign goods that arrive. . . .

There is no standard price for any article—the value being regulated according to the wants of the purchaser. Storage is very high. $1.50 per month for barrels and at the same rate for measurement goods. There are no fire insurance companies here and the holders of property must take their own risk. There is neither any fire department, and a fire once commenced would not stop till it had consumed the place entirely, the buildings being very slight they would catch like tinder. . . .

Many young men from New York, driven hither by the thirst of adventure, find that however pleasant in imagination, hardships are stubborn things to encounter, and that the hard ground does not afford so soft a bed as feathers, and consequently in actual battle they are easily vanquished. We have applications almost every day by clerks for employment. The labor at the mines is too severe, they would only give their life in exchange for the gold, or in the search for it, and of this they soon become aware. There are great many to whom the song "Sweet Sweet Home" never possessed such pathos as it does in California.

I am not of this number however. I am not disappointed in the privations and can endure them. I shall remain here some years. You know that when a man "puts his hand to the plough he must not turn back." I am glad that I came here and am contented to remain—whether it be for good or evil.

Chapter 2

The Ties that Bind

One of the distinguishing features of the gold rush, certainly an aspect that makes it unique among American migrations, is that for the most part the thousands of men and women who came to California did not intend to stay. This was not a movement of immigrants seeking to build a new life in a new land. It is clear from their correspondence and diaries that the vast majority of these people hoped to get rich—preferably quickly—and return home.

The temporary nature of their presence evoked a striking psychological response from the Argonauts. Had they been traditional immigrants they would have somehow managed an emotional break from family, friends, and all that was familiar, determined to make a go of it in their new home. They would have mourned what they had left behind and their hearts would have ached for family members never to be seen again in this world. But as they sent down new roots in the new land their mourning would fade and the aching turn to a wistful nostalgia for what used to be.

For the new residents of California, however, the break with home was an open wound that would never heal—because they did not want it to heal. There was no question of putting the past behind them—what was past would be their future, and they felt a critical need to maintain a link with what they had left unfinished, awaiting their return. The strain was particularly great for husbands and fathers who felt guilty about abandoning their family obligations. They needed to maintain somehow a presence at the family hearth, to continue to fulfill the role of head of the household even though they were three thousand miles away. As the new world they lived in grew ever more bizarre, more filled with temptations and chicanery, as they were strongly buffeted by disappointments and crushed dreams, there was an even stronger need for reminders of a familiar world of quiet domesticity back home, awaiting their return. For those who were literate enough to read and write, letters became that indispensable link, a connection that for many became—in a very literal sense—a lifeline.

For women, both those who came west and those who were left behind, correspondence played an important role in helping to redefine their gender roles. Women who suddenly found themselves running farms or making family financial decisions at first looked to their husbands' written instructions for guidance.[1] But as time passed and the unavoidable lag time between letters became apparent, their self-confidence grew. They began to make decisions on their own and to assume a primary role that they had previously left to their husbands or fathers. For the women who traveled to California, letters helped to construct a temporary feminine milieu that would have been impossible to achieve otherwise, given the small number of female participants in the gold rush. These women might have been immersed in a brusque, overwhelmingly male environment, but a letter from a mother, a sister or a best friend could transport them for at least a brief time to a familiar world of feminine concerns and confidences.

In addition, the discipline of keeping journals and maintaining long-distance correspondence helped many pioneer women comprehend the enormity of their own accomplishments. What had been for them a very protected, circumscribed existence suddenly flared out into a world of life-or-death decisions, of wild economic swings, of daily encounters with strange cultures, of politics and commerce that were raw and raucous.[2] All this had a liberating but disquieting effect, and many women made sense of these changes through the process of writing it all down, their discourse giving meaning to their experience.[3]

The problem, of course, was how to carry on a correspondence from the edge of the civilized world. Prior to February 1849, there was no government-sponsored mail service between California and the United States. A letter writer wishing to send correspondence back east would make arrangements with a ship's officer to carry the letters and deposit them collect-on-delivery at the U.S. post office at his port of entry. For this service the post office would pay the officer two cents (provided the ship was American-owned), and the charge was added to the postage. The letter's recipient would then pay six cents if the letter was delivered locally at the port of entry, or the inland postage rate plus two cents if it was forwarded beyond the port. For mail leaving the East Coast the sender would pay the postage to the port of departure, and the ship's officer would deliver the letter to a customs officer or commercial agent at the west coast destination, to be held until the addressee arrived to pay the additional ship letter fee.[4]

The Treaty of Guadalupe Hidalgo made California a possession of the United States, and its inhabitants were thereby entitled to certain amenities provided by the U.S. government. One privilege Americans had come to expect was a reliable means of written communication. At the beginning of 1849 there were seventeen thousand post offices east of the Mississippi but not one officially established post office in California.[5] William V. Van Voohries was appointed to address the situation, with a mandate to "make arrangements for the establishment of postal routes, for the transmission, receipt and conveyance of letters in California and Oregon."[6]

Van Voohries arrived in San Francisco on 28 February 1849 as a passenger on the maiden voyage of the steamer *California* which, under the government contract awarded to the Pacific Mail Steamship Company, was supposed to be inaugurating West Coast mail service. In Van Voohries's first report to the postmaster general back in Washington DC he enumerated a few problems: 1) The *California* had failed to stop in San Diego or Santa Barbara as scheduled, so he still had in his possession the mail for those ports; 2) it was impossible to hire local postmasters at the rate he had been budgeted, since labor was in short supply and men could easily command five times the amount working at other jobs; and 3) the property values of potential post office sites were pegged far beyond the federal government's ability to pay. He hoped to convince a few established shopkeepers to open postal counters and to serve as part-time postmasters. He also suggested that plans for other California post offices be dropped, and that all mail be delivered first to San Francisco, since most of it was destined for the Bay Area anyway. Van Voohries had planned to send this report back to Washington on the return trip of the *California*, but the U.S. mail steamer was stranded in port when its entire crew jumped ship and headed for the gold fields. The report was sent back on a Peruvian ship.[7]

Van Voohries needn't have bothered. Before his official report had even reached Washington a new postmaster general had been appointed and Van Voohries was terminated and replaced by R. T. P. Allen. Allen arrived in San Francisco on 13 June 1849 to discover the same chaos that Van Voohries had encountered. He too saw that the major problem was the absence of a network of post offices in the hinterlands, which caused the mail to back up in San Francisco. With the influx of Argonauts in full flood, a single steamer that arrived on 2 August 1849 brought eighteen thousand pieces of mail to join the thousands of letters already sitting unsorted.

Allen rolled up his sleeves and went to work. He dropped plans to establish post offices in Santa Barbara, Los Angeles, and San Diego, and turned his attention instead to Benicia, Sacramento, Stockton, San Jose, Vernon, Coloma, and Sonoma. He hired postmasters at salaries above the established limit and set up temporary emergency arrangements to move the mail out of the city and into the hands of the miners in the gold fields. In return for his energy and resourcefulness in getting the mail out, Allen was severely reprimanded by the postmaster general in Washington for failing to follow rules and regulations. He was informed that his temporary arrangements, however expedient and efficacious, were illegal, and that his authorization of expenditures above the budgeted amounts would not be honored by the government. Allen was chastised for his disobedience in failing to establish post offices in the coastal ports—regardless of whether or not they were actually needed. In fairness to the postmaster general, the real problem was an inadequate post office department budget. Congress was willing to appropriate money for a postal network that linked the easily accessible California seaports, but balked at the high cost of providing service to the inland regions.

Meanwhile the tide of letters grew ever more daunting. In one month—October 1849—13,362 letters and 15,571 newspapers arrived from New York State alone.[8] Long lines formed at the post office in San Francisco with the arrival of each steamer. Some men would stand in line all night when a delivery was scheduled; late-comers would offer a packet of gold dust in return for a place near the beginning of the line. The mere word that a mail steamer had entered the Golden Gate could provoke pandemonium.

George Law, whose United States Mail Steamship Company held the government contract for mail service between the East Coast and the Isthmus, realized that the Pacific Mail Steamship Company was unable to keep up with the volume of mail on the western leg, and offered his company's services to the San Francisco postmaster. He too was allowed to carry the mail, but on the condition that the sender indicate on the envelope that he or she wanted the letter to go out on one of Law's ships. This was a clear violation of the Pacific Mail Steamship Company's exclusive government contract and the postmaster general quickly quashed the plan, decreeing that all mail that was sent through the San Francisco post office had to go out on a contract mail steamer only.

The hunger for mail was so insatiable that it led to the establishment of an institution unique to gold rush San Francisco: letter bag operators. For a small fee these entrepreneurs would deliver a letter to the next outgoing steamer (contract or noncontract), thus bypassing the bottleneck (and monopoly) of the United States Post Office. Some letter bag operators required senders to bring the letter to their offices; others set up mail boxes around town and picked up outgoing mail on a regular schedule.[9] Their fees were added to the legally established postage (forty cents per half ounce), but they did a brisk business with San Franciscans who wanted their letters to go out as soon as possible.[10]

It is not surprising, then, that the topic of mail plays such a prominent role in gold rush correspondence. William G. Brown's worried plea to his wife back in Iowa—"Dear Margaret, I feel there must me something wrong. . . . *Write* me soon"—is typical of the agitation felt when time passed without a word from loved ones. Anxiety also reigned back home, when months passed with no word from California. Benjamin C. Howard failed to appreciate the anguish his parents must have felt when they were mistakenly informed that their son's ship had sunk off Valparaiso. (A tardy, jocular letter finally arrived to lift their mourning.) Letters could also bring Argonauts the news of the death of a family member: Jonathan Locke's mother, Josiah Griswold's two children.

Good or ill, the news that letters contained linked the recipient with the daily life he or she had left behind. A letter was an intimate talk with an absent friend or a longed-for spouse. A letter was like holding in one's hands a piece of home. Very quickly mail became more precious than gold.

Robert Smith Lammot

Letter to his father
15 December 1849

As soon as we went on shore we went on to the Post Office and took our place in the line to the window. One man who stood at the foot of the line called to another who was near the head to change places with him so as to let him have a chance soon for his letters. "What will you give for my place?" Said the other, "Fifteen dollars." "No, I'll take 25." "No, I won't give more than fifteen." Mr. Price tells me that it is nothing uncommon to see a man at the foot give one near the head from $20 to $50 for his place in the line.

John McCrackan

Letter to his family
25 June 1850

I am seated, my dear Mother and Sisters, to commence my letters for the mail, which will leave in the Steamer on the 1st of July, and in accordance with my usual plan, after saying I am (through the blessing of our Heavenly Father) enjoying perfect health, proceed to give you some insight into the secrets of time, since I closed my last. . . . In looking over the list of arrivals published in a City Extra, I saw the name of Lt. G. H. Gorden, U.S.A. Expecting letters by him as well as being very anxious to see him, I made every possible effort to do so, but he could not be found at either of our Hotels, and a search about the city proved equally fruitless. Still I was hoping he would find me out and with this idea, I remained quite contented, expecting to see his card on my table whenever I entered my room after a short absence.

The day passed off, and the next, and next. Neither have I heard from him at this time, and cannot imagine what has become of him. I thought if he had letters for me, he would either have delivered them in person or placed them in the Post Office. This latter I thought quite probable, as he had undoubtedly the intention of visiting his brother at Columa, still he may not have letters for me, and I await patiently for them to turn up, as they will one of these fine days if they are in the country.

The mail steamer *California* arrived on Sunday morning and brought up a mail of one hundred and sixty-five bags. No letters were delivered till this morning (Tuesday). I was up at five o'clock and took my position in the line, there then being about one hundred ahead of me. Office opens at 8 o'clock, about which time a friend passed me who had just been inside the office, and gave me the delightful information that "there was a letter for me from New Haven," and I stood the next hour out very pleasantly, relieved of the uncertainty we all feel when we present ourselves for letters.

About nine o'clock a nice fat letter was handed me. I hastened to break the seal, but after finding you were all well, I proceeded to my breakfast, where over my chop and omlet, I reveled in the contents of that sweet and sacred budget. They were all from my dear Lottie, No. 28, 29 and 30, as late as May 5, although the last letter was not dated and perhaps it might have been much later, as I see the Postmark is May 13th. But more anon. I must answer these in another sheet.

I cannot help telling you the offer made me for my chance at the [post] Office. I was within one of the delivery [window] when a person presents himself and offers me sixteen dollars for my place, but I noticed his remark only by saying as many hundred [i.e., sixteen hundred dollars] could not keep me from my letters ten minutes, and he turned to make an attack upon some one behind me. There must have been six hundred persons in my line from K to Z this morning and about the same number in the A to K line. So, as you may imagine, my breakfast this morning was a very sweet one.

John McCrackan
_____

Letter to his sister Lottie
25 February 1850

We have indeed had a busy day. The Steamer *Oregon* arrived on Friday morning from Panama, bringing dates from the States up to Jan. 17th. The steamer *Unicorn,* which arrived on the 15th brought no mail, so you see we have been a long month without letters. The *Oregon* brought "ninety five bags." These were delivered at the P.O. on Friday morning, and this (Sunday) morning the Office was open for delivery. Thanks to the kindness of Julia's brother who was assisting in the office, I received your sweet long letters early this morning. You know not what it is to have "a friend at court," as they say. I read but part of their contents when the church bell summoned me to the honor of God, and on my return my time between service to four o'clock was occupied finishing and rereading two or three times. On my way to church, I passed the long line of expectants [at the post office]. They form from the Cove and take up the whole street with their numerous windings. They are obliged to stand from five to six hours, often, before their turn comes around. This is very unpleasant, but what will not one do to get letters from dear ones at home.

Henry Didier Lammot

Letter to his father
26 January 1850

We received your and Dan's welcome letters by the last mail, and have yet to get Mother and Annie's. The *North American* has not yet reached us. The Post Office here is conducted in a rather strange manner. You can get no letters out for three days after the arrival of the Mail Steamer, while they keep the Newspaper window closed for a week. You can form no idea what pleasure it affords us to read and re-read your long letters. They brought us right back to home and all our dear friends. . . .

It is very amusing, and if you ever should happen to take a trip to sea (which I don't think will ever happen) you would find it to be [the] case that as soon as the skipper gets on his black suit, shaves and as the sailors say "gibs his land tacks aboard" he is an altered man. While in Mr. Winston's employ I had occasion to be [back] on board the bark *Maria* pretty constantly. Why bless you, nothing was good enough for me. It was, "Mr. Lammot this" and "Mr. Lammot that." "Mr Lammot, you will stay to get dinner, or stay all night and not go ashore in the rain?" &c &c. Well, all that was very good, but he forgot while at sea he would never speak to us. When I say "never" I mean seldom, and when he addressed me it was, "Lammot," which was brought out with a growl which sounded like any thing but what it was intended for.

William G. Brown

Letter to his wife
5 June 1849

I have not received any letters from you since we left Panama. They were written on the 15th of March. I was in hopes I would have got some letters by the mail that come up with us on the [steamer] but it is not all opened yet, and will not be for several days. I am still of the opinion that there must be letters in this mail for me, but we will leave for the mines tomorrow and if the[y] should not be opened by that time, I shall not get any. I am anxious to hear from you. We have been some two months longer getting here than we expected, on account of being detained in Panama. We shall probably be ten days yet getting to the mines. The weather is said to be exceedingly hot in the mines in daytime, and cold at night. It is quite different at this place: there is almost continually a wind blowing, which makes the weather cool, and the nights are very cool.

I feel exceedingly anxious to hear from you and [would] give any thing in the world for a letter. I have not received a letter yet from Ralston, which makes me think there is something wrong or neglected. I have written regularly, about every two or three weeks, and if you have not been more lucky in getting them than I have yours, you will know how to appreciate my feelings. I expected to have received several letters from Ralston, as well as yourself. If I could just get one line that would let me know where you are and how you are getting along. . . .

Dear Margaret, I feel as though there must be something wrong or I would get a letter. I will keep writing every opportunity, whether I get letters from you or not. I hope you and the little one are well and comfortable. If I thought you were not, I would be uneasy. Breakfast is ready and I will close. Our breakfast is composed of beef steak and coffee and bread. We will leave today, the sixth of June. . . . This letter was written on a trunk in the tent, and it's doubtful whether you can read it or not. Kiss the little [one] for me and take good care of yourself, and I will return as soon as possible. *Write* me soon.

John McCrackan

Letter to his sister Lottie
27 January 1850

I am seated, my dear Lottie, at the close of a very busy day, having just finished "a glorious good dinner" to have a quiet chat, so now give me your hand and we will commence at once. . . . Your last letters were so acceptable, dear Lottie. I had determined to get my letters if I had any, so as to answer them by the Steamer which leaves here on the first of February, and in order to accomplish it, I dressed myself about five o'clock on the morning in question and proceeded to the [post] office three hours before it opened, but even at that hour

I found about sixty persons ahead of me in the line. However, I stood it out most bravely, through the rain which fell in perfect torrents, but which I could effectively defy.

About nine o'clock I left the office, having been richly repaid in getting your sweet letters. I wended my way direct to my breakfast room, where I could be as quiet as possible. This was but a few steps, and they were passed with a bound, and a hop, which alone prevented my opening them in the street. Seated in my quiet corner, I was soon lost in the reading, and when I had finished, my mutton chop and chocolate had long since lost their heat. While a second order shared the same fate, having become lost in a second reading. Words cannot express, my dear Lottie, how delighted I was to recognize once more the marks of your pen, to read once more the warm and affectionate impulses, to trace again the pure and beautiful language expressing a "sister's love," and to enjoy once more that sweet and holy communion enjoyed only by souls that love.

Jonathan F. Locke

Letter to his wife
31 October 1849

I have arrived here at last safe and sound after a tedious passage of 236 days. Our Brig not having any damage or accident worth mentioning, you may imagine my feelings when I learned that reports have gone home that we were certainly lost. I have hopes that some of my letters have reached you, in all of which I assure you that, although many things seemed conspired against us, yet we had one of the best sea boats that ever weathered a storm. . . .

The mail is about to close and what I write must be done quickly. There is a great deal of bustle on board and I find it difficult to proceed on what to say. You write you were all pretty well, for which I am most thankful. I am glad to hear that our children are doing pretty well. Tell J[osephine] that I expect she will exert herself to do her whole duty and not be discouraged. I cannot get George [their teenage son] to write to all of you. He is well and grows amazingly. I hope his health will continue as good a[s] it is now. . . .

When I think of you and the children, how I wish I could make you acquainted with my exact circumstances and feelings. All I can do is to continue to trust in the goodness of God, who has been my support and my strength. Yes, let us still confide in him. You must be satisfied with a few lines, as my time for writing has expired. George sends his love. Give our love to all our friends. Let our mutual prayers daily ascend for our preservation and our reunion under prosperous circumstances. . . .

P. S. Your package of three letters and envelope cost me $1.65. Put on a thin envelope. You will get them at the bookstore.

Benjamin C. Howard

Letter to his father
6 January 1850

There is one report that I hope did not reach home, that was, the following. The Barque *Sarah Hooper* arrived on the 3d inst. The Captain of her went on shore to Macondray's Office and reported the Ship *Thomas Perkins* [Howard's ship] sunk off Cape Horn. Then was very much surprised when he saw Capt. Rogers on shore. We passed him off Staten Land, the next morning Cape Horn hove in sight and he was just in sight astern. When the gale struck us we were obliged to run before the wind four hours to take in sail, and he thought we went down. He also reported us sunk at Valparaiso. We beat him 43 days. Ha ha.

Henry DeWitt

Letter to his brother William
24 January 1850

From what I hear you seem to be quite put out because I have neglected to write to you. I know I ought to have writen to you before but my time has been so much occupied that it was impossible for me to do so.

I heard all about your *love scrape* long before I received your letter containing the news. Charles Mintum (who, by the way, was built on a small last) came into the store and told all he knew about the affair—and he with the help of Arthur Ebbits have continued to spread it among all our acquaintances. In fact, Arthur appears to know more about it than I do. Mag [his brother Alfred's wife] and myself are axious to learn all the particulars. Your dear Mary's—Kate's—Kitty's or Betsey's Father is I understand now here, and his business will prevent his returning untill two years from this. So you see, there will be no necessity of your rushing the business. We all exspect (if we live) to be home by that time, and therefore we do not exspect to miss the fun. When you write do me give me more of the particulars. Has she got the *dinero*? Her Father I no doubt will make a pile here.

Uncle John arrived here safe and well. The boxes were opend yesterday—and my fixings were handed to me. You ought to have written to me and given me a full description of the clothing as regard fashions. I have not tried on anything yet except the boots, which fit *excelent*. I intend to put them all on next Sunday and, together with that hat, I flatter myself that I will cut quite a respectable appearance for a retail merchant. . . .

Do not encourage W. Parkins to write to me as it is impossible for me to write to him. Tell him that my correspondence of my own family takes up all my time. . . .

Do not forget to give me the particulars of _____ when you write. If you wish it, I will act as your agent out here (in regards of influencing the Father). I will only charge you 10% per ct *on the profits.*

Anne Willson Booth

Journal
15 October 1849

Uncle Wes came off from shore this morning, bringing letters from home brought over by Mr. Daugherty, which were very welcome, although of a much less recent date than those we received last. Jemmy Mitchell's letter informs him of the death of his Grandfather, which does not seem to surprise him much, as he was generally sick, Jemmy says. . . .

We are looking daily for the arrival of the Steamer *Unicorn*, which is expected to bring the mails up from Panama. I hope we shall receive a budget by her, although we can not expect any of a more recent date than our last. Still it is always a pleasure to read over what we have not seen before. When this mail shall have arrived, I shall begin to prepare letters for home. Sometimes I feel disposed to sit down and write to each and all of my dear friends, and it is only the fact of there being such enormous postage on letters between here and the United States that deters me from this. Some one has been kind enough to send me 1/2 dozen bottles of Ale, for which I am truly thankful.

Jonathan F. Locke

Letter to his wife
15 November 1849

Last evening I received your letter of August 21. With what pleasure I read the first part of it[s] contents. Then imagine my feelings when you merely refer to the death of poor dear Mother. Oh, I have only to bless the dispensation of Providence, who has taken a suffering, care-worn mortal, one of his children, to his mansions of rest. I cannot mourn as one without hope. I cannot complain, but I should feel happier had I been with her in her last moments. You say you have written two letters beside the one I have just received. The one I have not received gives the particulars, I suppose, of Mother's last moments.

Josiah Griswold

Letter to Benjamin S. Hill
29 December 1849

Your welcome letter of July, Sept. and Dec. I rec'd the 13th inst. I also received one at the same time from my family under date of Oct. 16. These letters announce to me afflicting and mournful news, in the loss of two dear children. You, My Brother, have not I believe mourned the loss of any thus far, and I hope the day is far distant when you will have cause to pass through so great tribulation and anguish of heart. Oh, how bitterly have I wept and with what poignancy of grief have I lamented their loss, to feel and know that on the twelfth of March last I bade an eternal adieu to them, that they have gone without resting their eyes on their Father, who should have been there to relieve, if possible, their sufferings, and to bless them ere they died. Tis this, My Brother, that has grieved me, and caused me to regret that I left my humble but happy, happy Home. In mourning for them, I have been admonished to bear with fortitude, and with the eye of Faith look forward to a union in another and a brighter world above. From thee, my friend, I have had support and kindly encouragement in your letter that is now before me. Throughout your letter there gleams the sparks of friendship and goodness of heart, and trust I have profited by your counsel and well-timed words of consolation.

Edward Austin

Letter to his brother
8 November 1849

I was never so anxious as I am about your letters. Every hour seems two, and if I had not received Mother's and Jim's, I do not know what I should have done. The cholera has been so severe in the States, I opened their letters with a nervous hand I assure you. Has Lucy returned yet from her summer retreat? How is that Baby? Does it grow well and is it a pretty child? I suppose it will have its Mother's red cheeks. Give it a kiss for its Uncle Edward.

How is that old flame of mine, M—— R——, is she caught yet? I hear she is getting fat. Serves her right. I could have kept her lean. Between you and I, George, I should have stuck to my business better and never failed if it had not been for that affair. I should not have spent so much money either. I wanted excitement and that was all that kept me alive. I have now, I believe, got over it and just begin to feel mad about it. I will not say I hate her, but after I think it all over, I think she served me a shabby trick, and shall take some way to let her know it when I get home.

Anne Willson Booth

Journal
12 October 1849

We have had an unlooked-for but joyful treat today in receiving letters from home, that came by express. Thankful do I feel to hear all are well so far. We are informed that our letters by the *Austen* had been received.

Oh! I cannot express the emotions of delight that fill my heart upon hearing from my loved Parents, sisters and child. Surely there is no comfort equal to it, and the pleasure I derive from this event only reminds me of how careful I should be to improve every available opportunity by writing to them, knowing their solicitude to be as great as ours. First of all, I had a letter from my beloved Mother, the sight of whose handwriting caused the tears to flow. I love her more dearly every day, and it is my constant prayer that we may be permitted again to meet. Dear Mother, your mind has been much troubled I know. Dear Mary and dear Bell are over their trials safely, for which I thank God; many an anxious thought I have had about them. They have daughters too, which is I suppose a source of joy. I wish dear Bell had called her little girl after me; how I would have loved it. I expect there will be quite a stock of nieces and nephews when we return home.

John McCrackan

Letter to his family
25 December 1849

Christmas Day, and I not with you, and yet, and yet, I am with you. Yes, I feel it, I know it. I am present although absent. I am with you at the festive board, and the family altar. I am seated where I see your bright and lovely faces and there I hear your kind and endearing words. Many, many a merry Christmas dear ones, do I send to you upon the wings of love. My spirit joins you in the festivities of this holy and happy season. It leaves its wandering tenament and seeks its earthly home and resting place where, with kindred spirits, it revels in the fullness of happiness.

I attended church this morning and listened to a very good sermon from our clergyman, the Rev. Mr. [Flavel S.] Mines. Our church was very full and the service of course most impressive and beautiful. I am regularly installed in the choir and never till now did I seem to appreciate the pleasures and privileges of our church. Deprived as I have been for so long of its services it seemed like getting home once more after a long and painful absence.

I have used every exertion to appear happy and enjoy the day. In my imagination I have returned to you. I hear the warm greeting and have felt the sweet kiss. I listened to the kind solicitations and anxious remembrances and heartfelt prayers offered for the absent ones.

John McCrackan

Letter to his sister Lottie
16 April 1850

Yesterday after breakfast, I started with a friend named "Sheppard" of Baltimore (who is in practice here and will probably be taken into the firm of Brooks & McCrackan), on an expedition of "office seeking"— not in the way of political appointments however, but looking at offices, it being our intention to change our locality the first of next month. While about to cross a street I felt a hand on my shoulder, and on turning, you may imagine my surprise to recognize Edward Hotchkiss behind me. Our interview was very short while standing in the street, but parted with the understanding he should dine with me at 6 o'clock. He spoke of seeing you all but a few days before he left, and of course I was perfectly delighted to hear you were all well, and it indeed seemed pleasant to look upon his familiar face. He said you would not send letters by him, yet he had a package of "Newspaper slips" which he would hand me when he came to the office at dinner time. And this he did when he came to the office about five o'clock.

I must return many thanks for your *thoughtful kindness,* my dear Lottie, yet most of the "Congressional proceedings" are received here by the papers, and get them in half an hour after the Steamer arrives. Hotchkiss dined with me, passed the eve with me, and [I] gave him half of my bed last night. Of course I had many, many pleasant enquiries to make of him regarding friends, and asked him two thousand questions, and it was so delightful to see one so directly from home. He arrived in the *Tennessee,* also Scranton of Fairhaven. I was of course quite disappointed he did not bring letters but, as he said, he presumed it would not be allowed by the company. Yet as it proved, there was no trouble attending his landing, and he brought quite a large number of letters to persons here. However I was assured by him that you had written me, but they had been mailed, and of course I should receive them by this mail.

I was up this morning at five o'clock. The morning was bright and but little wind. I with others took my stand at the [post] office to get my letters, but after standing there till 8 1/2 o'clock, I was informed there were no letters for me and I left really disappointed. However, I kept up my spirits, returned to my office and renewed my business. I had occasion to go to the post office about noon, when to my delight I was delivered two letters from home, of the 7th and 12th of February. These letters acknowledged the advances sent by Judah and it was indeed pleasant to know you had heard of my arrival, that I was in good health, &c. Your letters, my dear Lottie, were truly sweet and interesting, so full of that lasting love and affection, which in this distant land draws me near home, and the dear objects of my thoughts and dreams, and then to know you are all well seems the greatest relief.

John McCrackan

Letter to his sister Mary
12 May 1850

I am seated, my dear Sister, to answer your delightful letter of March 19th and 23d, which was Oh! so acceptable, and so unexpected. The mail which arrived on the 8th inst. brought but a few bags, and I little thought when I presented myself at the "Bone Office" I should receive letters, and how my heart thumped with joy as I searched my pocket for a small gold piece. How insignificant seems the postage, if it were ten dollars an ounce for every letter, how readily would I pay it to hear from the dear ones in my own distant home.

John T. Rundle

Letter to his sisters
20 March 1850

I hav not had a leter by male cince the twelfth of october I hav negleced ritin wating for you to wright but I am tard of wating so I hav writen I want you to wright and let me now how you ar gitting a long and tel me all the nuse I wan you [to] direct my [mail to] San Fransisco california in care of the cargo[?] joint stock I think that hear is sombody by the same name of my self and gits my leters. . . . I dont think of nothin else at persan you mus not do as I hav dun a bout riting but right evry male and I wil do the same so giv my lov to all . . . so good by

John McCrackan

Letter to his sister Mary
14 April 1850

I am writing on the evening of one of the most exciting days we have had for a week. . . . As we were leaving the church, I joined a lady of my acquaintance and stood upon the steps looking upon the beautiful bay at our feet and then extending our gaze upon "Mount Diablo," which was very prominent from our high position and rendered still more conspicuous as the smoke issued from its mouth, and hung in dark masses in the blue heavens above. This Mount is volcanic and has been burning most freely of late, at night the effect being of course very beautiful. As I was saying, we had just withdrawn our eyes from this dark object to descend the hill, when my eyes were attracted in another direction by the outline of some dark mass, which as it appeared from behind the high head land, proved to be the long looked for and anxiously expected Steamship *Tennessee.*

Our little city, which has been on the "qui vive" expecting her for ten days past, was in ten minutes time in the most perfect state of excitement, about which time (for comparatively but few knew of her arrival till then) she fired two salutes. These salutes completely electrified every one, sending the blood into every vein at the thought of "Letters from Home." I can give you no correct idea of the scene of the remainder of the day. I think no steamer has created so much interest. Although not a regular mail steamer, yet she was to bring back mails, three of the *Ohio,* and *Crescent City.*

In ten minutes after the gun was fired (for we stood looking upon the scene) our beautiful bay was perfectly alive with boats of all sizes and shapes, from the creek skiff and yaul, to the gig and launch. All were in motion, straining every nerve upon the oar to distance a neighbor in this merry race, and by the time the Steamer had dropped anchor and "swung to" the bay was perfectly black with its "swarming myriads." As you will imagine, this was a very pretty sight. While along the streets of the city which our elevated position commanded, men were seen running about in the utmost confusion. Already satisfied with our prospecting, we continued our walk conversing of home, but neither very talkative me thinks.

John D. Mitchell

Letter to his family
23 January 1850

Cold and rainy but I do not care, as early this morning I went to the Post Office and stood three hours waiting for it to open, and one hour after it opened I arrived at the delivery box when hurra, hurra, hurra, three times three, I received a letter from John Harrison in which MAB had written, another from Catharine, Maria and Mother, together with 1/2 sheet from Anthony. I tell you what, it done me good after standing four hours in all and then received them. Ginger, I can't tell you how I felt. A man did offer me $10 for my place after I got within 12 of the delivery box, but I told him I would not sell out for 50, and if any one had offered me $1000 for my letters before I opened them, I mean I would not have taken it. Jehosiphat, you can't imagine my feelings at the present time.

Jonathan F. Locke

Letter to his wife
30 April 1850

We have just finished our cradles (Mr. W[hitehous] and myself), not to rock babies in but to rock out the oro (Spanish for gold). I expect they will be troublesome comforts. There will be more work in it than the ones we left at home. Never mind, if they only do something for the help of the home manufacture. I hope at any rate they will help us to a small "pile" any how. I have no idea how long it will require us to satisfy me, but as I have often said before, if our lives are spared us I shall take time rather than return empty handed. There are very many who get next to nothing. We may be among that number. Then, as I have said before, there are so many who squander their gains and perhaps go home penniless, or go back to acquire more, or hang about here as idlers or, what is worse for industrious mechanics, will work for anything rather than return to the mines. . . .

I am glad Josephine does well (as I think she does) at her school and at her Uncle's. I feel much obliged to them. Willy wrote me a letter. I must speak a word to him.

Now Willy, my son, you are doing very well at your school and do you take care of Johny. He is younger than you, and I know you will not run away from him and plague him. You love little sisters too, and try to make them happy.

Now Johny, where are you? I can't see you. Are you behind the door, or out in the barn? Well, I guess mother can see you if I can't. Now, both of you boys, how do you do? What makes you open your eyes so wide? Well now, if I had a great piece of candy, you would look more earnest. Well, be good boys and mind your mother. I will come home as soon as I am ready.

And where is little Mary? Is she feeding the chickens? Oh, I guess she is climbing into Mother's lap. Now, if I don't give you a kiss it will be because I can't. "Oh, when will Father come home?" Don't say that. Be a good little girl. I am going to rock the cradle to get some gold if I can for little Mary, a cradle that looks something like the one little sister rocks in, only it has a sieve instead of a baby in it.

Little Harriet, I can't say a word to you, but I send you all a kiss. Yes, Mary the elder, lots. Now Mary, for the mines. "Now comes the try to win." Well, I am anxious to be off. I a[m] disappointed in not getting a letter from you before I go. However, keep up good courage. I am sanguine in my expectations, but not extravagant. I shall carry your likeness to remind if I needed it. . . . I feel thankful to the kind friends who surround you. God bless you all and keep you safe for always.

Chapter 3

O, Don't You Cry for Me

Though the vast majority of Argonauts setting off for California fully intended to return in a few months or years, they were all aware that they might never again see their loved ones. Life was particularly precarious in America during the nineteenth century. The journey before them was filled with hazards regardless of the route chosen: poisonous watering holes, potentially hostile Indians, early mountain snows, venomous snakes, ravening animals, exotic diseases, foundering ships swamped by storms at sea or smashed by rocks within sight of the Golden Gate. Moreover, those left at home were subject to an ongoing barrage of life-threatening challenges, the most common of which were the epidemics of fatal diseases that swept the country with alarming regularity, killing by the thousands and striking particularly hard at the very young and the elderly.

With cruel irony, just as gold fever began spreading throughout America a pandemic of Asiatic cholera entered at the ports of New York and New Orleans. The first worldwide outbreak of cholera in recorded history, in 1817, had little effect on the United States, but the second and third pandemics, in 1832 and 1849, killed an estimated 150,000 Americans. The 1849 outbreak lasted six years—the entire gold rush period—and subsided only in 1855.[1]

Asiatic cholera is an acute bacterial infection brought on by the bacterium *Vibro cholerae.* It is spread almost exclusively by fecal-oral contact and is particularly prevalent in areas of poor sanitation and inadequate personal hygiene. Infection induces violent diarrhea; the resulting rapid dehydration can be fatal, particularly for patients who are already weakened because of age or otherwise poor health.

On 9 November 1848 the packet ship *New York* left Le Havre, France, carrying 250 passengers, mostly German refugees fleeing the revolutionary tumult that had set the cities of Germany ablaze. Seven people on board died of cholera before the ship reached New York harbor on 1 December. Forty more died within a few weeks; by the end of the next summer, five thousand New Yorkers had become victims. A second ship, the *Swanton*, left Le Havre two weeks before the *New York*. When it reached New Orleans it, too, proved to be a carrier. In 1849 nearly four thousand people died of cholera in New Orleans; before the pandemic subsided one-third of the city's population had succumbed.[2]

The migration westward drew contagion into the heart of the country. Cholera infected passengers on virtually every boat making its way along the Mississippi, the Ohio, and the Missouri Rivers.[3] As mentioned earlier, St. Louis, St. Joseph, and Independence, Missouri, the primary gathering places for westbound wagon trains, were centers of the contagion. Many unsuspecting Argonauts set out only to succumb along the trail.

The American medical community was ill-equipped to battle the pandemic. Little was known about the etiology of cholera, and while poor sanitation was suspected of playing a major role, little could be done to ameliorate the situation. For immigrants crammed into city slums, for passengers on months-long voyages aboard crowded ships, or for those who used temporary trailside latrines and washed utensils with little or no hot water, knowledge of how the disease was spread would have been of little use.

In San Francisco, medical practitioners of all stripes were faced with the problem of too many people too poorly housed in too small a space. Impure drinking water was the primary culprit, causing widespread dysentery. Between 1848 and 1850 five to ten deaths per day were linked to the poor water supply.[4] As the transportation hub of the region, San Francisco took in passengers from ships arriving from around the globe, many of whom carried smallpox, cholera, and typhoid, and it was to San Francisco that sickly miners came when they were too weak to stay in the gold fields. During the particularly cold and damp winters of 1849 and 1850 consumption and other pulmonary diseases were widespread. Easy money and loneliness also contributed their share to the misery: the largest number of hospitalizations were for the treatment of venereal disease.[5]

The city of San Francisco was slow to provide government-supported medical care. The U.S. Navy commandeered one of Thomas Larkin's sheds to serve as a hospital in April of 1847, but it was not until December of 1849 that the city contracted with a private hospital to provide medical services. The State Marine Hospital, an institution supported by state funds, was established in 1850 because it was felt that the city should not have to bear the full expense of caring for the large number of nonresidents and transients. "Pest houses" were set up San Francisco in 1850 for cholera and in 1854 for smallpox.[6]

Most hospitals, however, were privately operated. Providing for the medical care of members became one of the most important functions of the numerous ethnic benevolent societies that sprang up to provide fellowship and material support for the wide range of foreign nationals gathering in San Francisco. The French, Swiss, Jews, Chinese, and Germans had their own hospitals or other medical care facilities where members could go to receive treatment according to their own traditions, provided in their own languages.

For those who could afford it, medical care provided by physicians in private offices was the option of choice, and there were many from whom to choose. An estimated fifteen hundred doctors arrived during the gold rush period; as early as 1850 the market was completely saturated, and physicians had to turn to other trades to supplement their incomes.[7] This surplus of medical practitioners helped alleviate to some extent the medical crisis (though doctors were ineffective in addressing the main *causes* of illness), and the absence of large hospitals was not high on the list of civic complaints lodged by the citizens. In San Francisco, as in most of America in the mid–nineteenth century, hospitals were places of last resort, to be avoided if at all possible.

Elbridge Gerry Hall

Letter to his wife
30 June 1849

I have no *news* to write, but cannot let the opportunity pass without writing to my own dear wife. I have hired a store and may now really consider myself an inhabitant of San Francisco. I have to pay 150$ pr month rent for my store—and was offered 200$ pr month for it the day after I rented it. I take possession next week and shall then have a place where I can feel a *little* more at home. There is now in the harbor about one hundred vessels and they are daily increasing, as the hands desert as soon as they arrive and wages are so high that but few are able to pay the exorbitant wages charged. Many kinds of goods are selling at wholesale at much less than cost in the States.

You may think it a little strange that we need a fire to sit by this evening being the last of June but such is the case. The weather is very cold in the afternoon and evening—but I think it will suit me very well. I had a very severe cough when I arrived here but it has now entirely disappeared—and I have gained ten pounds in weight since I have been here, which makes me about as fleshy as last winter, and I never had a better appetite (considering the fare) than I have at present. There is many that are going home, but they are generally men not calculated to take the world as it is. No one need come here with the expectation of enjoying the luxuries he can procure in the States.

I have not heard from the men that I have in the mines but expect to very soon. I send you in this a small lump of Gold which I paid an Indian 4$ for—it will probably be worth 5$. You can keep it if you wish or dispose of it as you think proper. I shall send Franklin a small piece in my next. I have written Mr. Thayer to send you from 25 to 50$, (I sent him 1075$) as soon as he receives my letter—which I hope may answer you for spending money until my next. As there is not paper money here, it is difficult for me to send direct to you, but if I should not send you by the next steamer, I will send you a draft the steamer following. I hope you have received the letter forwarded by Captain Treadway from Panama. You will probably receive my last letter from here (which went by steamer *Panama*) about the time you do this, which I send by my friend Mr. Hazard from Staten Island.

I hope, dearest, you are enjoying yourself with our *dear Parents* and friends. How I would like to drop in even if I could not stop but a very few days. I look back with much pleasure to the few short weeks spent with my *Dear dear* wife and forward to the time when there shall be no necessity for our separation even for a few weeks. I hope I may succeed in my undertakings, and think I shall. I hope to be remembered by you and our dear Parents—and you may depend that *you will be* by me.

Elbridge Gerry Hall

Letter to his wife
1 July 1849

I have been to church this forenoon and heard a very good discourse from Rev. Mr. Wheeler. There is ministers here from the Sandwich Islands and Oregon. I suppose they have to follow their flocks. . . .

I am in hopes to hear from my dearest this week and hope to hear good news. In answering this please write all the news and what changes have taken place &c &c &c. I suppose it will be the middle of August by the time you receive this, and I shall expect an answer by the 1st Oct, as I hope the steamers will run regular after this. I cannot even imagine the time that I shall return, but it will be as soon as I think it for our mutual interest. You know that I would like to be with you but I feel my poverty keenly and am willing to make personal sacrifices of comfort for the sake of making up what I have heretofore lost. But all other sacrifices is as nothing compared to being absent from the one who is so *truly dear* to me.

Tell Mother I should like to hear from her. Give my love to *our family*—and dispense with love and respects to others as you think proper. In my next I am in hopes to be better able to write an interesting letter, as I shall then have a place to sit down and write, but at present am oblig'd to hold my paper in my lap and sit on my bedstead. A brother-in-law of ex-President Tyler is in an adjoining room sitting on a floor writing. So you see what kind of *luxuries* we have in the Emporium of the "Pacific".

Margaret DeWitt

Letter to her mother-in-law
30 July 1849

You may imagine how delighted we were to receive our letters by the Steamer *California*, and at the good news they all contained of the good health of all, with the exception of Father. We were truly sorry he had been so miserable, but as Helen wrote he was much better, we hope ere this he has fully recovered, and made a nice long visit in the country. I should think the change of air would greatly renovate him.

It was just three months from the time we left home that we got letters, and I was beginning to feel quite anxious for their arrival. I received a fine parcel of letters from home, also a very affectionate one from Helen Chambers, which I shall not have time to answer by this Steamer. Henry [her brother-in-law] only got two—one from Theodore and his Father. It is too bad some of the others did not write him. They must treat him better or I shall have to lecture them for their inattention. You, I know, are very excusable (and Helen too) but *those brothers.* If they were only near enough—Henry and I would both give them a talk.

Henry is very well, and seems contented and happy. I believe he intends writing you a long letter if he has time. They are all very busy—and work very hard—but it seems to agree very well with them, and all enjoy perfect health. Alfred [her husband] was quite sick for a few days last week with Dysentery. Called in Dr. Turner, who gave him something that soon relieved and he is now quite well. I felt anxious about him at first, as that disease prevails quite a good deal, and a number have died quite suddenly. I think the water here is not healthy and causes a great deal of sickness. Mrs. Frank Ward died quite suddenly of that complaint. She had not been well for a week or two—and neglected herself—was taken very ill on Friday night and died Monday. It is a very sad thing—and has cast a gloom upon all that knew her, her short residence here having endeared her to all. Her husband feels deeply, and it will be sad news to go home to her friends. . . .

The climate is so very changable that unless a person is very careful as regards clothing and diet, they are very apt to be sick. We have been very much favored in having such good health, and I hope we may continue so. I have been quite well, with the exception of a few days—something like chills and Fever—but by taking it in time, soon broke them after a few hearty shakes and am now perfectly well, and as usual enjoy everything. A great many have fever here, brought on by exposure and over exertion.

I am happy to say I have a very good Irish woman living with us. She came this morning. I have been alone just two months, and had plenty to do—I can tell you. Still I enjoyed it and got along very well, but they all thought it was too much for me, and Alfred wanted me to have a man come and work, but I thought I should rather wait till I could get some nice American servant. This woman has been 10 years in America, and came out with her husband, who is going to the mines, and she wanting a good home was willing to come for sixty dollars a month—for one month. Then I expect she will want higher wages. I hope by that time the price of labor will go down. Most everyone is paying 100 per month. At Mr. Gillespie's they pay 100 a month to two servants and give out washing—and their family is no larger than ours. This woman is a good washer and ironer, which is a great thing.

The expenses of living here are enormous—and then you are not near as comfortable as at home. We have five without the servant, and I believe Alfred intends to have the rest eat here too. I shall now have time to do some sewing. Before I had but very little, as generally I was too tired when I got through to do much. Dress makers here get a good price for their work—they ask 10 and 12 dollars to make a perfectly plain dress, and 3 and 5 for fitting. I am glad I can make such things myself, or it would be rather expensive. I wear thick clothing all together—rarely a calico as it is so cool the latter part of the day, they are uncomfortable. Dark delaines and merinos are the only comfortable kind of goods for ladies, and I think it is cheaper to dress warm than to pay the Doctors. I think the intense hot weather we had at Panama was enough for one season, and I like this climate better than if it was hot—only it is so dry, and the high winds which blow every day make it more so. Yet if it was not for the wind, I think it would be very unhealthy, as it seems to blow away all impure air.

I must [not] neglect to thank you for all the nice things which you put up for Alfred—and came safely by the *Ocean Bird*. The Ginger cakes are delightful and taste as fresh as when first baked. The sweet meats very fine—and whenever we have them for tea, you get plenty of compliments paid to your superior skill in preparing them—and the pickles all very nice—especially the stuffed *peppers* and *butternuts,* which kept better than any other kind. They are perfectly delightful and a great treat—I can tell you. You would not think your labor in preparing them lost if you knew how much we value them, not only on account of their goodness, but that you made them, and they have such a home taste. They were put up with so much care—and so nice—it must have been a deal of trouble.

Henry and I [are] most always longer at the dinner table than anyone else, and often have a good long talk about you all. I often wonder if you think as much of us, as we do of our dear friends at home. You must always think of us as being contented and happy and never feel anxious about either Henry or Alf, as I have them both now, and will always do every thing I can for the happiness of both. They are both very kind and do every thing they can to make me happy. Henry seems not at all homesick, and I hope will get along as well as we all wish. He has grown quite stout and looks very well.

I shall have to close. Give much love from *us all* to all at Home and accept a large share for yourself and Father. Good bye, Dear Mother, that you may all be kept by him who never slumbers or sleeps is the sincere wish of your affectionate Margaret.

Henry R. DeWitt

Letter to his mother
31 July 1849

I have writen to you by every mail giving you a full account of my journey. My travels have been a great benefit to me, having seen & learnt considerable. I soon found out after being away a short [time] that to get along well I had to keep my eyes open—and that I hardly knew as much as I thought I did. However, I got along exceedingly well for a new beginer.

You will I suppose before this reaches you hear of the arrival of the *Ocean Bird.* Your preserves did not come out in very good order a few of the jars being broken but those that came whole were excelent and are considered quite a dainty. The choisest of the pickels (Butternuts) fortunately was in good order. Margret thinks a good deal of them and are put on the [table] only on Sunday, and then no one must eat more than a half of one, some of the sweetmeats were fermented but Margret used them for making pies. . . .

It is now after 11 oclock having no other time to write as it is against all rules and regulations of this store to write during business hours. Even if it were not, the arrival of the *Ocean Bird* has given us so much to do that it is impossible for us to write any other time. As for Alfred's writing, it is out of the question as he can hardly answer his business letters. He is now writing. I exspect it will be daylight before he gets through.

I begin to feel quite at home here, Margeret being like a real sister to me.

Lewis & Myself have made up a room in the store with canvas the door being made of two strips of calico and good seeling made of canvas. I have an excelent bedstead & mattrass, a good fether pillow & blankets. 10 o'clock hardly finds me out of bed. I have made no associates here and do not intend to and therefore I spend my evenings by going to bed. . . .

I will send Pa six of the latus *Alta Californian* [newspaper] if I can procure them. D[e]W[itt] & H[arrison] have subscribed for 2 Sanwich

Island paper[s] but have not recd any since I have been here. If we get any I will secure some and send them on. My love to all.

John Tolman

Journal
8 September 1849

For three days past our sick friend has seemed brighter and we had strong hopes of his recovery, but last night he was rather restless, sweat freely, and this morn at 7 o'clock his spirit took its flight. He apparently suffered but little except from weakness. Fr. Whitimore about half an hour before his death informed him of his situation, but he was so very weak he made no reply and seemed but little affected. Soon after his Uncle (Mr. A. Loker) asked if he had any word to leave to his wife or parents. He wished them good by, and tried to say more, but was too far gone. He died without a struggle. I stood by him and spoke to him but he could not reply. He was the first person I ever saw die.

Anne Willson Booth

Journal
22 September 1849

The novelty of being safely moored in harbour prevented me from sleeping last night. Going on deck this morning, I was much struck with the strange appearance of every thing around us—high hills covered with a low green herbage, tents pitched here and there, the men around them differently employed, some washing, some cooking &c &c. These are persons just arrived, and waiting for conveyances to the mines. . . .

The harbour looks beautiful. It is thought there are upwards of 300 vessels here. About 1 o'clock, we received our letters by Capt. Codsman. Were rejoiced to hear all were well. Dear Lizzy tells me, my darling boy has been ill. Oh! I wish I could have nursed him and attended to all his little wants, which none but a mother can anticipate or supply. Poor little fellow, he wanted his Aunt Lizzy to write a note to his Papa and Mamma, not knowing how far away they were. I feel grateful to the Almighty, that he was so kind as to restore him to health. How I long to see him, no one can ever know. Bless him and preserve him, most heavenly Father!

Anonymous

Journal of a voyage from New Bedford to San Francisco
26 September 1849

I saw two vessels today with their flags 1/2 mast indicating [a death]. One of the corpses passed near our ship in a boat towed by another enshrouded with the American flag. Death is busy among the Californians. The climate is anything but healthy to North American newcomers. . . . Edward, the "Good Samaritan," compelled his brother-in-law to be taken to the Hospital—at an expense of ten dollars per day—depositing before he could be admitted one hundred and fifty dollars—and then could be allowed to remain only ten days. An awful place for a sick person it must be admitted. I doubt if he gets well.

E. A. Upton

Diary
15 December 1849

It is now raining again. Every little scratch or bruise one receives in this country is very apt to become a bad sore. A few weeks ago a flea bit me in the night on the leg near my foot—and in scratching the place I started up the skin, causing the blood to start a little. It is now a very bad running sore and my entire leg is affected.

Anne Willson Booth

Journal
30 September 1849

Mrs. Taylor is quite sick to day again. Her health is much impaired lately, which she thinks is entirely owing to living so long on shipboard. Their house will be ready I hope in a very few days.

Our Cooks have left us now, so it is quite desirable to reduce our family as soon as possible. The children are a great annoyance. It generally happens, when Uncle has company in the cabin, they both have a spell of crying, which makes it anything else than agreeable. Mr. Wright, one of our passengers, is very sick also, suffering from a severe attack of diarrhoea, which disease is very prevalent here. The water is thought to be unwholesome and should not be drank, it is said, without a little brandy. There were six deaths yesterday in town.

I have no doubt, the sickness is owing as much to the irregular manner of living as to any injurious influences of weather or climate.

Anne Willson Booth

Journal
1 October 1849

We are daily expecting the arrival of the steamer from the same place, by which we expect to receive letters from home. I sincerely hope that we shall not be disappointed; our anxiety being very great. Uncle obtained a paper yesterday, the "New York Tribune" of July 17th in which we learned the Cholera was making fearful havoc in some of the western cities. In Baltimore [her hometown], there were 26 cases and 8 deaths in the Alms House. We are filled with apprehension and dread to hear that some one dear to us has fallen a victim to the terrible scourge.

In this paper, we also learned the death of Mrs. [Dolley] Madison. Poor lady, she lived to a good old age, and a considerable share of this world's honours have been hers, yet, she at last was called upon to pay the debt of nature, and become an inmate of the charnel house, where there is no distinction. I saw that the *Louis Phillippe* had sailed on the 10th July for this port, under the command of Capt. Benthall. I wish her a safe and speedy arrival, and hope to receive particular information by her of things at home. We have several sick persons on board, all suffering from diarrhoea. If the cholera should break out in this place, it would be terrible indeed. The habits of the people are so irregular, their diet and water unwholesome, the climate is hard to get accustomed to. The mornings are damp and cool, at noon it is very warm, the evenings are always cold and render thick clothing necessary.

William F. Reed

Journal
14 September 1849

It is now evening and I must relate a little incident which has this moment occurred. Capt Smith wished to fill a lamp and seeing a canister similar to one commonly used for oil (our articles are scattered in all directions around the tent) seized it and attempted to pour out some oil, holding a lighted lamp within an inch of the nose of the vessel, but no oil would run. Upon which he examined the contents and found it gunpowder! The fact of its being caked saved us from being blown to pieces. O! this is a great life to lead. I enjoy it much. Accounts from the mines continue to be favorable in the general, although we occasionally see a poor individual who has been up and returned sick, and sick of the country with perhaps hardly enough to carry him home.

Anne Willson Booth

Journal
October 3, 1849

Occurrences on board are somewhat monotonous, and each day's events are but a repetition of the preceding one. There is no particular news afloat in the City. . . . It is said there were four deaths in one single encampment during yesterday, but little notice is taken of these occurrences. The immediate companions of the deceased procure a coffin and quietly inter the remains without any farther ado. There was a very sudden death on shore yesterday evening; that of a man who started to go to the Post Office from the beach, and fell dead instantly. I did not hear what cause was assigned. Many are becoming disgusted with the place and are making preparations to leave it. A resolution I think very nonsensical; for who could expect to find a second Paradise in California?

Anne Willson Booth

Journal
6 October 1849

This is another beautiful morning. The weather is quite mild for Oct. The sickness in town continues unabated, but is mostly confined to persons living in tents, of irregular and intemperate habits. The water is highly impregnated with mineral qualities, and is said to be a productive cause of the prevailing disease. Persons are returning from the mines every day, and each one gives a different account of the state of affairs. All agree however in saying, there is much sickness about those regions and that physicians are reaping a fine harvest.

Anne Willson Booth
_____

Journal
8 October 1849

It is so very dark to day, we can scarcely see without the aid of a lamp. . . . I dreamed last night we were all at home, having returned suddenly, and although my joy was very great at finding myself again surrounded by my loved family, still I could not help regretting our having returned without accomplishing the object for which we came, and was glad to find on waking it was all a dream. Poor Lizzy Collison was in this dream—how I would like to hear from her.

Anne Willson Booth
_____

Journal
10 October 1849

The sun rose clearly this morning, and appearance seemed favourable for a beautiful day; by 9 o'clock, the sky became overcast, and large drops of rain began to fall, which continued to increase throughout the day. They say the mud on shore is almost impassable, and that pedestrians have to be careful in order to retain their foothold. I can readily believe this, knowing the immense quantity of dust and sand about the place. If this should be the commencement of the rainy season, we shall have a dreary time of it, as it continues all through the winter months. Those who know from experience say however that these are mere showers, that when the regular rains set in we shall begin to think of a second deluge. Uncle Wes returned from shore filled with disgust at the mud and discomforts there. He came across some of our folks who are encamped about in tents and found them almost drenched with the water. I do not know how they can expect to retain their health in all this exposure. . . .

I am beginning to feel anxious now about our own situation. We have not yet decided upon any plan for the future. Mr. Booth and I would like to be at housekeeping; but the price of ground is so very high that it seems hardly worth while to incur the expense, Again we are disappointed in not hearing from home. The Steamer brought no mail and we have not been able to obtain a single item of news. Mr. Booth returned to the Ship this afternoon quite unwell, having taken cold from being exposed to the weather.

Anne Willson Booth

Journal

11 October 1849

Mr. Booth remains on board today, being too unwell to go to work. We have just heard of the death of old Mr. Shipley of Baltimore, who came out with his son in the *G. H. Brown*. He died of asthma, we are told, which disease he has been suffering from a long time.

It is reported, there are six deaths from Cholera on board of a vessel just arrived from Panama. If it should once obtain a footing here, great will be its havoc. The habits of the people, variability of the climate and filthy condition of some portions of the town, all conspire to render its progress inevitable. We procured a New York paper of the 16th of August by the steamer just arrived, which informs us the Cholera had been at work throughout the United States, but might be considered as being on the decline in that City. We searched eagerly for information concerning Baltimore, but were much disappointed, there being not a single item of intelligence of any interest to us.

Capt. Hugg and Capt. Waterman of Baltimore have just called. Uncle Wes being ashore, I was obliged to do the honours of the Cabin. They say I have acted wisely in remaining on board the ship, there being no place on shore half as comfortable. Capt. Hugg seems to be entirely disgusted with the country, and says, if it were not for the gold, he would vote for its entire obliteration from the map of the civilized world. It is said he has not reaped the golden harvest that he anticipated before leaving home, and hence his dissatisfaction. So prone is mankind to allow external circumstances to take the hue, whether lively or sombre, of their own luck or their own thoughts.

Anne Willson Booth

Journal

20 October 1849

I feel today a dejection of spirits, which I cannot get over, notwithstanding all my efforts to do so. I attribute it to my dream of last night, about my darling boy. I thought I was about to dress him when I discovered an eruption on his body, which we all pronounced as being symptoms of scarlet fever. Of course, I was much alarmed, so much so indeed, that I awoke, and have not been able since to banish the painful feelings about my beloved child this dream has occasioned. I feel sure, there is no one more free from superstitious dread than I; yet, impressions will sometimes remain inspite of us, and cause us to feel an intense anxiety concerning the object of them. What would I not give, if it were in my power, to know how he is today, as well as all the rest of my loved kindred.

Oh! it is sad, it is painful, to be thus separated from so many tender ties, and at times, I find it difficult to repress the emotions of sorrow which fill my heart when I think of the separation that divides us. My feelings cannot be described, neither can they be imagined, except by those, who have been similarly situated. Sometimes, I feel it to be a luxury to abandon myself to the indulgence of brooding over the scenes of my home, and the memory of those beloved ones, I feel so near my heart. . . .

Yet—I am not dissatisfied, or repining at what I know is inevitable; and at times I feel it a comfort to put my trust in God, believing in His infinite wisdom and goodness. To His care I submit the lives of all my friends knowing He is able to preserve them: for this end I sincerely pray.

Anne Willson Booth

Journal
25 October 1849

[D]uring the night, Mr. Booth awakened me by making quite an ado in his sleep, moaning and sobbing piteously. Supposing him to be under the influence of the nightmare, I aroused him, and it was with difficulty that he told me, he had been dreaming about our poor, little George. He thought he saw him strangling and he was unable to assist him. So full of agitation was he on waking, that he could scarcely realize it being all a dream.

We laid awake till morning, talking about the darling fellow. Oh! how we both long for him. I tell Mr. Booth, if we should remain here long, which will probably be the case, he must let me take a trip across the Isthmus to see my loved family and bring our darling Boy. Dear little fellow, he can never know the tender anxiety we endure for his sake. I pray the Good Parent of us all to watch over and preserve him from every harm, and Oh! may He in His goodness but permit us once more to be restored to our child, our parents and sisters.

What a heaven on Earth may we not enjoy in hope and anticipation of that happy event. I am content to live and for a while endure the bitterness of separation. . . . It has been a severe trial to my feelings, and still continues to be, but I hope for brighter days to come, when we shall all be once more together. Till then, we must endeavour to do the best we can.

Henry E. Murray

Letter to his brother
13 November 1849

I now take pen in hand to inform you of my helth I have ben sick the most of the time since I landed I am all most discorage in the first place I was taken with the blodey disentary that wastted me disc[h]arging nothing but blood and slime I thout I should dy here but thank god i am alive yet since i got over the disentary i undertook to work and I worked a few days and got sick again and am fair from being well now my not being able to go to the mines i have had the horrors the worst kind I cannot go now becaus the rany season has commenced about a week a go it rains all most everyday thare is not much chance to woork if i felt able I do think this is one of the *unhelthyist* places in the known world but thare is money to be made here in Sanfrancisco. . . .

i am not able to woork now and I dont know wen i shal be i have worked wen i was not fit i am that week that i cant walk a hundred yardes with out seting down to rest the wether is very bad the mud is a most knee deepe in the streets they fairly waid I never saw a sitty grow as fast in my life more than one half of the [buildings] have been put up sinc i landed. . . . it is wet and bad sleeping in these tents if one gets sik it is a chance if they ever gets well Since i have i would a giveall the mony i ever had or ever shoud have but now as bad a[s] i feel i should want somthing handsom to leave be fore i make a triel for gold i am bound to give it a fair triell or leave my bones here. . . .

horace runels has ben sik ever since he has ben here he has not earnt a dollar david pots a tending a store he has what i call a good chance he saves half the profits i would like sush a channce my self but i have had bad luck i hope it will turn soon when you write to me let me know what you are all a bout home. . . . Well my dear friends i wish you all well yours most affecionate brother and friend

Anne Willson Booth

Journal
31 October 1849

Dr. Hardy is better to day. He is constantly begging me to write to his mother and inform her of his illness. I tell him it would be cruel to do so, before she would receive the letter, he will be quite well, and forget all about his sickness. Well then, he says, I must write to his Uncle, Dr. Edwards, who is in Congress from Ohio. If he persist, I will write to satisfy him, but will not send it, as we all think he will soon be well.

DeWitt & Harrison

Letter to Peter DeWitt, Esq.
27 February 1850

We enclose with this our letter to Mrs. Hannah Archer informing her of the death of her son Jonathan, also his watch, rings, papers, and Bible taken from his trunk, and some gold dust which was found in his pocket, and we are informed by his friends was dug by him at Buzzards Bar, North Fork American River. His companions informed us that they were living in a log house (built by themselves) some 100 miles from this place [San Francisco] on the Sacramento River, and engaged cutting wood, and that the land around them of the distance of 5 miles was overflowed with water to the depth of a foot and over and that it was impossible to dig a grave at that place. They therefore brought his body to this town and placed it in our charge. We had him placed in the burial ground and a board with his name painted on it put at the head of the grave, the burial service was performed by our pastor Rev. Mr. Williams.

The expenses of bringing his body to this place and burial amount about $130. We have sent his clothes and trunk to auction and will forward the account by the next Steamer that the amount may be placed with John DeWitt & Co. for our a/c.

We forward this accompanying package by Mr. John DeWitt, who returns on this Steamer.

Margaret DeWitt

Letter to her mother-in-law
28 February 1850

Uncle John leaves tomorrow, and we feel sorry to part with him. We have enjoyed his society much—hope he may have a safe and pleasant passage and find you all well and happy. You may suppose I feel very unfit to write letters, after the sad tidings I have received this last Steamer. Yet I can not bear to have a mail leave with out at least a few lines from me. The *Oregon* arrived Friday 22nd and the next day I received a letter from Father enclosed in a note to Alfred—also letters from my sister Joanna and Father—giving the account of the illness and death of my dear sister Helen. Dear Mother, this news has made me very sad. I feel crushed, and it is a very heavy trial. God has supported me, to him would I look in every affliction. He alone can heal the wound his hand has made. I know I have your kind sympathy, and endeavour to feel submissive to God's will.

The news came so unexpected—every letter told of improved health, I was so in hope we would all be spared to meet again. She was a very dear Sister and is indeed a great loss, but we cannot mourn for her. She died as she had lived, a bright Christian. She is happy now, this comforts me so much. She is where there is no more suffering, sorrow and sin, among the saints at rest.

Could I have been at home, I think it would not have been so trying. This is the first sad news I have had since I left, and I feel it very much. I feel so sorry for dear Edward and my poor Mother and Father—indeed for all, for they have sustained a very heavy affliction. But they all know where alone to go for consolation. May this trial be sanctified to us all. Alfred is very kind and feels much for me, and all my friends sympathise much with me, and I know it is all right and feel sure that our loss is her great gain. Yet I cannot help feeling much. I was so happy and contented before—now I feel so very very sad. I feel so much the want of my dear Mother and sisters. It would be such a pleasure to be with them and talk over these sad events. It is nearly two months since she died, and I have but just heard the news. The distance never seemed so great as now. But it is all right—and I am satisfied that I am here and hope it will be for good.

John McCrackan
_____

Letter to his family
17 February 1850

I think I have learned a few principles as to the mode of living here, and they are these. First, have a good dry bed, and enough clothes. Keep your feet dry and warm. Eat the very best food you can get, and take occasionally a little stimulus, either with or after your dinner. Avoid coffee, drink chocolate once a day, drink as little water as possible and then I recommend a lump of sugar in it. With all this, to watch your self narrowly and see you do not abuse nature in any way. You know not how fully I believe in these few practical rules. I am aware of having done much good by giving them to friends, who have been sick "so long" they are dispirited, and think they never will recover. I had a call from a person by the name of "Minot" some few days since, he is from New Haven. He had been sick so long and never expected to be any better. I questioned him at once and, as I expected, found he was drinking coffee twice a day and eating no meat, because he heard meats were not good for him. I gave him some "Ideas"—sent him home to practice them. I told him to drink porter, eat meat three times a day, and leave off his [illegible] coffee. He came in a few evenings since and wanted to pay me for my advice. We get the very best English porter and ale here, and in great quantities. It is sold for eighteen dollars a dozen [bottles]. I only wish I could send you a basket. This is always my drink, if I take anything with my dinner. We get very good wines and brandies here, and cheaper than in the U.S.

John McCrackan
_____

Letter to his family
8 May 1850

On Wednesday the 1st we were moving some of our things into our new offices, although I could not be about in consequence of a slight indisposition which had given me a little trouble for a day or two, and I thought it most prudent to keep my bed. About noon a package was handed in by some unknown hand, and it was discovered by someone entering the room, who read the direction to me signed by Mr. Silliman, and "it was not to be opened till I am dead." By this I knew he must be ill again, although I had seen him but a few days previous and he was much better and promised to leave his tent and take a room near the center of our city.

I started immediately taking with me a Physician, and together we search "Happy Valley" for his tent for three hours, when my strength failed and I was obliged to return, after procuring a man to continue the search till he found him, when he was to inform me, but to find him if it took a week! You may think it strange one could be so difficult to find if he was in a tent. But let me tell you, "Happy Valley" (which is about a mile from the city) is of itself a city of tents covering a mile and half square, and I had not the least idea in what part to find him. Beside[s] the whole Valley is a perfect desert of sand, and one cannot take a step without going over ankles, and as you will imagine it is very unpleasant wading through it. My exertion proved too much for my feeble condition, and I took my bed again. The day passed and the next, and no news from the Valley. On the day succeeding I was up, and about night I was fortunate enough to discover a man who could give me the desired information. He had seen Mr. Silliman, he was very sick, and soon concluded he must be moved and appointed the following morning to move him. This intention was frustrated, for the next day (Saturday) we were visited by the dreadful fire and could get none to assist.

On Sunday I was called to go to the Mission of San Raphael, but left an order to have him admitted at my own expense, which however was not done till I returned, though only for a few hours, to see if it had been done and how he was. Finding he was still in his tent, had him moved directly to the Hospital. He had for two or three days refused all food and was taking nothing but the most powerful stimulus, which in his condition having diarrhea and dysentery must soon prove fatal. He seemed a little recovered and his mind free, seemed happy, and left directions with me. He seemed inclined to sleep, and after remaining with him an hour or so I left him feeling and knowing he was in the best of care.

On my return from the Mission the next day the poor old man was no more. He had died but a few hours after I left him. His funeral, as he requested, was plain and conducted with a view to economize as far as consistent his little property. In his letter to me appointing me administrator, he gave me a full account of his effects, instructing me to inform his family and friends of his death &c, and this is a sad duty indeed. I have been the greater part of today collecting his things, the most valuable of them have been seriously injured by being exposed in his tent. I found among his things the miniatures of his several daughters, also of his wife.

It is dreadful to think of his coming out here to suffer so much, and to die at last. Had he lived, this month I could have given him all the writing he could and thus he might have earned sufficient money [as a law scrivener] to take him back to his dear family. It will be a severe blow to them, and Oh! how I regret that mine is the sad duty to open their bleeding hearts. May Heaven guard and protect, pity and relieve them in their affliction, and give consolation to the Widow and her fatherless children is my oft repeated prayer.

John McCrackan

Letter to his family
15 June 1850

We have all been severely afflicted and still continue so by the illness of little Willey Brooks. He was taken about a week since, and has been very ill, every day becoming worse. Mrs. B. has always used Homeopathic Treatment, but there appeared no medicine in my chest which would reach his care. She was obliged to abandon the practice, and employ a regular Physician, since which time although the little fellow did not appear decidedly worse. Yet the Dr. gave but little hope of his recovery. Mr. B. has been confined with him constantly, as one or the other are obliged to hold him constantly.

I went on board to see him on the eve of Thursday (day before yesterday). I learned from Mr. B. he had little or no hope of his recovery, and when I entered the saloon and saw the hopeless mother, she was seated on the sofa, holding Willey and in the depths of despair, schooling herself to the dreadful truth that he was to be taken from her. I could not give her much consolation, although her earnest inquirys evinced her desire to draw something favorable from me. He did not appear changed materially and had little the appearance of a sick child. But before me I saw a mother's heart, bowed down by the most intense agony, holding her feeble infant to her breast with that convulsive grasp that seemed to say they could not part, and the fate of her child must decide her own.

We have long been warm and very dear friends, the most convincing proof of which was the outpouring of her almost bursting heart, upon seeing me. She is a young mother, Willey being her first born and with a fresh, beautiful face even in despair. She stirred the warmest feelings of my nature, never before have I sat by the side of one so utterly hopeless, called to part with one dearer than life to her, her first born and best beloved. Willey has been her idol and I have often said to her she was too fond of him, rude words for a mothers heart, and so she seemed willing to believe, but what could lessen her love, how could she control it?

I saw the moment my eye rested upon the little fellow his symptoms were "dropsical," yet the Dr. called it "Choleric infantum." I remained with them all eve—and night. The Dr. said that night would be a very critical one with him, and so I remained. He rested well the first of the night, but toward morning commenced these fearful symptoms, the rolling of the head and eyes, accompanied with his mournful cry. Toward four o'clock he became more quiet, and for the first time recognized me. He however did not appear very much pleased, although he looked at me as much as to say he was "so sick."

His mother and father both got some sleep, and when I left him yesterday morning I thought him rather better than he was the eve previous. I need not tell you, my dear mother, of what emotions a "mothers heart" is capable. You have stood at the silent grave, and watch[ed] it close upon dear forms, bright hopes and long cherished anticipations, and your oft chastened spirit has been won to resignation and submission by the severe visitations your Heavenly father in his good will and pleasure has showered upon you, afflictions which were made to answer his just end of winning bright spirits to his "Heavenly Home".

John McCrackan

Letter to his family
16 June 1850

This letter should have been commenced this afternoon, which I passed in an almost fruitless effort to get sleep, of which I was deprived Saturday eve by watching with little Willey Brooks. After ending my letter No. 66 yesterday, we dined, when I went on board the *Balance*. Willey just at that time was very restless and seemed to be suffering from cramp. We made use of the usual remedies, but they afforded no relief, and I took the skiff and brought off the Physician. He was at length quieted and passed a very comfortable night.

I remained to assist Mrs. B. and allow Mr. B to get sleep, of which he had been deprived for some time, both have been very much confined, the little fellow obliging some[one] to hold him constantly. Saturday a Mrs. Tuxbury was on board all day, and thus Mrs. B had the opportunity of getting rest. When I left the Ship this morning at seven o'clock he was very much better, he knew me perfectly and seemed to be quite pleased to be with me. I do not think him out of danger as yet, but we entertain but little doubt of his final recovery.

John McCrackan

Letter to his family
25 June 1850

Little Willey is now almost recovered, while mother and father are almost sick with constant watching. The little fellow noticed me among the first moments of returning consciousness, raised his eyes and made an effort to extend his arms, thus signifying his intention or wish to have me take him. I did so, and with his arms placed about my neck and his little face resting against my cheek he continued in my arms for some time, and it was such a sweet, pleasing incident, equally to the parents as myself. This was last Saturday (22nd). Since then I have not been on board, but hear from him daily.

Anne Willson Booth

Journal
17 October 1849

Nothing has occurred to day that is worthy of note, I believe. The weather continues delightful, and the work of discharging is nearly completed. The ship is already taking in ballast as fast as room is made to put it. Uncle Wes thinks to get away from here in about three weeks. He does not expect to go to China now, consequently will reach home much sooner than he would otherwise. How I dread being left here in this forlorn place. But such is my choice, and I am willing to abide by it. Yet I cannot help wishing sometimes that we had accomplished our object and were ready to return home in the ship. I sincerely hope however that in a very few years we shall be again at home. Indeed I may say this is my determination, for if successful we shall be prepared to return. If not, this place will have no inducements for us.

Anne Willson Booth

Journal
18 October 1849

Six months have now passed away since we left home and friends; and, Oh! how long the time appears when I recall the day we bade adieu to many a kindred tie that bound us to our dearly loved home. How eventful to us have these last six months been, and how replete with interest too. As my friend Mr. King and myself were conversing together on this subject last evening, we both remarked that we should always have something to think and talk about in after years, if we should be again permitted to return to our homes. Many an interesting incident has occurred, which will always be remembered with lively interest. Even this short lapse of time has effected many a change and been marked by many an event of joy to some, and of sadness to others. Who can look forward to the termination of another six months, and say what shall be its changes? Most fortunately, no one has this power! I think it one of the wisest ordinations of an ever kind Providence, in thus withholding from us, poor mortals, the power to foretell future events. This knowledge would not increase our present comfort, or prepare us in any measure to avert whatever evil may present itself, but, on the contrary, would only serve to incapacitate us from the enjoyment of present benefits. No, I would not if I could peer into the dark vista of the future or penetrate its gloom. Happily, it is a sealed volume forbidden to mortal vision, and only known to Him who tells us: "Sufficient for the day is the evil thereof."

Jonathan F. Locke

Letter to his wife
17 November 1849

George [their son] is cook for our mess at present. I fear however he will not give satisfaction. He does not fancy the business. I think I can make him earn something, for he is very hearty and stout. I find some trouble to manage him but I think he improves a little of late. He is truly beset with a thousand temptations. I have strong hopes that he will come out right at last. I cannot induce him to write as yet, but he promises now we have some conveniences to commence soon. . . .

Tell Willy and Jimmy to be good boys and help mother and I will send them a piece of gold soon. I wish I could see them trotting about.

Tell them father is living in a cloth house when it is not half so cold as it is at winter [illegible]. Tell Jonny I guess he will see me again if he is a good boy. If he and Willy goes to school and learns fast, how proud I shall be when I come back and find they know so much.

You must keep up your courage and you will get along with the children well enough. I have perfect confidence in your abilities to perform all that is required regarding the children. As for me, I came out here to get something to pay my debts and something for your and the children's comfort and education. I could enjoy myself if I knew you were all well.

Caroline Stoddard

Journal
15 December 1850

The schooner *A. Emery* is now lying near us, commanded by Capt. Galagher, bound to Oregon with passengers. He was formerly a Unitarian minister, who I have heard preach in Fair Haven, we, that is Mrs. Stott, John Merrill and myself hailed them, to know if they would sell us some coacoa-nuts—purchased six at 12 1/2 cts apiece.

Caroline Stoddard

Journal
19 December 1850

Fears are entertained here, for the safety of the Sch. *A. Emery,* it is thought she foundered in the gale, we had on Tuesday—and all on board perished.

T. Warwick Brooke

Letter to his mother
9 February 1850

I fear this is the last time you'll hear from me for some months. When next I write I trust to tell you of good dollars won by good hard work. We reached this place on Tuesday—the weather has cleared up within the week and folks are all turning towards the mines. I have had great difficulty in finding anyone to whom I had letters. Bradley and Warren are both reported to have turned home. There are scores of papers and letters lying for Barclay at the Post [Office]. Butler King isn't here. Dr. Ver Mehr is the only being with whom I have fallen in—he is a very pleasant Evangelical French or rather Belgian, and his wife is very nice good natured being. I assure you, after all the "roughing" of the past two months an hour's chat with gentlefolk is something better than plum pudding.

Of all adventures by flood and field you shall, if it please the good God, hear from me when I am with you again. How precious to me from day to day that word "meet again" is. I have no space to tell you. It is, however, the main spring of my existence now and the source of my perpetual good spirits—nay, I verily believe of my health too. . . .

When I shall receive the letters which are on their way for me I know not—but write, please write and tell me everything. Dear people, how I lie and think of you at night, stretched on a good plank bed—dirt! I never knew what being dirty was till now! I think of the good bath-room and clean water and plenty of it! Well, never mind. I'll have a patent shower bath of my own up in the mines. But I must make a short note of this. . . . I think of you sleighing. Oh! I didn't know when I was happy—but no regrets! I look forward! . . . And now, dear Mama, to catch you the very biggest rock in the whole digging and bring it back alive and tame.

Chapter 4

Madmen, Drunkards,
Murderers, and Whores

It is axiomatic that the American West was a violent place (though historians now disagree on how much more violent it was than the rest of the country at the time). This almost legendary wildness was to some extent a self-fulfilling prophesy, as early on the mythmakers portrayed the region as lawless and unforgiving and the westerner as "a man of rough habits and violent disposition."[1] The meek and dutiful therefore meekly and dutifully stayed back East, and only the extroverted and adventuresome were inclined to kick over the traces and head out into the unregulated unknown.

Violent crime was almost commonplace in the nineteenth-century American West, particularly in boomtowns like San Francisco. Shootings and stabbings were reported with alarming frequency, usually committed by males under the influence of alcohol, in a saloon or nearby street, most frequently after dark. The victim was usually an acquaintance of the murderer and the dispute usually a minor one that had escalated thanks to an excess of whiskey and bravado. Friday and Saturday nights were particularly deadly.[2]

The West attracted young men of high spirits who, even if they were married, tended to leave their wives back home and enter a life of enforced bachelorhood. Of the eighty-nine thousand Argonauts who arrived in California in 1849, 95 percent were male.[3] This selective migration created a cohort of immigrants who were of an age and gender most inclined to violence, and placed them in an environment that was both unstable and transitory. These young men tended to be heavy drinkers who were hypersensitive to slights (real or perceived) and who relied on firearms to bolster their self-image. They had little invested in whatever community structure the town boasted and—even more deadly—they suffered from the usual young man's disbelief in his own mortality.[4]

Into this volatile mix of alcohol, lead, and testosterone, gold rush San Francisco infused a singular strain of melancholy. Unlike the young men who ended up in Dodge City or Tombstone, the Argonauts were motivated primarily by a desire to accumulate quick wealth and then to return home as soon as possible. They were not, for the most part, driven west to escape an unsatisfactory home life or to seek out adventure beyond the reach of parental control in one of the wild, wide-open towns that dotted the American West.

Most Argonauts came from closely integrated communities, either from crowded urban neighborhoods or from rural farms populated by extended, multigenerational families. They were accustomed to an environment in which everyone knew everyone else's business. In San Francisco, however, they found themselves in a situation in which there was no authoritarian father, no doting mother, no highly principled sister, no admiring kid brother, no indulgent but easily shocked sweetheart. There was, in short, no one to monitor their behavior, whether to censure or to praise. In California no one knew what they were doing and, what is more, no one cared.

Some Argonauts attempted to create a sense of community by traveling with relatives or neighbors, and many formalized this structure by incorporating themselves into legally established companies. Few of these companies survived the first few weeks in California, however, as they came to the realization that panning for gold was very much an individual endeavor. Those who went into commerce or the service industries also quickly learned that doing business in San Francisco, with its wild fluctuations in supply and demand, required a degree of on-the-fly entrepreneurship that was difficult or impossible for large enterprises to manage.

Nevertheless, individuals still sought the social company of their compatriots (Boston men preferring the company of Boston men, or at least Massachusetts men or—as a last resort—other New Englanders), but even these bonds proved to be ephemeral, and some men failed to connect with others at all. Living without privacy in a flimsy tent or in a narrow berth of a canvas-sided flophouse, many found themselves surrounded by humanity but paradoxically alone. Adding to the disorientation was the utter randomness of fortune: the stranger to one's right might suddenly drop down dead while the stranger to one's left might just as suddenly become fabulously wealthy. Hard work or merit seemed to have little to do with success or failure.

The gold rush attracted many men who lacked the maturity required to deal with stress and the sudden loss of community structure. They were the group most likely to become alcohol or drug abusers, to commit suicide, to become insane, or to succumb to a variety of diseases associated with the squalid living conditions. Men in the prime of their lives poured into San Francisco in 1849; within six months one in five was dead. So high was the mortality rate that insurance companies refused to write any new policies for Californians.[5]

Death in San Francisco came from diseases that coursed unchecked through the sprawling tent city. It came from exposure to the elements during the rainy winter of 1849 to 1850, and during the following summer when a damp, cold fog wrapped the city like a shroud. It came from prolonged drinking bouts encouraged by the ubiquitous lure of alcohol (six out every hundred Californians were involved in the liquor trade).[6] It came from shootouts in the gambling halls and muggings in the streets. It came also in the form of suicide for those who could not cope with unrealized dreams or a sudden reversal of fortune.

How was it that so many healthy, adventuresome, hopeful young men simply fell apart in San Francisco? Recent studies of post-traumatic stress disorder may give a clue. Psychologists have begun to study the damage caused by life-threatening or identity destroying stimuli that exceed the brain's ability to cope.[7] In many ways the Argonauts present a classic case: months spent en route under the most trying conditions, followed by immersion in an uncaring world gone crazy in the pursuit of wealth. Many immigrants were constantly battling exposure to the elements, unable to afford decent housing or adequate food, torn between the hard, risky venture of panning for gold and the slow, steady accumulation of savings in humiliating jobs that were no better (and frequently much worse) than what they had left at home. Many felt keenly that they were disappointing their families or sweethearts by not becoming, as they had boasted they would, instant millionaires. Loneliness and frustration led to drinking binges, and the profits of months of labor flew away within minutes at the monte tables. Constantly assailed by ill-health, danger, and disappointment, many simply lost their grasp on life.

The gold rush itself might be viewed as a risky endeavor that attracted men who were already of a self-destructive bent. The transfer to California involved multiple losses: loss of a community of loved ones, loss of shelter and reliable medical care, loss of family savings spent in outfitting the traveler. Lost, too, were the ritual structures that can help an individual deal with loss. As one study of suicide on the frontier concludes, "Migrants tended and tend to be people in search of transformation. . . . To the extent that transformation is either restricted or impossible, the guilt for having rejected past values and rituals intensifies as the dream of self-transformation fades. In any case, fantasies of self-transformation always carry with them a burden of self-rejection and to a certain extent of self-hate. Immigration and migration exacerbates all of these problems."[8]

Individuals who were strong enough to stand up to the humiliations and disappointments of the surroundings encountered other threats to their personal safety as well. In the early months of the gold rush a strange dichotomy of crime existed: personal property could safely be left unattended but human life was highly vulnerable. Particularly feared were the "Sydney Ducks," supposed convicts from Australian penal colonies who preyed upon the unwary.[9] Historian Hubert Howe Bancroft, looking back on the San Francisco he had personally experienced, drew a dismal (if melodramatic) picture:

> At the corner of Pacific street stood a four-story building adorned with balconies, wherein the City Hall had found a halting-place after much migrating, in conjunction with the jail and court-rooms. The opposite block, stretching toward Montgomery street and at the foot of Telegraph hill, was filled with shabby dens and public houses of the lowest order, frequented by sinister-looking men and brazen-faced females, who day or night were always ready either for low revelry or black crime. The signs above the drinking-houses bore names which, like Tam O'Shanter, Magpie, and Boar's Head, smacked of English sea-port resorts, and within them Australian slang floated freely upon the infected atmosphere. It was in fact the headquarters of the British convict class, whose settlement, known as Sydney Town, extended hence north-eastward round the hill. It was the rallying-point for pillaging raids, and to it was lured many an unwary stranger, to be dazed with a sand-bag blow, and robbed, perhaps to be hurled from some Tarpeian projection into the bay.[10]

Living in San Francisco required a combination of street smarts and tough business acumen, as well as a blind eye when it came to the folly of one's neighbors. Particularly during the years of 1849 and 1850, when the hope of easy riches and a quick trip home were still

high, citizens were able to adopt an urbane disinterest in the under-belly of the city. Eyebrows were raised and heads were shaken, but little movement was made to reform the community's vice, probably because what was happening at the monte tables was not that much different from what was happening in the gold fields or being trans-acted over the "respectable" shop counters. It was *all* a crap shoot. Since San Francisco was not viewed as anyone's permanent home, and since there were so few women and children in need of protec-tion, little effort was made to draw a curtain of respectability over naked vice.

Gambling halls—such as the Bella Union or the Palmer House—were the largest, most lavishly decorated buildings in the town, and most were clustered around the Plaza (Portsmouth Square). Though they were usually constructed of little more than a slight wood frame covered with canvas, they boasted fine furniture, loud music, im-ported liquor, and beautiful women—all of it illuminated by dazzling oil lamp chandeliers. When viewed from the street on cold, foggy eve-nings the tent saloons glowed like giant Japanese lanterns. Quickly they became the social centers of town, and few of the men huddled in rough tents or crowded rooming houses could resist the lure of their warm hospitality.

During the gold rush the entrepreneurial spirit was so paramount that everything—including sex—was reduced to a commodity, sub-ject to fluctuations in market demand and the quality of the goods be-ing offered.[11] With the skewed ratio of men to women in the popula-tion it was inevitable that prostitution would flourish; among the forty thousand immigrants who arrived by ship during 1849 were seven hundred women, mostly prostitutes from Mexico and other La-tin American countries.[12] The earliest years of the gold rush in San Francisco have been characterized as a "period of free competition" for aspiring prostitutes, and the wide-open town certainly provided many opportunities for economic advancement for any woman bold enough to seize the occasion.[13] In the same way that the lowliest New York City bank teller or clerk could within months own his own fi-nancial institution in San Francisco, the most destitute Parisian streetwalker could, with diligence and a little luck, own her own sa-loon or brothel.[14]

Prostitutes were certainly economically mobile (if not socially ac-ceptable), particularly during the first years of the gold rush. In the grand tradition of supply and demand, prostitutes and saloon owners formed a symbiotic relationship, each exploiting the opportunities presented by the other. Sexually available women brought in gamblers and the gamblers with the most money frequented the most elegant saloons. Consequently there was stiff competition among the prostitutes for securing work at the few places that attracted the high rollers, such as the Bella Union and the El Dorado, while on the other hand the smaller establishments competed among themselves to employ the most desirable women in order to enhance their commercial draw. A woman who was reasonably attractive could make a lucrative arrangement with the proprietor of one of the lesser establishments. In addition to the salary she received for serving as a waitress, a hostess, or as merely an alluring piece of room decor, she was free to make any private arrangements with the customers once she completed her work shift. Saloonkeepers might offer her a free room on the premises to use for such encounters, or rent rooms by the hour to the clientele.[15] After 1852, when men seized control of the sex trade in San Francisco, a prostitute typically forfeited most of her earnings to her pimp or the brothel owner, but during the early years the majority of the profit was hers. With a market price of anywhere from two hundred to five hundred dollars per night, a prostitute could earn enough in a short time to open her own establishment.

Two groups of prostitutes were excluded from this picture of prosperity: Latinas and Chinese women. As has been noted, the first prostitutes to arrive during the gold rush were from Latin America. Unlike their peers from New York or Paris, most of these women arrived as indentured servants, pledged to work for at least six months in the little cantinas and fandango parlors that sprung up at the foot of Telegraph Hill in a neighborhood known as Little Chile. They might dream of one day gracing the elegant Bella Union, but in reality they had little chance of rising above the squalor in which they lived since they rarely received more than a dollar per sexual encounter. Contrary to the general respect shown "the fairer sex" in San Francisco, Latina prostitutes were held in low regard and were contemptuously referred to as "greaseritas."[16]

The situation for Chinese prostitutes was somewhat more complex. A few Chinese women came to San Francisco on their own initiative in hopes of making a larger profit from their prostitution than they were able to make in their homeland, but most of the young girls were sold into the sex trade by destitute parents. One daughter was able to send back as much as two to three hundred dollars after only seven months in California.[17] Almost all of the Chinese prostitutes came from the peasant class of Kwangtung in southern China, and arrived with few skills and little education. In San Francisco's Chinatown they were known as baak haak chai (one hundred men's wife).[18]

Probably the first Chinese prostitute in America was a twenty-year-old woman from Hong Kong named Ah Toy, who arrived in San Francisco in late 1848 or early 1849 and immediately opened business as an independent prostitute in a small shack on an alley off Clay Street above Kearny. So successful was she that by 1850 she expanded her business, adding two recently arrived Chinese prostitutes.[19] Ah Toy's clientele were primarily non-Chinese and comparatively affluent, and she was soon able to open her own brothel.[20] It was reported that she was so beautiful that men would wait in a line a block long and pay a full ounce of gold just to gaze on her face. Also rising from a humble beginning, Lai Chow began her career in San Francisco as one of two dozen twelve-year-olds shipped from China in a crate labeled "dishware." She was able to make enough money to open a brothel, and in turn smuggled in girls of her own.[21]

Chinese women were quickly objectified into sexual fetishes, primarily because there were so few of them. The 1852 California census lists only nineteen Chinese females, compared to 2,954 Chinese males.[22] Since most Chinese male immigrants were either unmarried or had left their wives at home in China, it is likely that most or all of the Chinese women in this census were prostitutes. For Anglos who had never in their lives encountered an Asian, the combination of exotic appearance and seemingly universal sexual availability made Chinese women both highly desired and socially scorned.

Vice and violent crime grew unabated in San Francisco during the early years of the gold rush, but in the letters and diaries both are treated almost as charming local color. "Good" women such as Anne Willson Booth and Caroline Stoddard were able to write about the depravity with a cool and sophisticated detachment, rhetorically lifting their hems to walk gingerly past the mire. Edward Austin sent his family a suspiciously detailed account of the goings-on in the gambling dens, while assuring them that *he*, of course, had not succumbed to temptation. Strange, sad figures appear in these letters and then vanish as quickly as they did in life—"young Gardiner from Salem, Mass." who is carried to the hospital and dies there, insane.

Crime increased and became more violent as the easy placers

were stripped clean and the hunt for gold became more difficult and more costly. Men found it harder to adopt an "easy come, easy go" attitude toward their riches, and with the raised stakes came a new level of viciousness and mayhem. This trend was challenged by the Vigilance Committees of 1851 and 1856, but even then the reasons for wanting to clean up San Francisco had little (if anything) to do with moral outrage at the parade of rampant sin. For men of the cloth, however, San Francisco's flaunted immorality represented the nadir of civilization. As the pioneer Methodist minister Rev. William Taylor proclaimed, "The city of San Francisco may, with propriety, be regarded as the very citadel of his Satanic Majesty."[23]

Henry R. DeWitt

Letter to his brother William
18 June 1849

I had a very pleasant trip up from Panama. Win Parkins' friend Mac-Ivain is the purser of the *Panama*. He is very unpopular, and was flogged once or twice coming up in the steamer by some of the passengers. Maybe you remember some time ago one night when we were up in Union Park. Win introduced us to [a] young man by the above name, this purser is the same one. I did not know him till he mentioned the fact of his meeting me before. It came all right to me. . . .

H. Whitimore is here and I [think] he will never get out of this alive. He has severe attacks of the inflamations of the bowels. He hardly recovers from one attack, then he's taken down with another. He means to return if he ever gets well enough. Dr. Hudard['s] son—the one that came out with Col. Stevens—got drunk and shot an Indian, for which he was sentenced to wear the Chain and Ball for two years. I heard that he has excaped. The Indian he shot was not killed.

George Ginnes [?]

Letter to John Harvey
21 July 1849

You will be no doubt somewhat surprised when I tell you we have dissolved our Company, and every one digs upon his own account. It is following in the steps of all other Companies, it ascertained beyond a doubt to my mind that it is impossible for large Companies to operate in the mines, and as for mutual protection—it is all moonshine. Gold is plenty enough without murdering people for it, and I have no doubt but you will receive as much from the men as you ever anticipated. I do not doubt but every man will do what is right with the one who put a fortune in their hands. James Rundlet Jr. has been drunk 1/4th part of his time since he left home. He is a poor miserable goat. Not so with Mr. Phipps. I think he is destined to be a man.

William J. Towne

Diary
22 July 1849

Cooked some fritters for the first time. A man shot himself.

J. K. Osgood

Letter to George Strang
23 August 1849

I am sorry that Sherwood ventured to come, as the place is a perfect Hell in dissipation. Gambling is carried on at all hours of the day and during Sunday, the evening of which the rooms are generally crowded. Have no fear of my falling into this vice or into intemperance, I think that I can resist both.

Alfred DeWitt

Letter to his brother George
28 August 1849

The gamblers are reaping a rich harvest and many a young man who never resorted to such places at home, after being here a few months is found at the tables throwing away his earnings. To show how profitable the business has become to such characters, they offered Mr. Ward $3000 a month for his dwelling house, to be used for that purpose. He refused it and said that he would burn the house down before he would let it to them. Many of those who have been fortunate in collecting gold become so excited after their sudden gains, that they are easily drawn into the meshes of the card playing gentry, and of course their money soon vanishes.

Edward Austin

Letter to his brother
24 September 1849

[Send] enough cherry boards for a good bar to the two story house. That house will rent for 60$ per day. Some fancy paper—say, some hunting scene or something like that—which will set it off to good advantage. I believe I wrote for paint and oil. The invoice I ordered before of tumblers, decanters, &c will answer for the fixtures. I am to have nothing to do with the concern except collect the rents. And also send a few chairs—say, one dozen like those I had in my country room. Send out a few—say, four or six—chaste pictures of naked women with good frames. I put this in separate so that you can keep it "shady"—don't let the folks know any of this, not even Lucy, although I do not have any thing to do with it and would not, they might think hard of it. . . .

I believe Frank can get any amount of goods, and tell him not to be bashful, I know the ropes of this country and the business. I have been in the country as long as most any one from the States. I arrived early, and should have been as rich had I funds on arrival. It is a hard place for one to accumulate money if he starts with out capital, but if you have money you can go it with a rush.

Oh George—it would make your eyes water as have mine, to see the noble chances slip by for a fortune, and you powerless for want of funds. If many had saved their money here and been prudent they could have gone home now rich. One young fellow in particular. He made $23,500 in four months in the mines up to last April. I saw him. Well, he came down to San Francisco and in five nights he was with out a cent, and had to work his passage up the river on the same vessel I came up on. He has sobered down and does not find it so easy to raise funds again. He has got now, he told me the other day, $1,400 and he was going to put it where the devil could not get it.

Anonymous

Journal of voyage from New Bedford to San Francisco
25 September 1849

Masury sorry he came here, can find no occupation. Told me his intentions were to go into a Salem house established here as a clerk— this was on the first of the voyage—he lied: there is no such house as he told us of in San F. And what is more, he has not the requisite qualifications. The fact has proved him to be just what a passenger told him he was: "a head strong reckless fellow—that he must have got himself into much trouble in his life—and that the remainder of his passage through it would be a flinty and a thorny one." Our captain learned on shore in conversation with a gentleman from Salem that he had a fine woman for a wife and one child, that they lived at his father's, that he abused his wife shamefully and gave them all a great deal of trouble, that they were all happier in his absence than when at home, &c &c. I think he has gone to Coloma—may his "roving commission" soon run out, [and] he become a better man. My cold is better.

C. C. Hyde

Letter to his brother
27 September 1849

But this *town is a town of itself not one of the towns,* a person can form no idea of it until they come here and see for themselves. It is jammed full of people from all parts of the world, and all classes, loafers, gamblers, gentlemen and labourers. . . . Gambling houses here pay the best rent, it is astonishing to see how much of that business is carried on here. Whole buildings are occupied for that purpose, having from three to six monte tables, two or three roulettes, and any quantity of other games in each. The monte tables have generally from $2 to $5000 of silver and gold on them all the time. These houses are crowded night and day.

A great many people are returning almost daily from the mines, who do not stay there two weeks. They say there is gold there, but not near as plenty as it has been, and it wants an iron constitution to be able to undergo the hardship of getting it. I saw a man last week who had just returned from the mines. He said he had followed lumbering in Wisconsin nearly all his life and he said that that was play in comparison to digging gold. There are men though who come down with gold, but they are generally of the rough class, that can endure any thing. The most of these fellows come down with it and stay just long enough to gamble it away and then they start for the mines again.

Thomas Reid

Journal

7 October 1849

This city is nearly as big as Pawtucket. They are erecting a great many new buildings. Carpenters get from 12 to 15 dollars per day. Lumber is very high. Labour[er]s get from 5 to 6 dollars per day; board is from 10 to 30 dollars per week.

The streets are lumbered up with goods of all descriptions. You can see piles of trunks laying about the streets, and great quantities of merchandise that will not pay for storing of them. I saw four or five thousand dollars worth of flour on the beach. It was Chilean flour, put up in bags. The bags were rotting off the flour on account of being exposed to the air.

The laws are very strict. For theft of any amount they cut the ears off for the first offence. The second, they hang him without ceremony. This law is a very good one, for a person can leave his trunk outdoors anywhere unlocked without any danger of anything being stolen.

I think that most all the hardest gamblers are busy to work with their gambling tools. I saw the noted Cris Lilly, the man that killed Macoy. He has made his independent fortune here. He is worth forty thousand dollars. He owns a splendid house. He keeps a house of prostitution, and makes a great deal of money at this business. He also is banker at a gambling game called monte.

It is estimated there is 20 thousand people in San Francisco. The people are thick as bees lounging about the streets. There is all nations collected here—Indians, South American, Spaniards, Mexicans, Yankees, English, French, and there is about a dozen of Chinese here. I saw them in the streets wearing their native costume.

Money is very plenty here. At most any gambling saloon there will be thousands of dollars stacked before the bankers. I saw some of the most miserable beings with their pockets full of gold and silver and betting their money high on the blacklegs tables. Fortunes are made and lost here in a day. When they lose their money, they go to the diggings to get more. They don't pay any respect for the Sabbath, for the gambling saloons are all open and busy to work.

There is hundreds of tents pitched about the city and along the beach. Some that arrive here destitute have to work here until they get funds to carry them into the diggings. I have saw, while four hours in the city, more money than I ever saw before in my life.

Anne Willson Booth

Journal
28 September 1849

Col. Myers dined with us to day. He is encouraged by the prospects here, and has rented a house in connection with several other gentlemen, for which they pay $16,000 per annum. They design letting out the different apartments, I believe for gambling purposes. The gambling place[s] are very numerous and, it is said, very attractive. A gentleman with whom I am acquainted lost the sum of $30,000. There is always a Spanish female at these places, I am informed, who sits at the head of the table and sings, plays the harp or guitar. When I was ashore, we passed many of these establishments, and I was surprised to see the heaps of gold and silver that were piled upon the table. There is no secrecy observed about them at all—the doors are kept wide open, every thing being exposed to public view. It is said, the most perfect order reigns throughout these establishments, and in this respect form quite a contrast to similar places in the Union. Indeed, morals generally are much better here than we were taught to expect. I had imagined an almost lawless state of society, in which crimes were perpetrated with impunity, but in this respect am most agreeably disappointed. Whenever a crime is committed, summary justice is at once executed, so that offenders are kept under by the fear of being lynched. Such a thing as theft, it is said, is not known at all. There is a large amount of goods lying about, and regarded perfectly safe. This is, at least, one pleasing trait.

Anne Willson Booth

Journal
8 October 1849

Mr. Taylor was on board this afternoon and informs us of Mrs. Reed being quite sick of the prevailing disease, diarrhea. We heard of one man being found dead in his tent, circumstances being such as to induce the belief he had been dead three days. It is remarked by all, there is much more dissipation about town now than there was when we first arrived—mostly confined however to the sailors, who constitute a large proportion of the population. When they accumulate a sum of money, they knock off work, and become victims to the various means devised by others to dispossess them of it. When their funds are exhausted, they are cared for by nobody, and if sickness overtake them, they are left to suffer and die.

Thomas Reid

Journal
9 October 1849

To day I went ashore for a couple of hours. I went down to what they call Sacremento Street. This street is full of gin shops and gambleing saloons. Some of the houses in the center of the city are made of canvess cloth stretched on light frames and furnished inside with splendid furniture. . . . Last night there was a man killed ashore by a chillian. The United States craft *Savanah* is here. One of her boats was ashore with a boat's crew and a midshipman, one of the sailors, jumped ashore and run. The officer fired a revolver at him but did not hit him and the sailor got clear but I think they will catch him if he stays in the city.

Anne Willson Booth

Journal
18 October 1849

There has been quite a melancholy occurrence in the harbour to day. Capt. Proctor of the Ship *Capitol* of New Bedford, in a temporary fit of derangement, jumped overboard and was drowned. He had been sick a few weeks, which is said to have been occasioned by difficulties that existed between him and his passengers. It is said they were a very unruly set, and harassed the poor man out of his wits. Capt. Proctor is said to have been about 25 years of age, very amiable and universally respected. It is a sad event truly, and seems to excite general sympathy and regret. The shipping have their flags at half mast head in token of respect.

Anne Willson Booth

Journal
20 October 1849

There is to be a fearful tragedy enacted in this harbour on Tuesday next. Five seamen belonging to the frigate *Savannah* are condemned to be hung for a crime committed a short time previous to our arrival, which was an attempt to drown one of the midshipmen belonging to the same vessel by throwing him overboard and rowing right over him. This occurred at night, while they were going off to the frigate. He soon became exhausted, and he was left, as they thought they had succeeded in executing their murderous intentions. Fortunately however, his cries for help attracted the notice of some persons on shore, who immediately came to his relief and found him in a state of exhaustion, from which he soon recovered and gave evidence as who were his would-be murderers. They were soon arrested and confined on board the frigate.

A court martial has been in session the last few weeks. This morning it was decided they should forfeit their lives. There are three war vessels in this harbour, each one is selected as the place this horrid affair is to be consummated. Mr. Taylor has been solicited to assist the other ministers in administering the ordinance of baptism and sacrament. Poor, misguided men. How my heart bleeds for them; what a horrible fate awaits them. Every one seems filled with horror at the awfulness of the deed, which is to deprive five human beings of life—while all agree that they deserve their fate, and justify the tribunal in their decision. Certainly, it was not owing to their clemency, that the object of their vengeance did not suffer the fate they intended for him.

Anne Willson Booth

Journal
23 October 1849

There is quite an excitement in the harbour this morning, this being the day on which the poor, unfortunate men are to be executed on board the war vessels. Boats are plying about in all directions, filled with persons anxious to witness the horrible scene. The surrounding hills are thronged with spectators, as well as the different vessels lying near those selected for the performance of the sad deed. At 12 o'clock, we heard the firing of a gun, which signified that one had paid the penalty of his crime. In a few minutes a second gun was fired. We heard no more. When our folks returned to the ship, they informed us that of the five men condemned to die, but two had met this fate, the remaining three having been reprieved in consequence of a confession made by the others of their not having any thing to do in the planning or execution of the crime they were about to suffer for. Then their lives are spared, but of course these men will be severely punished for lending their countenance to the rest, and then running away from the ship.

Christian Miller

Letter to his family
29 October 1849

Just before I arrived at this place five sailors were arrested for attempting to drown a port midshipman belonging to one of our men of war. Last week two of them were hung at the yard arms on the Frigate *Savannah* the other three were reprieved, but received about one hundred lashes each (their object was to get to the mines). It is all peace and quietness here and at the mines—and no danger from the Indians.

E. A. Upton

Diary
19 December 1849

A few weeks ago five of the crew of the *Savanah* were rowing an officer ashore in the port, and when about three miles from the ship and two from the shore, at a signal on[e] of the sailors instantly seized the officer and pitched him overboard. Another sailor then struck at him several times with an oar and hit him once on the head, but did not stun him, the officer succeeding in reaching a vessel in the harbor by swimming. The sailors have all been since taken in New York on the Pacific [New York of the Pacific, now Pittsburg, California] and brought back to San Francisco in irons, tried on board the Sloop of War *Warren* [?], and the sailor that threw the officer overboard, and the one that struck him after he was over, were hung at the yard arm. The other three were sentenced to work in irons three years without pay.

E. A. Upton

Diary
25 November 1849

A city ordinance is posted up for the first [of December] forbidding stores and shops being kept open, all gambling on the Sabbath forbidden and all music on the Sabbath, under the penalty of $24.00. Not much if [any] notice taken of it.

Benjamin C. Howard

Letter to his father
25 November 1849

I never saw such a place. They no more respect Sunday than any other day. I saw lots and *lots* of people as I passed [a]long, gambling, and such piles of money. . . . The other day I saw a little boy who certainly had not seen 10 summers, gambling with three or four others and seemed to be as old as any of them. Who should I see but Tom Brooks the City Marshall on the landing on Thursday looking as sober as a judge. He has not succeeded very well. He was dressed with big boots, a large yellow coat and a tarpaulin hat. He had just come from the mines and had two little purses in his pocket full of dust. . . . I never saw such a place for honesty in all my going a fishing. Nothing is stolen here. Onshore the people leave their duds all exposed, and they are not touched. Two men were hung a few days before we arrived on board the man of war——for attempting the life of one of the officers. It is useless for me to try to describe the place, it would fill a volume. It seems like great training day more than anything all the time. Capt. Tibbetts will tell you all about it. Excuse this writing for I am writing like smoke.

E. A. Upton

Diary
29 November 1849

Suicides are now frequent in the city, committed by those who have lost all by gambling or being disappointed in their expectations in reference to the mines.

Margaret DeWitt

Letter to her mother-in-law
30 March 1850

You remember Mr. Frank Ward, who lost his wife last summer. He has failed in business and it is said has lost every thing. This together with the loss of his wife had a great effect upon him and (it is supposed in a moment of derangement) he attempted to kill himself with a pistol. The ball passed through his eye and lodged, I believe, in the opposite cheek bone. Strange to say, it did not kill him and he is now lying ill with fever and it is supposed he will recover. It is said he looks frightfully. It is a very melancholy thing and has cast a gloom over all. He was a very high spirited man, but much beloved for many excellent qualities. This should teach us all a lesson—not to set our affection upon earthly riches, for surely they take to themselves wings and fly away. It was supposed last summer he had made a very large fortune, and I fear many others who have speculated will find themselves in the same condition.

Edward Austin

Letter to his family
29 November 1849

All cannot help making a fortune if prudent, all have much chance of being ruined, unless they can shun temptation. Large saloons fitted up with great taste—beautiful music and some 10 to 15 gambling tables occupying each one—are very plenty and in some streets the light lightens the street from the blaze within. Women sit at the gambling boards and deal the cards—and take the money with gracious smiles. The Spanish women come in to most of the saloons and make their bets with as much coolness as any of the men—and I must say that San Francisco is the most dissipated place in the world, and at the same time the most orderly and quiet. Dollars fly away and come and go and no one seems to mind it. Some are rich to day and poor tomorrow and so it goes on. Thus you will see that every inducement is held forth for men to play. This is mostly done by the Southerners and Western men. The New England men—I say it much to their credit—are not as a general thing addicted to play. The Boston boys are steady and seem destined to succeed, they all seem to be workers.

E. A. Upton

Diary
5 December 1849

A young man just returned from the mines with his entire summer's worth, amounting [to] 150 ounces gold, went into a gambling establishment and lost all but eight ounces, when his luck turned, and he won all back again together with six ounces in addition, when he quit saying he would break the bank. . . . I notice at many of the gambling tables women staking largely.

E. A. Upton

Diary

7 December 1849

A man just dropped dead in Wash[ington] St., the cause of his death as near as I could learn was exposure. His features wore the expression of extreme suffering. He was well dressed. His boots were pulled off by one of the bystanders and he was then lifted into a rough board coffin and with his clothes on, nailed up and carried off. This is one of the most loathsome sights I have yet seen. . . . Have just heard of the death of another of our ship's company, young Gardiner from Salem, Mass. He was sent a few days ago to the Hospital on account of his being insane, but it was the brain fever upon him, and he died in a few days.

E. A. Upton

Diary

14 December 1849

A serious row took place about 10 o'clock this morning in a gambling saloon called the "Bella Union," during which a young man from New York was stabbed in the neck, severing the main artery, and instantly dropped dead on the floor. I have just been to see his body, which lays in a back room of the saloon. The doctor had just finished sewing up the ghastly wound. He is a good-looking young man, and it is a sorry sight to see him stretched out covered with his own blood. The saloon is a very large hall and considerable numbers were there at the time, and it is surprising that no others were killed, as revolvers were freely used. I noticed a bullet hole over the large glass chandelier that hangs in the center of the saloon, which bullet went up through the hall above where there was a ball. I noticed two other bullet holes in the walls, and one through the floor. The stove was broken in pieces, chairs demolished &c. &c. Among others in the room at the time was a young Spanish woman gambling at one of the tables.

12 A.M. Very squally, much rain and hail, thunder and lightning. Have learned the young man killed this morning is called by name Reynolds, from Philadelphia. The young man that killed him, Withers of New York. W. also stabbed a man named Brady in the melee, two or three times, but not dangerously.

E. A. Upton

Diary
15 December 1849

[S]ummoned on a coroner's jury to hold an inquest on the body of Mr. Reynolds, who was murdered yesterday morning in the Bella Union Saloon. An inquest was held at the time, but was not at all satisfactory to the young man's friends. The corpse had been buried in the city burial ground, and we were obliged to travel to the ground about three quarters of a mile and have the body taken up. When we arrived, there was a man at work digging a grave, and in fact he is incessantly at work in this occupation. He told me he had covered over nine men yesterday in this place. I recollect this spot very well, as I passed this spot on a gunning excursion one morning when we first landed in Francisco, and I shot a lot of blackbirds here. Then, there was not a single grave here or any near here, but since I was here last there have been a *thousand corpses* buried in this very spot! Oh, thought I, how uncertain is life!

The grave digger was ordered by the coroner to open the grave, which he did in about half an hour. But it was very wet, and when the top of the coffin had been unscrewed and lifted off, the coffin was full of water. No part of the corpse was out of the water except the face. After we had heard the testimony of the witnesses and they had identified the body, it was again covered up, and we repaired to the coroner's office, and after remaining locked up a short time rendered our verdict, the substance of which is that "Reynolds came to his immediate death by a wound inflicted by one Ruben Withers, with a knife or some other sharp instrument." After each of us had signed the verdict we were discharged.

This is the first service I have rendered the Territory. We were occupied in this business about three hours, and it was a most disagreeable affair.

E. A. Upton

Diary
16 December 1849

Saw a young man last night "tap a Bank," as it is called. The Bank belonged to two Spaniards—the game was Monte. The young man in the first place lost all he had with them, several hundred dollars, and then put his gold watch into their bank. His luck turned. He staked largely—and in less than an hour he won all his own money back, redeemed his watch, and finally made a heavy stake which happened to turn in his favor and broke the Bank, taking every cent of the money in [the] Bank to pay him. He filled his handkerchief with gold coin, and the remainder in silver dollars he put in a large canvas bag which a friend shouldered, and they walked off leaving the Spaniards to make the best of their ill luck. The young [man] who won was an American and a New Yorker. The whole amount in the bank, gold and silver coin, was said to be $6,000.00. . . . The Alcalde offers a reward of $1,000.00 for the arrest of the murderer of young Reynolds, Withers. Gambling establishments all in full operation to-day accompanied with their various bands of music.

E. A. Upton

Diary
20 December 1849

A row took place yesterday among the gamblers in the Haley House, during which two barrels of a revolver were discharged, one ball taking a piece out of the shirt of a man and passed into the ceiling; the other passed into the ceiling injuring no one. The room was full at the time. One of the gambling tables was thrown over with several thousands of dollars in gold and silver coin upon it, which rolled in every direction.

E. A. Upton

Diary
22 December 1849

Mate had quite a scuffle with a boy who Capt. H. sent on board. He was extremely saucy to the Mate and refused to do anything he told him on board. The mate finally give him a smart box on the ears, when the boy immediately caught up a stick of wood and struck at the Mate, who foiled the blow and caught the boy in his arms—and told [him] to get his things ready instanter for he should now put him ashore. The boy said he would have him (the mate) before the Alcalde tomorrow sure for striking him, and after gathering his things together and cooly lighting a cigar said he was ready. The boy is about 15 years of age, and is literally a "spoiled child." . . .

I hear the merchants of the city have added $2,000 to reward offered by the Alcalde for the apprehension of the murderer of young Reynolds, making the reward offered $3,000. Another pistol was discharged to-day in one of the gambling saloons, but no one was hurt.

E. A. Upton

Diary
26 December 1849

Another man has been murdered between the city and the Dolores Mission, stabbed in 18 or 20 places. Three men were found dead in different parts of the city this morning—died probably from exposure. Mr. H. Reill found one of this three on Millers and Howard's wharf. He saw a man asleep, as he supposed, on a pile of boards. There were merchants, traders draymen &c all busy near him, but no one disturbed the man as they supposed him asleep—but Mr. R. thought he would look at his face, and lifted the blanket gently for this purpose, and at once saw the man was a cold corpse.

Oh the suffering, the horrid suffering in all its various phases that exist in this city! None but God knows or ever will. If a poor fellow is sent to the Hospital it is about the same thing as being sent to the grave-yard, as they give him little or no attention, especially when sent by the city. The city pays $5.00 per head a day for all they send, private persons are charged $10.00 cash per day.

E. A. Upton

Diary
29 December 1849

Met Capt. H. at Haley House. We went to the Ward House to dine, where we met Mr. Jones, Auction and Com. Merchant, and Mr. Plume of the firm of Burgone & Co. Brokers, which gentlemen sat down with us. Before we left the table a disturbance took place in the room fronting the dining saloon and revolvers and knives were drawn. Several gentlemen in the dining [room] exclaimed, "Do not fire this way!" and all rose to leave the saloon but were all obliged to pass through the front to get to the door. In pass[ing] through the room Mr. Jones made a joking remarked to Dr. B——, who coming the opposite direction the Doctor very foolishly took the remark in high dudgeon, and very severe allusions followed in rapid succession. Being one of the party, I ventured to interpose and having a slight acquaintance with the Doctor, I assured him Mr. Jones made the remark without the slightest ill will. "Well," said the Doctor, "if [it] *is* the case, I have nothing more to say"—but they soon were at it again, and finally Capt. H., fired with indignation at the remarks the Doctor made in reference to his friend, said he would slap the Doctor's face if Mr. Jones did not, and stepped forward to carry his threat into execution, but I caught him by the arm and literally dragged him from the House. It was with the strongest persuasions only that I could keep him from returning. Mr. Jones soon joined us however, having agreed to meet the Doctor on Monday next for satisfaction. The first trouble was quieted without bloodshed. About 4 1/2 [4:30] o'clock a man had a quarrel with another in the St. Charles and fired off six barrels of a revolver but no one was hurt.

Robert Smith Lammot

Letter to his father
30 December 1849

I have met several others whom I knew in Philadelphia, some doing well and others badly, among the latter is Rob. Milligan. Hard work does not agree with him at all. I suppose you have heard of the death of Frank Shubrick. On his way out here Capt. Harley, son of old Geo. Harley, took him under his care and every one thought him thoroughly cured of his bad habits, but last Monday he quarreled with Harley, came into town while it was on fire, worked hard, took a drink, and in the evening called at a friend's house nearly naked, and very drunk. His friend took him in, clothed him and started him off home, but on the way Frank sold all his clothes for liquor, staggered into a tent about three miles from town, and died during the night of deli[ri]um tremens. The coroners jury returned a verdict of death by apoplexy brought on by exposure. Little Sam. Nicholas is in a fair way of going the same road. Alexander and Tom Maslin—ditto.

Jonathan F. Locke

Letter to his wife
4 February 1850

This is a great country: surveyors turn teamsters, merchants, clerks and mechanics—diggers. Anything for money. I know brokers who are keeping eating houses, steady men turn gamblers. . . . By the way my neighbor . . . and his brother set up a gaming table the other day. The man they employed about it while they went to dinner took the bank—that is the money that was on the table: $200—and put aboard the steamer that was going up the river. They did [not] get him or their money, good enough for them. I hope they will lose more if they try the same way to get money. I care not how much any one loses in this way. Did I say any thing to you about the fire we had here that caught in a drinking and gambling place on the Square? There were lots of such places burnt. I should have cared little if they were the only sufferers. There was some 2,000,000 in property burnt. There are no public engines and but one of any kind at the fire.

T. Warwick Brooke

Letter to his mother
9 February 1850

I suppose I must tell you what a striking place this naughty town is, with its houses built in two days, its thoroughfares in which mules flownder belly deep in mud, of the "trottoirs" made of old staves, of the beautiful bay, and fine hills behind the town, up whose slopes shine numberless tents, of the fresh heavenly breezes, the fine days and cold nights precisely like an October in England. I am utterly disgusted with the town itself—gambling scrambling, raking, drinking. I long to be away from it, in the pure quiet country, where I can hear myself think and be at work. . . . No accounts I have read do justice to the spirit of recklessness about. Why, yesterday morning a dead man lay all drawn up as he died (probably from exposure while dead drunk) just ten paces across the street and there he lay for hours, and they say 'tis a common sight.

Henry Didier Lammot

Letter to his brother
24 February 1850

It is certain death here for a man to get drunk and lay out all night in the open air, while he could do it with safety if he were sober. There was a man found dead a night or two [ago] here just below us, who was in the habit of getting drunk and sleeping among some house frames, and the other night there was a hard frost, and he was found dead next morning.

John McCrackan

Letter to his sister Mary
27 February 1850

I have not said much about the mines in my letters, and [that is] because they do not interest me to any great extent. I was very much
amused however the other morning when at breakfast a ugly, dirty
looking boy presented himself at a table adjoining, and called for a
venison steak. Very soon I heard the waiter talking with him, and the
conversation was sufficiently loud to attract my attention. From what
passed I concluded this fellow must be the boy who recently found a
lump of gold weighing eleven pounds, at least there was eleven
pounds of gold, the lump weighed 18 pounds stone and all. I called the
waiter to me and asked him, he said yes. This fellow it seems found
this lump [and] was offered 2,800 dollars for it, which he accepted
and came down here to receive the money. It was bought for exhibi-
tion in the States, I believe.

Samuel C. Lewis

Journal
4 April 1850

Green [of Wells & Co. Exchange Office] at about noon today came into
the office and said he was going to Sacramento, to be absent some
time. I remarked to him that I had opened and posted up his books
and wished to have an understanding about salary before he left, and
the offer he made me was $100 to stay till he returned. Said there
would not be much to do during his absence. My reply was, that I was
looking for steady employment till fall or I would stay for $300 a
month, if he desired. Said he could not pay that, upon which I told
him I thought I had better leave. He urged me to remain at his offer. I
told him I could not (because I did not like the business he was engaged in). He has received the goods that have been seized by the
Custom House here for breach of the revenue laws and has loaded
the Schr. *Ferdinand,* Schr. —— and Brig *Charlotte*—all for Sacramento, and he intends to sell the goods up there and account for them
to *somebody* here as near I can make it out *at some price.*

I will not say more, than there will probably be trouble with the
Govt. or Custom House before the thing is closed up, as I told him the
only way the goods could be disposed of according to law was by Pub-

lic Auction. Said he cared not. *They* had given him the goods to dispose of and he was bound to make something out of them. The bulk of the three cargoes was rum, gin, brandy, ale and beer and flour—most part of the drinkables. He acknowledged to me that he did not know how to keep his accounts and was not will[ing] to pay. So I made out my bill—2 1/2 days @ $12 pr day, $30—took my money and *bade him good morning.* Have not seen him about town since and presume he has gone up the river.

Samuel C. Lewis

Journal
7 April 1850

Rain most of the day and streets very muddy. It is a strange sight to pass along the streets and see the drinking and gambling houses crowded with persons, and a band of music stationed in the long room of 70 or 80 feet long and 35 or 40 wide, on this day [Sunday], but such is the fact. To be sure, all the usual occupations (or mostly so) of business are suspended on the Sabbath as they are in our cities at home—but the gambling and drinking houses know no Sunday, and as a band of music is playing martial music in the rear, one cannot hear anything that is said, but [the] room [is] crammed full, some pushing for the bar for grog and some pushing for the gambling tables. I am told the authorities do not interfere to stop it, and believe it to be the case—but I hope the time will soon come, when a city government becomes organized, that some measures will be adopted to stop the nuisance. It's quite enough to see the sight on week days.

I intended to have gone to meeting today, but the rain and such prevented. As I should have to look some time to find the place where the Presbyterians hold meetings, concluded to give it up till next Sunday, and spent a dull day . . . some time spent reading the (Eng.) Episcopal prayerbook and at 9 o'clock go to bed.

Caroline Stoddard

Journal
5 December 1850

From there [the wharf] we walked to Portsmith Square and here what we saw defies description. The largest buildings are occupied by gamblers in large saloons, which as we passed by, we saw filled with men and boys—tables covered with gold and silver in piles, beautiful music in most of them, and of course a bar, and shocking as it may appear a woman sometimes attending them, as we saw in our walk the most frightful set of desperadoes of every country. It is said there are seven thousand convicts from Sydney N.S.W. who help swell the list of vagabonds. Every week, or night rather, there are one or two shot in these gambling establishments. The wonder might be, that more do not fall victims in these horrible places.

Caroline Stoddard

Journal
6 December 1850

In our walk this afternoon, passed the Eldorado, a very large building said to be the most famous Gambling house in the city. The streets in the evening are quite worthy a walk thro. They are brilliantly lighted (that is, the saloons) which are crowded to excess, and always accompanied with excellent music to toll the unguarded passers by into these horrible dens of iniquity.

E. A. Upton

Diary
18 December 1849

Have now taken up my abode once more on the ocean. Have a very comfortable berth in the cabin. Glad am I to get out of San Francisco once more, for it is literally a pandemonium on earth—murders, suicides, gambling, drunkenness—and in fact the whole catalogue of the blackest vices riot in San Francisco.

Chapter 5

The Phoenix Rises

When word of James Marshall's discovery of gold reached San Francisco in May of 1848 the village quickly emptied. By the time the rains set in the following autumn and the gold seekers returned home, they discovered quite a different place awaiting them. Already by the end of 1848 the streets had begun to fill with immigrants, all come "to see the Elephant" or experience the phenomenon that was being talked about worldwide. San Francisco property owners discovered their personal worth had increased by far more than the little bags of dust they had carried down from the mountains. Within a year lots were selling for ten times what their owners had originally paid for them—and that was only the beginning of a crazed period of land speculation.

As Hubert Howe Bancroft poetically described it, "Stretching its youthful limbs in the gusty air, San Francisco grew apace, covering the drift sand which was soon to be tied down by civilization, carving the slopes into home sites for climbing habitations till they reached the crests, leveling the hills by blasting out ballast for returning vessels, or material for filling in behind the rapidly advancing piling in the cove."[1] Montgomery Street, once beachfront property, became the central thoroughfare of a sprawling new town.

In 1839 Jean Jacques Vioget was hired to draw up a street plan for Yerba Buena but the resulting "ragged, irregular delineations" proved unsatisfactory, and in 1846 Alcalde Washington Bartlett asked Jasper O'Farrell to resurvey the newly named San Francisco.[2] The resulting plat was completed in 1847, supposedly based on the model of the city of Philadelphia.[3] It employed two sections of right-angle grids, with the streets running north/south and east/west above Market Street, northeast/northwest and southeast/southwest below. In its strict geometry it made no acknowledgment of the various hills that punctuated the area, but most of O'Farrell's attempts to adjust the lots to account for the terrain were opposed by Bartlett and other property owners. The resulting triangular lots and irregular T-intersections were awkward for horses and buggies and proved to be traffic nightmares with the arrival of the automobile.

Drawing up a plan for the streets of San Francisco was the easy part, however. Translating the lines on paper to the jumbled hodgepodge of wooden, brick, and canvas buildings proved to be the challenge. Street construction consisted of labor-intensive grading, planking, and sewering. The city paid for one third of the expense and levied the remainder against the property owners whose lots fronted the streets under construction. In an effort to cut costs the city fathers specified use of the plentiful supply of wood rather than stone, brick, or other more expensive (and more permanent) materials. Unfortunately this meant that when the city burned—as it did six times between December 1849 and June 1851—the civic improvements burned too.

When grading operations required the use of filler of some kind, road crews turned to the piles of unwanted goods lying about the shore, materials abandoned because no current market existed for them and the cost of their storage was prohibitive. Into the muddy holes went tobacco, iron, sheet-lead, cement, beans, wire sieves, and salt beef. When the perishables decayed the sidewalks caved in.[4] Fluctuations in the price of goods at times made improvised foundations more valuable than the buildings they supported. Some chili beans that were sunk to make a street crossing on Broadway would have made their owner a fortune only a few weeks later.[5]

The proliferation of flimsy canvas-and-wood buildings presented San Francisco with a severe fire hazard, but it was not until large portions of the city were razed by the Christmas Eve fire of 1849 that any serious effort was made to provide fire protection. In January of 1850 the city council appointed F. D. Kohler as Chief Engineer and charged him to organize a fire department. Kohler formed three volunteer fire companies and equipped them with hooks, axes, and other implements, but after an initial burst of enthusiasm interest flagged. When a huge blaze broke out on 4 May 1850 they were of little use. During the following month efforts were renewed and Kohler finally established a series of volunteer fire companies, each with men drawn from the same former locale: Company 1 and Company 2 were all New Yorkers, Company 3 were all Bostonians, etc. This regionalism provided a certain esprit de corps but it also led to clannishness and petty rivalries. Companies vied to outdo one another with the fitting and decorating of their fire stations. The furniture alone in Sansome Company's firehouse cost five thousand dollars and it was equipped with its own library.[6]

Each time the city burned it was quickly rebuilt, usually of more-permanent materials. Canvas walls gave way to wood, and wood to brick. Those seeking ultimate security against destruction by fire— such a J. G. W. Luyster, who wrote to his mother of his recovery plans—built with iron, little realizing the dire consequences of such a choice. Heinrich Schliemann, the excavator of the ancient city of Troy, visited San Francisco and witnessed the conflagration of May 1851. In his published diary he recorded a vivid description of the carnage:

> Neither the iron houses nor the brickhouses (which were hitherto considered as quite fire-proof) could resist the fury of the element; the latter crumbled together with incredible rapidity, whilst the former got red-hot, then white-hot and fell together like card-houses. Particularly in the iron-houses people considered themselves perfectly safe and they remained in them to the last extremity. As soon as the walls of the iron houses getting [sic] red-hot the goods inside began to smoke, the inhabitants wanted to get out, but usually it was already too late, for the locks and hinges of the doors having extended or partly melted by the heat, the doors were no more to be opened. Sometimes by burning their hands and arms people succeeded to open the doors and to get out, but finding themselves then surrounded by an ocean of flames they made but a few paces, staggered and fell, rose again and fell again in order not to rise any more.[7]

Of the three fires described in the letters and diaries of the present collection, the December 1849 blaze was believed to be accidental but there was strong evidence that the conflagrations of the following May and June were the result of arson. Though fire remained a constant fear it seemed to have little effect on the optimism of the city's inhabitants. John McCrackan wrote of the festive scene as bystanders were encouraged to clean out the contents of an endangered wine shop; each San Franciscan involved prided himself on the connoisseurship revealed by his wine of choice.

Business flourished in spite of (or in some cases because of) the recurring destruction, so much so that the demand for ready currency outstripped the supply. From 1849 on, coinage companies established offices in San Francisco and they remained in operation for the next ten years.[8] Even locally minted coins were not enough to satisfy the frenzy, however, and it was not uncommon for shopkeepers to accept Prussian florins, Indian rupees, French francs, and English pounds. When established currency was unavailable, raw gold dust wrapped in little paper packages became acceptable legal tender.

Though a few clipper ships had been constructed prior to 1848, the gold rush created both an urgent need for the sleek, fast vessels and the money to pay for them. A clipper ship was able to cut the long voyage from the East Coast from six months to a dizzying eighty-nine days. San Francisco's harbor, protected behind the Golden Gate, was large enough and deep enough to accept the world's entire tonnage and the city quickly became the hub of transportation for the West Coast. By 1850 it was connected by regular stage service to San Jose, Monterey, Santa Barbara, Los Angeles, and San Diego.[9]

Isolated on the tip of a long peninsula, San Francisco soon found itself challenged by East Bay rivals when engineers began drawing up plans for a transcontinental railroad, but in 1849 and 1850 there appeared to be no obstacle too daunting for the "Metropolis of the Pacific." Optimism for the future flew as high as the semaphores that crowned Telegraph Hill.

Augustus West

Letter to Peter DeWitt
31 August 1849

I have long since promised myself the pleasure of writing to you, in acknowledgement of your many esteemed favors of remembrance and regards so kindly extended since our sojourn here in this distant but none the less interesting country—and tho so long apparently remiss in doing so, I can but hope that even now I am still welcome, engrossed as I have been for months past in the exciting scenes and stirring events that have collected around us on every side, and at the same time an active participator and, as you may imagine, not a disinterested one.

I assure you that apart from those claims of a business character, I have had but a scanty respite to gratify the many wishes that I entertained to indulge myself in this more social and pleasing manner. But

I am happy to say that now we have become more settled, and our affairs more in system and order, and duties that were at first without method are now defined so that I trust you, as well as many others, will hear from us two pioneers, rather more frequently. Both Alfred [Peter DeWitt's son] and myself have had a goodly share of this world's toil and trouble upon our hands, and with the inexperienced assistance we have had, you will readily conceive that our labors were but slightly lessened. If we have been fortunate perhaps in exceeding the expectations of our numerous friends, or if we have been successful in discharging the trust reposed in us, it has been accomplished, I may say literally, by the sweat of our brows.

Yet this is no more than all have to do at this time who would succeed and secure to himself a support for the future. This is truly no place for idlers or indolent men, and they make a great mistake who come out here bouyed up with the fallacious hopes created by the thousand and one rumors they hear of, about high rates, high prices &c; and how many are disappointed and become disgusted with the country, with themselves and everything else. And I dare say that ere this you may have heard the sorrowing representation of some unfortunates who, unfitted to combat with the realities that meet one here face to face, have sought again their less exacting homes. Instances easily occur that go to prove with how little reflection they embark to this country. Almost the first question asked is, "Well, I suppose there is plenty of gold?" You have "good times," "making money," "getting rich"—supposing all a natural consequence, without toil or effort. Alas, they find the big lumps as well as the small are not to be had alone for the going for, and smarting hands, aching heads and sore limbs are more usually the results.

The mines still continue to yield abundance, and parties are fitting out to gather their share of the glittering dust, while others are returning quite content with getting back and satisfied, as tis termed, with the *Elephant.* Most of the associations have dissolved partnership and started on their own hook. Strange as it must seem, the old maxim of "Circumstances alter cases" annuls all previous engagements and of course breaks up, I may venture to say, every mining company that arrives.

Still there are many that are successful and who realize their expectations, but tis generally those of the hard working class, brought up to labor, tough as pine knots and case hardened. The Oregonians are the ones who make the most, for they can labor and toil and have no longings. As a class, I think they are the roughest, most hard working and penurious set of men I have ever seen—quite free from excess of any kind and saving to a penny, and I doubt if they have even an idea of what the comforts of life are.

Our City is growing up like magic, peopled with natives of every country, and engaged in every profession and I question if there is ought that could be started that would be new. Our streets are fast becoming lined with houses—all stores or grogshops or eating houses. Even the old sign-board is seen here and there to attract the passer by of "Cakes & Pies," "Pies & Cakes," "Hot Coffee," &c. During the day all is life and activity, wagons and carts, wheelbarrows, peddlars, musicians, and all sorts of things jostle you on every side. It is really wonderful to witness the great changes since last fall upon our arrival. One would scarce know the town, and at night when lit up by the numerous lights from the many dwellings that are scattered over a large space, presents to the eye a bright scene of a large City. Our harbour too wears the same busy, thriving look, quite in harmony with the confused appearance of the town—covering the whole front of the town, 6 and 7 deep, and so close that the eye can scarce find a break in the long line, and the many lighters passing to and fro from point to point along the beach, all tends to impress the stranger with the idea that this is a great place, tho a perfect anomaly to them.

But the papers you receive will give you a more general idea of our city than I can. But suffice it to say it has no equal for its age. Consider, but scarce nine months have elapsed and ships from every part of the globe almost, now lie in its harbour. Merchandise, also from every port, both Home and foreign, are now in the market, and tho the business is now at the present time in my opinion at its lowest ebb, the time is fast approaching when it must assume a more healthy state. The state of the market here when known in N.Y. must cause a check as a general thing upon further shipments—and a revulsion in affairs must be the result. Notwithstanding the general stagnation in business, still scheming and speculation is carried on. To this there is no check and tis most surprising to see how successful are the operators. The state of scarcity here is hard to define, made up as it is of every material. I can only say that for its composition it does credit to the town. All is peace and quiet and no cause for apprehension. . . .

We are all well with the exception of Henry [Peter DeWitt's younger son] who has a slight bilious attack, but he will be up again in a day or so. He is doing well with us and I find him a great assistance in our business. I can hardly say what I would wish to of our household affairs, but suffice it to say as far as I can speak we have a happy time of it and enjoy the comforts of Calafornia with good zest. It is now 12 o'c. Bidding you and all good night, with my best wishes for your continued health and prosperity. Believe me to be yrs truly Augustus.

Anne Willson Booth

Journal
16 October 1849

Another bright and beautiful day. As the wind set in from the sea this afternoon, the dust began to fly again. Since the heavy fall of rain a few days ago, we have not been much annoyed from this cause. It is dry now however, and has again become troublesome.

Mr. Daugherty came on board last evening and remained all night. Our visitors all say these are more comfortable quarters than can be found on shore any where. Uncle Wes dined with Wm. Buckler a few evenings since at his Hotel and says the fare was very ordinary indeed and badly cooked, for which he pays $40 a week. I often wish we may succeed in obtaining a house and the necessary articles of furniture, so that I could accommodate a few particular friends. I have already promised several that if we should go to housekeeping, I would do so. It would be pleasant to me, although laborious. There is no such thing as help in this country—unless obtained at an enormous price. One lady told me she considered herself highly fortunate in securing an assistant at $50 a month.

Mr. Booth is trying to secure a lot, that being the greatest difficulty. If he should succeed, he will put up a small house. Uncle Wes has been kind enough to offer him four of the state rooms that were put up between decks for the use of the passengers. Mr. Kellon took the other two, and has converted them into a shop for himself on a part of the lot belonging to the Methodist Chapel. He is very kindly exerting himself in order to obtain a lot near there on favourable terms for Mr Booth. It is a very pretty location, being elevated considerably above the business part of the town, is healthy, free from dust, and overlooks the harbour. I much regret that we did not bring a few articles of furniture with us, such as bedstead, chairs, tables and cooking utensils. Every thing of the kind sells enormously high here, so it would be impossible to obtain them. I can however do with but little at present.

Anne Willson Booth

Journal
17 October 1849

Mr. Booth has been offered a lot on very favourable terms and is allowed a few days for decision. It is 21 feet by 120 for $300, in a good location which can not fail to improve, being a little distance from the business portion of the City, and better suited for a residence. Mr. Booth seems to have set his heart on housekeeping, but there are so many difficulties to be obviated, I cannot see the way clear. After purchasing the lot, the expense of getting up even the smallest kind of a tenement is enormous. Mr. Kellon has put up the state rooms he purchased from the ship and the cost was between 7 and $800. I am not willing for Mr. Booth to incur the expense, unless we can have one or two spare rooms for the purpose of accommodating a few boarders, so that I can contribute my quota towards accumulating something. Uncle Wes seems to think the state rooms will not make a house that will protect us from the dampness during the rainy season, and says he would not be willing to leave me in such a frail tenement. Mr. Morris and Mr. Reynolds, his partner, are willing to put up a house for us and board with us, but Mr. Booth is afraid to incur the expense, which, I am afraid, would act as a drawback upon him. Uncle Wes thinks we had better keep quiet until Capt. Smith comes down again, which will be in a few days, as he thinks it probable we may be offered inducements to go up to Bodega. I am ready and anxious to embark in almost anything that may be profitable.

George May

Letter to Joseph S. Curtiss
20 November 1849

You will have rec'd my last informing you of my arrival before this reaches. I regret to say that the prospect of doing anything at our contemplated [plan] is forbidding, that both Randall and myself judge it not best to make a trial at it. First we are too late—the time for commencing the coining business is past. There are already four establishments of this kind in California now, only two of which are doing a profitable business. One is Moffitt & Co., the other the Miners Bank, both of them (particularly the latter) with large capital. Had we arrived at the time contemplated we might perhaps have succeeded, but it is certainly too late now.

There are some dozen small concerns which left the States for this business that have abandoned it altogether. All the large merchantile and other business houses from motives of interest use their influence against it. It is more for their interest to buy the dust and send to the States than give circulation to coin made here. Unless therefore it be done by a league with some of these large establishments (which we cannot make) it is difficult to get much circulation for such coin. The agent of an organization for this business with a capital of some $20,000 has recently arrived from New England. He is [a] personal and intimate friend of mine and tells me it is quite doubtful if they attempt it all. Moffitt & Co. and the Miners Bank have considerable in circulation. The former has obtained his circulation principally through the gamblers, who circulate more money here than any other class of men. The latter is a heavy concern owning a large amt of real estate and which redeems its coin with government coin when called upon to do so.

John McCrackan

Letter to his sister Mary
9 December 1849

A gentleman offered me a salary of six thousand a year to go to "Pueblo de San Jose" about sixty miles south of this. He was a Lawyer. I have determined to practice. A friend in the Legislature (which will meet in a few days at "San Jose" the Capital of the State) promised to get me the appointment of District Judge if I would go to Monterey. Lawyers, I believe, are doing the best regular business here. Sam Clarke is in practice here and doing very well.

You have no doubt heard of Professor Shepherd. He came out here with the idea of making his "eternal fortune" picking out the best places for miners, but he soon found any body was as well able to judge as himself, for the very reason none can tell—it is all luck—and so he turned team driver, and I believe he made some money at that. "O what a fall was there my countrymen." It is most amusing to see how men get on here. I went into an eating house the other noon, and as I was not waited upon immediately I rapped with my fork. A person answered my call. "What will you have, sir?" The voice was familiar. I looked again, and recognized an old New York friend named Birge. We were both very much embarrassed, although I thought I was much more than he. He gave me in a few words his history since we parted, which was in the Steamer at Sandy Hook. He was then on his way to Liverpool, and intended passing two years on the Continent, which it seems he did. He had started for California overland. They had suffered intensely and were obliged to leave everything on the road, arriving here without a penny. His first job was the melancholy one of digging a grave, for which he got twenty dollars. He came to this eating house for food, and at last got the situation which he now holds for two hundred dollars a month. This is the regular wages.

"Do you see that man," said he, pointing to a waiter that that moment passed us with a plate of beans. "His name is Goodwin, a graduate of Cambridge." Thinks I to myself, "Sich is life." Birge said, "Do you know the celebrated Dr. Watson of N.Y.?" "Only by reputation," I replied. "He is our cook," said Birge, and so it is, my dear Mary.

Men do any and everything honorable here to live and get money. You see a New York exquisite up to his knees in mud and mire trying to extricate his mules. Either the harness has given way, or the load is too heavy for them to draw. Carting has been very good business. I thought quite seriously of going into it at one time myself. They pay a man to drive a cart fifteen and twenty dollars a day, which the proprietor can well afford then he gets from five to fifteen dollars a load, and all he can do at that.

It is now the wet season here and the streets are almost impassable, such mud and filth. Men wear none but the high-legged boot here, with their pants inside. Here boots sell from fifty up to one hundred and fifty a pair. The india rubber is generally used, for which you pay four or five ounces. It seems so odd to deal in gold dust. It is done up in a brown paper and in quarter or less quantities. Some packages are marked on the outside so much, fifty or one hundred dollars as the case may be. Silver, half and quarter pieces, are done up in five and ten dollar packages, marked on the outside, and are seldom opened or counted and in this way pass through twenty hands in a day. We never see silver less than a quarter. There is no use for it. You can buy nothing for less—a cigar, [a] quarter, a lemonade, or any kind of drink, a quarter. And you have no idea how honest the people are here. There seems but little use for locks and bars.

We have a very generous importation of French, German and Spanish, many of whom will perhaps make this country their home. There are also some sixty or seventy Chinese here, some engaged in building, while others are engaged keeping an eating house. This is my usual place of dining, and the cheapest place in the City. You pay one dollar and a half, and eat all you please. Other houses charge so much a dish, and at such prices that with an ordinary appetite you would pay two dollars. These Chinese are very enterprising. Their cooking is good and the food very clean. I observe one requires a great deal of animal food here. There is such a constant war to the system. There is a large supply demanded. Beside the beef is mild and of course much lighter in its nature.

E. A. Upton

Diary
10 December 1849

Had the curiosity to enquire the price of cabbages as I was passing a provision store to-day—was told $3.00 per head, and they were rather ordinary. Oranges are selling at $1.00 each. I saw to-day a brown bear that was dressed for sale, also at a provision store. The bear was shot just across San Francisco Bay and weighed 350 lbs. I procured one of his claws. The fat on its back was about 3 inches thick. The meat was selling rapidly at $1.00 per lb. I ate a steak cut from this bear. Tasted some like pork.

E. A. Upton

Diary
22 December 1849

I find the perusal of *Nicholas Nickleby* extremely interesting. I have had an interesting conversation with several young gentlemen from London to-day on board (part of whom are going down the coast with us as passengers) in reference to Dickens' works. They all spoke in the highest terms of them, but said that if I would fully appreciate his well drawn characters, I must live in London a short time. One of the gentlemen spoke very highly of Mr. Dickens, having met with him many times on various committees, &c.

John McCrackan

Letter to his family
24 December 1849

This morning at four o'clock a fire was discovered in a large building known as the Exchange, and by the time we were aroused on board the ship it looked as if all San F. were afire. The boat was manned, and we proceeded to the shore and such confusion. The buildings generally here are built very light and are as nothing before the flames, which by the time we reached the Plaza were destroying the Parker House, one of the largest Hotels in the place, and then came a dragging out and such destruction you cannot imagine.

The streets, which are a foot deep of mud, was perfectly heaping with all kinds and descriptions of goods. Besides gold and silver which was melted up. The loss must be very great. The fire was stayed by resorting to powder, blowing the buildings up. This endangered the lives of many. Two were killed, while not a few had their limbs broken and burned. Several wine stores were selected to blow up and the people were invited to go in and help themselves, which of course they accepted without waiting for a second one. Some with boxes of claret, some with baskets of Champagne—while others were using their best efforts to get out a barrel and all seemed to evince some pride and taste in their choice. They continued busy at this till the authorities gave signal to clear the building, and the next moment the frame work was [blown] high in the air and the fleeing multitude dodging the pieces which reached the ground from all directions.

I shall send you a [news]paper giving you a full account, as it will perhaps be more vivid than any I could give. Had there been any wind the whole city must have been destroyed without doubt. Water is very scarce here and none could be obtained, indeed we have no fire engine to through the water, if we had an abundance. This whole block which has been destroyed will be rebuilt before three weeks have passed.

E. A. Upton

Diary
24 December 1849

Mate has awoke me telling me the city is all on fire. I instantly issued from the cabin without dressing, and the vast sheet of flame that was eating everything combustable before it made a most splendid appearance viewing it from the harbor, but unlike any such occasion in the Atlantic cities, not a bell was to be heard, not a single stream from an engine to be seen.

6 1/2 [6:30 AM] the Mate, one man and myself are now leaving the vessel for the shore. The fire commenced in Dennison's Exchange, a large building devoted to gambling from top to bottom and which was burned to the ground. Next, the Parker House, which was soon destroyed, together with the large building on the corner adjoining called "El Dorado," large gambling establishment. The Haley House and the Bella Union were on fire several times. The large Plazza [Portsmouth Square] was filled with men and goods of every description, although it was hot as an oven. The fire spread rapidly down the Square to Montgomery St. and it looked curious enough to see so many thousands of men compelled to stand still, look on and see the fire burn, not having a single engine, hook or ladder at their command to work. Several buildings were blown up, but this experiment was not managed judiciously and did no service. I saw my trunk, chest and &c. stored in a store on Montgomery Street were in danger and after much difficulty I finally persuaded a drayman to remove them to the wharf, paying him $8.00—distance to wrf. about 800 rods. Goods were being removed from all the stores far and near and draymen were in great demand. The mud in the streets in many places over the hubs. It was a profitable speculation for the drayman, this fire. I noticed one man being born on a litter from the fire, said to have been hurt either from the explosions of powder or some other cause. Many more were hurt. Almost every store that was burned contained more or less powder and liquor, and explosions were taking place every moment, some of which were tremendous. I never was at a fire where there was so much danger of life, but have not yet heard of anyone being killed.

Finally a private engine brought from England and owned by two English merchants was brought to the scene and did good service. The fronts of all the stores on Washington St. presented a curious appearance after the fire, being all hung with blankets and every color and variety of dry goods, most of which were partly burned or scorched to a crisp, the men not being able to keep them wet enough. Merchants were flying from all parts of the city with their safes and large sacks of gold dust to the Custom House, which is fire proof and has a large number of excellent safes. During most of the time, I stood on the piazza of this building which is quite elevated and commanded a perfect view of the conflagration, saw the police arrest several for stealing goods.

11 o'clock. My foot has become so painful from the chafing of my large boots I am obliged to go on board our vessel again, first having sent my baggage on board by two of the sailors in the long boat. The fire, I think, will soon stop on Montgomery St., there being no wind. If there was a high wind, two thirds of the city would be burnt, as the fire has its own way. This is the first fire of any account that has happened in this city—and it will probably open the eyes of the city authorities to the great importance of establishing an efficient Fire Department immediately.

4 o'clock P.M. It has been a very mild and pleasant day—the thermometer now indicates 74 above. The fire is still burning but will [not] spread any farther at present.

7 o'clock. I can still see the light of the fire, and the smoke from the deck.

Robert Smith Lammot

Letter to his father
30 December 1849

Last Monday morning as I was dressing myself preparatory to going to work I heard a cry of "fire" and on looking out I saw the Parker House in flames. Harry [his brother] and I got to work instanter to carry our things away, for we were within twenty yards of the fire. We took them down to the wharf and one of us stood guard over them the whole day. As more than nine tenths of all the houses here are wood, the flames spread very rapidly and it was only by blowing up three or four and pulling down others houses that the whole city was saved from a general conflagration. As it is, there were some dozen houses destroyed, among them the Parker House, El Dorado and other large gambling establishments; but such is the enterprise of the people of this town that before the Parker House was done burning, contracts were made for rebuilding it, and today—six days after it was destroyed—there are six large houses roofed and weather-boarded in and four others in process of building on the ground that four days ago was a heap of blazing ruins—beat that in the East if you can!

Robert Smith Lammot

Letter to his mother
24 January 1850

For the first week you can scarcely conceive of two more unsettled, bothered, disappointed individuals than Harry and I were. I had the azure demons to perfection. Here I was, in a strange place, business comparatively dull, rain every day, at an expense of twenty two dollars a week for board and lodging, (where, by the way, I was almost eaten up by fleas) and meeting hundred of persons who were heaping maledictions on the country and every thing connected with it. Mr. Winston alone gave me comfort by telling me it was always the case, and that as soon as I got accustomed to the high prices—and found employment—I should feel better satisfied, and he judged rightly.

I trotted about town in style hunting something to do, but the thousands of applicants gave me no chance, and so I made up my mind to go to Pueblo San Jose (the seat of government) to try and obtain a situation under the State Surveyor. I went to the wharf, made a bargain with the master of a small boat who plied between San Francisco and San Jose, which is about 70 miles distant. I then went to Mr. R. M. Price to get a letter of introduction to someone there, when Mr. Price told me he heard that Judge Bryant wanted an engineer to lay out and superintend the making of two streets down in the lower part of the town [San Francisco].

Accordingly I posted hot foot to hunt up the Judge, whom I found just going in search of someone. I told him my business and referred him to Mrss. Price and Winston. He then showed me what was required of me and asked me what charge I would make. I told him that I was newly landed and of course ignorant of what would be a fair remuneration, that he might fix the price himself and depend on my using every means in my power to push forward the work and give satisfaction. He then offered me fifteen dollars a day, with an assistant whom I might choose at twelve pr. diem, which terms I accepted and offered the situation of assistant to Mr. Graham (our supercargo) who had been an engineer for a number of years on different railroads, one in Georgia, from which he had returned but a few months before we sailed. Mr. G accepted, and gave up the control of his business to Mrss. Winston and Simmons, to take the place.

My work commenced the following day (Bill's birthday by the bye) and has steadily gone on since that time, with but one or two days intermission on account of bad weather. I had to run the lines, fix the grades, employ hands, keep their accounts and pay them off—having between eight and ten thousand dollars placed in my hands for the purpose. A few days since, having expended all the funds in my hands, I made a report of our doings &c. which I presented to the Judge, who was appointed by the company to attend to the matter. He complimented me very highly on the way I had conducted matters, as did several of the gentlemen interested—all of whom said that there had never been such an amount of work done before in California for so little money &c &c. I think I must have blushed *some* when they told me all this, but as I had no mirror present, I cannot positively assert that such was the case. But you may suppose that it was all very gratifying to me.

I had at different times as many as 137 men employed at once—in different parties, working on six streets, some of which were over half a mile apart—so you can perceive that it kept me pretty busy running from one to another. I finished two streets, and had four others under way when our funds ran out. The City Council then immediately made an appropriation of $6000 to finish the work I had on hand—and told me to go ahead and that when I had finished those they would open other streets and keep me in work.

Mr Graham and I have gone into partnership in the business under the firm of Graham & Lammot, Surveyors, Engineers & Draftsmen!!! That is, we divide all profits and each pays his own expenses. We have had some small jobs which did not interfere with our regular work and paid a good sum to each. For instance, he took a contract the other day to grade a lot for a man who wanted to build a house for which we charge $100. We laid out the work, employed a few hands and after paying expenses, had about fifteen dollars each clear profit for two days work, in addition to our regular pay.

Yesterday I finished a draft of the City of Suisun (which by the way, contains only one house except on paper) for which I got fifty dollars—three days work. Harry, as soon as he got through the job Mr. Winston set him at, came to work under me at $4.50 a day until I find something which will pay better to do. The work is easy and healthy, shoveling sand, or cutting off brush wood from the line of the road, which agrees with the shaver so well that he has grown so fat his clothes will scarcely fit him; he weighs something over 145 lbs. solid flesh, however, I suppose he has informed you all about that. . . .

So you see, dear Mother, that your boys are doing *"pretty consid-erable well,"* and hope to continue so.

Robert Smith Lammot

Letter to his brother Dan
13 January 1850

I should have written to you before, but my time has been so much occupied with work that I have actually had no time. After the first week ashore, I found a job opening three or four streets, which pays me well, and at my room we have no place to write. This is written on a checker board which I hold on my knee, while three or four per-sons are talking away as fast as they can; so if you perceive any inco-herency in my letter you can know what to attribute it to.

It is impossible to describe San Francisco—it is altogether an inde-scribable. Wooden houses, brick, frame, Chinese, zinc, iron, leather and canvas—indeed anything that can make a covering is used to shelter the thousands who are thrown in here. Of all this medley there are not strictly speaking ten houses which would be considered inhabitable in the States, yet they are rented at enormous prices. . . .

Mr. Graham and I are associated together as Surveyors, Engineers & Draftsmen. No capital is requisite, and we divide profits. I am em-ployed at present in opening and grading several streets, the first work of the kind ever done in this place. I, myself, threw out the first spadeful of earth from Bush St., San Francisco—the first street that has been graded in California. Since I first commenced (about 3 weeks) I have opened five streets: viz. Sansom, Bush, First, Market and Mission, and property on those streets has risen to nearly, if not quite double its value before. As far as I have gone, I have spent about $10,000, which is generally acknowledged to be a wonderfully small sum for the amount of work done, and my friends tell me that it will be the means of our getting as much of the same kind of work as we want. I hope it may.

Drafting is a good business, but I have had no time for anything else. Sundays we generally devote to writing letters, making up ac-counts &c., for I have to keep the accounts of all my men (137) and pay them all off &c. I shall, the first leisure day, take a ramble around the adjacent country, so as to be able to give you an idea of it, as well as to satisfy my own curiosity on that point. The climate is far more agree-able than I had expected to find it: it rains, to be sure, during the winter, every few days, and sometimes for a week on a stretch, but then the intervening ones are clear and warm as our May weather. The grass always green, and the birds singing in a way that reminds one of home most wonderfully. On the other hand, while it rains, it *does* rain in style and *then* the mud! "*My good gracious*"! it *is* muddy "*to a degree.*" If I should "make my apparel" every time I got up to my knees in it, or splashed from head to foot, it would take up most of my time in dressing. It is really insufferable, and what is more, dreadfully hard on clothes. Our every-day rig is a colored flannel, or hickory shirt, army pants, our blanket monkey jackets, and felt hat, with a pair of our heavy boots drawn on over the legs of our breeks. On Sunday we vary our costume by having the aforesaid shirt *clean* and the mud scraped off the boots. Without exaggeration, nine tenths of all the streets in San Francisco are in a worse condition than any hundred yards of road you ever saw in Delaware County [Pennsylvania].

I saw a man try to cross Montgomery St. (the greatest business street in the town) where there were no bushes laid down nor boards to walk on. He was about half drunk or he would not have attempted it. He floundered in up to his waist, then up to his neck, and had not some persons thrown him a rope, he would have been smothered. This, however, was the worst hole in town, but I have many a time gone up to my knee by missing the board, which was itself half buried, and often seen mules and horses, sometimes six or seven at a time in one square, up to their bellies in mud, while their drivers were endeavoring to extricate them by putting pieces of scantling under them as pries. . . .

Washing and ironing cost from 6 to 7 dollars a dozen. You will laugh I am sure, but actually the cheapest and best way that it is done here is by having the clothes sent to the Sandwich Islands! There is a man here who takes the dirty clothes, makes you out a bill of lading for them, insures them, sends them there, brings them back for about two or three dollars per dozen—about half of what it can be done here for. But you must be tired of this rigmarole of things which you see much better described in the papers and, like the Mexican War, is so oft repeated and so much of it, that it ceases to be interesting. . . .

As soon as Hal got through his job with Mr. Winston he came down and I set him to work shoveling sand on the road. It is a good, dry, healthy employment, and $4.50 a day is a good deal better than loafing. By the way, I have a curious collection in the 137 men I have at work: lawyers, doctors, dentists, jewellers, officers of the army, masters and mates of vessels, and one man who was a member of the Wisconsin Legislature.

John D. Mitchell

Letter to his family
16 January 1850

Two slight shocks of an earthquake was felt here to day. I myself noticed the shaking and told Billy of it. He also felt it.

Robert Smith Lammot

Letter to his father
15 February 1850

The Steamer *Unicorn* which arrived here a few days since brought no mails, on account of her being a foreign bottom. Consequently we were deprived of our usual semi-monthly intelligence from the Atlantic side. *We Californians* are in hopes of a speedy reform in the mail department, so that we may get our letters within a week after their arrival here. As for newspapers, no such article have I seen since I became a resident of this place—with the exception of the Pacific News, Alta California, and Placer Times and some old Philadelphia papers that we brought with us. . . .

Now I will give you an account of how affairs stand with us here. We made about $300 or $400 on the goods we brought with us. I have lent out $500 to Hob Smith on good security for a month or two at 4% a month, which I can have at any time. Mr. Graham and I are in partnership in the surveying and engineering business—which pays so well and keeps us so well employed that I have but little time for drafting—though I have done a little at it during my leisure moments and for which I was well paid, say $50 for a draft which would take three days to make. . . .

The greatest difficulty we labored under was from not having sufficient instruments to work with. The compass I brought out, tho' a good instrument, is not sufficiently accurate for our purposes, which threw us out of a good deal of work, but a lucky chance has remedied all that matter. A few days ago a gentleman came up on to the street where we were at work, and in the course of conversation, we mentioned the disadvantage we were under from the want of instruments, etc. "Don't let that worry you," said he, "I have them and will lend you those you want, and you can have them for perhaps three months, and by that time probably your own may have arrived from Philadelphia." Accordingly, the next morning Mr Graham and I went to the gentleman's lodgings and got a transit compass and level—two of the best instruments in the country. The gentleman was Lieut. Blunt of the U.S. Navy, and the instruments are Uncle Sam's so you may suppose they are fine ones. We gave him a receipt for them, and are to use them until some vessel arrives from the United States, which has the Coast Survey party on board. Is not that a streak of luck? . . .

Harry and I have just finished chopping a lot of wood to last us a day or two—which will account for the irregularity of my hand writing. While we were at it a young man of my acquaintance passed the house with bucket and tea kettle in hand. "Wouldn't folks at home laugh," said he "to see us employed in this way?" "Go it," said I, "we're in California now, and can do any thing that is honest, so that it pays."

Henry Didier Lammot

Letter to his mother
22 February 1850

I just happen to think that this is Washington's birthday. All the vessles in the harbour have their flags flying in honor of the "Father of his Country" and the U.S. Sloop of War *Falmouth* has just fired the National Salute (21 guns). The Mail Steamer arrived this morning, so in about a week we may expect some letters, for it generally takes about that time to sort them. This is Friday. Well, perhaps they may open the post office on Monday. . . .

If you should see a plan of San Francisco and should look at the corner of First and Market St. you will see the position of the present residence of your sons. After a while I expect we shall move out to *our house* on Mission St. (ahem).

A day or two ago as I was walking out Mission St. I saw some men at work round a string, and on going up I found some gentlemen *washing gold* out of the sand. They got out during the day near 1/2 oz. of gold, so it is all over town.

John McCrackan

Letter to his family
17 February 1850

Take a look with me at San Francisco from my building lot in "Vermin Place." Vernon Place [Marcy Place], as I have before told you, is a
small knoll, large enough however for four building lots. Behind it
the land gradually rises till [in] about a thousand yards, it reaches the
summit. You follow this line of high land laying directly back of Vernon Place and to the Westward, you follow this line northward, when
the land suddenly rises to a greater elevation ending in a very high
graceful hill. You see its rounded and easy outline in bold relief
against the sky. Here and there are men or cattle climbing its gentle
sides, and their position is so perfect, you can see their every movement and feature.

Upon the very highest part you see a gathering in a spot which at
other times would be conspicuous, it being marked with a cross. This
spot, my dear family, is dedicated and consecrated to the "Masonic
Fraternity," a place selected by them to bury their brothers whom
they are called to part with here. Even now as I look upon that little
band, I see a movement. They separate and in turn each deposits a
sprig of evergreen upon the rude coffin, after which the prayer is said,
the farewell taken, and the brother is left in his glory. The procession
is formed and as it turns to leave the grave, your ear is saluted by the
thrilling dirge that makes its way into the silent valley below. Such
was the scene this noon.

Could we trace that beautiful hill northward, we should find it
gradually losing itself on the Bay shore. We will now return to Vernon
Place. You can trace the outline that bounds the horizon westward as
it turns southward, rising as it approaches the point directly south
from Vernon Place, and then forms a counterpart of the hill described
on the north. This high hill south, however, is gradually lost in the
beautiful table land of the Mission Dolores. Thus, you see, Vernon
Place is the center of a beautiful little cove of the hills.

Now then, we will go east, and let us go carefully lest we lose or
neglect to notice the many prominent objects. Vernon Place is framed
upon the summit of a hill, small in contrast with the many larger
ones bounding it on the north, west, and south, and yet the hill is sufficiently large enough to induce one to believe it will always remain.
The descent on the east and south, and indeed north, is very sudden

into a beautiful valley, which is now richly carpeted with the rich green grass. Here and there are houses erected, or about being finished, giving it a busy and lively appearance. This valley is but a few hundred yards long, and let us trace it. We find it winding around the base of Vernon Place, then taking a sudden turn, turning the corner of a church, it soon finds itself in what is called Broadway. Now it seems to me as if this valley were there just to "show off" V. P. to advantage.

Now let's look a little beyond. With our eyes we cross this valley, [and] ascend the hill opposite (directly eastward). This hill gradually rises till it forms a summit spoken of in the south. As you look eastward upon this hill, you see two churches, beside[s] the one in the valley. Two are Episcopal. I attend the one on the hill. It is small, but being neatly painted, it presents a very pretty appearance. The bell is hung by the side, supported in a high wood frame. This hill is much lower than Vernon Place, and consequently does not obstruct the view of the city.

Now look at San Francisco. How like patch work it is, buildings of all kinds and descriptions, and many of the streets, being narrow, are hard to discover here. As we stand on this hill and look north, we escape the protection of that beautiful hill, and here we trace an even valley winding about its base, which we follow till we meet the blue waters of the Bay flowing up to meet us. The windings of the bay southward are lost for a time by a very high hill which stands on the verge of the Bay. That hill is northeast from Vernon Place. Upon the top you see the Stars and Stripes, here a person has opened a stand for refreshments, and thus attracts the idle or the curious. From this place you see the whole Bay, north and south, as well as the city. It is rather a bleak place for a residence.

This hill slopes gradually southward to the streets of the city. The slope is very regular, and consequently not unpleasant to climb. Let us return to Vernon Place and after looking for a moment at the mighty improvements going forward (such as building government warehouses and wharfs), do look at the innumerable number of vessels of all sizes in the Bay, and indeed we do not see them all, for some are behind that high hill in the northeast. Some of these large ships are stripped and hauled upon the mud, and used for store houses. This will be the case with the *Balance* [McCrackan's ship]. Here and there you see several small steamboats darting about among the ships, and these little busy creatures earn more money for their owners than could be imagined.

Just beyond the vessels eastward, and apparently in the very center of the Bay, is a small island, the resort mostly of sea dogs and birds. The northern extremity of this is at the mouth of the Sacramento River. When directly back of this island (although there is, I presume, a vast gulf between), you trace from the very Ocean a dark irregular line of hills. If you look attentively you will see how they seem to rise one above the other, each growing of a deeper shade while it towers above its neighbor. You will see on the top of the highest of these hills layers of snow, which in the clear sunlight form a beautiful contrast with the dark sides below and the bright blue above. These high hills produce pine (redwood) trees one hundred and fifty feet high, by thirty and forty feet in diameter. This I believe, although [I] have not seen them.

Deer, elk, beavers, grizzly bear and all kinds of game are found here. You can form no idea of the quantity of game we have here, and the most beautiful and really gorgeous plumage many of the birds have. It is a rich country for the naturalist. The highest of them is said to be fifty miles hence. It leads you to the beautiful valley of "San Jose" and "Santa Barbara." I have conversed with men who have been over there employed cutting wood, and they say very frequently when the sun has been warm and bright over them, they could see a heavy vapor hanging about our hill tops over the city. This we expect now, as the spring has fairly come at last. The weather is said to be very uniform, in summer, very. The morning thick and foggy till about ten o'clock, when the sun condescends to smile. It continues very warm and pleasant till noon, when a cold wind springs up from the west and increasing in violence as well as temperance, till by eve it blows a small gale. It goes to rest generally however, with the sun. The night dews follow, and are very heavy. These a person must avoid if he will keep his health.

John McCrackan

Letter to his sister Lottie
16 April 1850

We are all taught to realize here in this new country the true value of health. Besides the want of care and comforts, one's business suffers so much. A fortnight sickness and confinement here is like being on the bed of sickness a whole year any where else. We are so progressive, one must be up and about constantly to keep pace with the "march of the times." Within a week the state of things may change, and render the rich poor or the poor man wealthy. All is activity, enterprise, industry. How any young man of true enterprise can remain at home quietly and view this glorious little state starting into existance without a desire to take part in this mighty enterprise, is unaccountable to me. I feel, indeed I know, I could not content myself at this time to look quietly on these things in my distant home. I should be perfectly miserable. This is the place for a young man. We all have a fair and equal start, all are young men together, and although I have no "political aspirations" and probably never shall, yet I am here in this wonderful country, and play my humble part (for there is no such thing as exclusiveness here) in this great dream.

Hotchkiss mentioned one or two young lawyers who were thinking seriously of coming out, and although we have a surplus of lawyers here in San Francisco, still this surplusage will be disposed of in the millions of new river towns and cities that are springing into existance like mushrooms. Their chances are very fine, and most desirable, and I have been sadly tempted to accept a "Judgeship" in some of them, and the only argument that effectively silenced these longings has been the thought that by living in these far off cities I should deprive myself of the pleasant communication with you all. Not entirely, but it would be so long before I could get my letters, and instead of my letters reaching me in forty five days from their date, it would [be] nearer a hundred. I am determined to live where I can get letters from you all as soon as they arrive, and in case I should be recalled, it could be done without loss of time.

I am confident that by industry and perseverance, together with good habits, I can accumulate enough to return before long, at least on a visit. My late severe loss will induce me to take a different course, and either transmit my money home or place it where I can have it constantly in view. But enough! 'Tis the fate of many others. It was made by the dash of a pen and lost in less time. I have one consolation, my dear Lottie, not one penny have I squandered, not the first cent has been expended for amusement. I feel that every dollar saved brings me nearer you and home.

The enormous rent I have been subjected to has really eaten up the business the last two months, [but] will be dispensed with in a great measure after next May. We shall take two beautiful offices (they are now being fitted up for us) for less than I now pay. . . .

We shall have our offices very nicely fitted up. After which I will appoint some day, and give you an invitation to our very snug quarters. I shall be particular to appoint a pleasant day and trust there will be no excuse. You must come. I shall take such precautions as will prevent your excuse about the "night air," "hot room," &c &c. I promise to give you a "musical treat" and as much cider as you can drink. I'll have sugar and rice for Sarah, seven cups of hot tea for William, lots of tomatoes for Mother, strawberrys for Mary, corned beef and cabbage for your own sweet self, and baked beans for all. Now is not that a "set out"? The company are politely requested to bring their silver forks. What a time we will have to be sure. I shall be as expeditious as possible, as I am in a perfect flurry to know how "things will look." I want the whole matter kept perfectly secret till the invitations are given out. "Oh! How it will astonish the Browns and the Joneses." I hope you will not think me rude or exacting when I request you will wear your "lucky red dress." I'll get you to mention this to the Lanmans, who I shall probably invite, as they might think it queer in me. In conclusion, I will only say get rid of your colds and don your sweetest smiles.

John McCrackan

Letter to his family
8 May 1850

You will have undoubtedly have heard before receiving this of the disastrous fire that very nearly swept our little city on the morning of the 4th inst.—and, of course, will be very anxious to learn if "Gothic Hall" [the building housing his law practice] is still standing, and so I take pleasure informing you immediately the "Gothic Hall" is still standing uninjured, while all around is desolation. Our beautiful offices fortunately are still the same, though of course made more valuable and conspicuous by the ruin before them.

The fire broke out about four o'clock in the morning in a large three story building known as the "United States" devoted, like all our large and expensive houses about the Plaza, to drinking and gambling. Mr. Sheppard and self gained the Plaza in ten minutes after the alarm was sounded, and yet so rapid was the fire that in that time the U.S. was perfectly enveloped by the flames, and the large buildings on either side already burning. This would seem incredible but from the fact that they were lined with cotton cloth, upon which is placed painted paper, and of course no time is required for the flame to reach the roof. The frame work is very slight to the best built, and to look upon one while in process of erection you would think our ordinary afternoon wind would carry them away.

We were early upon the ground, and yet many were there and all apparently stupefied, stood gazing upon this truly awful sight. No one offered the least assistance to save property or even life, while the flames were making fearful strides towards a large beautiful building which fronted on the Plaza and which has been about a month in finishing, (a very long time with us in Cal.) This building promised to be quite an ornament to the city, being one hundred and sixty feet, by forty-two, four stories high, and has cost sixty-five thousand dollars in cash to complete, even at our now very low prices of timber. The first floor on all sides was sided with most beautifully painted wood paneling, the ceiling fresco, and the most expensive furniture, mirrors and bar fixtures. This house had the day before been finished, and was on this day or eve to be opened for the first time, on which occasion they gave a champagne supper, free to all and everyone. Of course, this house had caused a great deal of talk, and every one seemed to feel a secret wish that the person who had got up this splendid affair might succeed. And here this building stood just finished, and in a few moments more would be food for the devouring element. No wonder people gazed. No wonder they stood listless and stupid with the prospect of this structure being destroyed, and yet no mortal hand could save it. All saw and felt this while yet the fire was three doors off. Still, no one was moved to rescue any of the beautiful and expensive fixtures. In ten minutes more this building was fired, and in twenty minutes more most of the timbers were blazing in heaps upon the ground.

After the fall of this house people came as it were to themselves, and began to look about upon the ruin, as well as to ask, "Where is this to be stayed?" And well they might, for it was fast spreading in every direction, and threatened the destruction of the entire city. Mr. S. and self left the Plaza in order to get near our offices, and the next half hour we were engaged removing a quantity of very beautiful "China goods,"—silks and shawls of the most costly kind—which had been cast into the street. I presume Mr. S. and self must have saved twenty thousand dollars worth by our own exertions, some being as expensive as four and five hundred dollars a piece (and our market here is perfectly flooded), such as would cost at home one thousand and fifteen hundred dollars.

I will not pretend to describe to you the scenes that were enacted, some painful and some most extremely ludicrous, and yet people generally seemed to be in most excellent humor, and after the fire really got to be frightful, they began to work in right good earnest, although without fire regulations of course we labored under great disadvantages, as men worked without proper organization.

Find[ing] the fire making rapid progress towards "Gothic Hall," we took our station near, that we might be prepared to remove our things. When we got to our building we found that those having offices there—all but us—had removed their things, their rooms being quite deserted. At this time our destruction seemed inevitable, and we commenced to move our trunks and get other things ready to take out at a moment's warning. After which we returned to the front stoop and concluded our arrangements, and so soon as the large building on the corner opposite should take, we were to remove the rest of our things, as that building must destroy us, and our only hope was that it might be saved. Adjoining it towards the fire was a brick building "Howard House," and next to that a large long building which at that time was taking fire. The whole strength and power, physical as well as water power, was thrown forward to protect the brick building, as upon our success in that place consisted our hopes in regard not only to Gothic Hall, but the whole block to the water, and perhaps even the shipping in the harbor.

I need not tell you how we battled the flames inch by inch, for a full hour on that spot, at one time almost indeed quite in despair but on we worked, holding the fire in check till a small engine came to our assistance and we came off conquerors. This is but a faint outline of this dreadful scene. I have not described the confusion of men and tongues—Spanish, Dutch, Jews, French, Celestials [Chinese]—all excited, all talking, and some perfectly crazy with excitement. I saw three men rescue a noble dog from a store which the faithful animal refused to leave, even when he was completely surrounded by fire and his beautiful coat burnt to a perfect crisp. I send you papers giving you full particulars. The number of buildings destroyed is near four hundred, and the estimated amount of property is four million, burning the same old ground over as the fire in December, yet that was only about one quarter as large.

About ten o'clock we breakfasted by invitation at the Bay Hotel, and it was very fortunate, as we should have gone without but for that, as many of our best eating houses had been burnt. The few that were left were not capable to answer demands. The fire in other parts of the city was fortunately stayed, in some instances by blowing up buildings and then again by pulling down, although as you will see by the diagram . . . all but a few buildings out of the three blocks . . . were destroyed, and these blocks as you will see are the very heart of the city. The loss has been very much greater than can be estimated with any degree of certainty. It has been a sad visitation, and we shall not recover from it for some time.

You will see on the diagram "Dunbars Bank," which escaped. This is a very funny affair, being nothing more nor less than a good sized brick safe, with fire ventilations, large enough however to admit of several men at a time. This was built some time after our last great fire, and has been opened regularly every day since, receiving deposits, &c. After breakfast in visiting the ruins I saw this bank open and crowded with people. On the outside on the wall was a paper notice "Dunbar's Bank open as usual," and it struck me as being very funny. This bank, as you will see, is in the very heart of the ruins, and no building standing within one hundred yards of it.

But I must mention our enterprise. In my walk about 10:30 o'clock I saw in one instance they had actually hauled the timber and the sill was actually being laid for the new house, and that was even while the fire was still burning in one section. I have heard of several instances where contracts were made for rebuilding by persons when it became evident their buildings must go, even while they were yet standing. By night of the day of the fire, two new buildings had been finished, and were in full blast. You will say, "What kind of buildings could they be?" They were frame tents covered with canvas, and these will not be rebuilt till next fall, when brick will be less expensive here.

On my way through the burnt district from dinner this eve I presume I counted fifty good frame buildings going up. Many will be done this week. There is nothing like our enterprise here. However, I do not think they will again erect as expensive wood buildings as those destroyed. It is quite impossible to get them insured. . . . This late fire has made money in great demand. There was a large quantity of gold melted in the fire. I saw them taking it from among the ruins. I did not tell you what a time we had at the time of the fire with gunpowder. There was a great quantity, every store having one or two kegs. You could hear them "pop off" at intervals, throwing the fragments high in [the] air. The powder prevented many from working at the fire, who otherwise would have done so, and it really was very dangerous. It seems almost a miracle none were injured by it, and all day after the fire you would hear frequent explosions of powder from among the smoking embers.

Margaret DeWitt

Letter to her mother-in-law
15 May 1850

Since I last wrote this City has been visited with a very destructive fire which broke out on the morning of the 4th between 3 and 4 o'clock. It commenced in the same place (a gambling house) that it did last winter and destroyed most of the gambling place, together with many fine stores and other valuable property. It raged so violently we feared at one time it would extend as far as DeWitt & Harrison's store and in case it did our dwelling house and all would have gone. As it was, we were in great danger from the burning cinders which flew in all directions. All were a good deal excited—and fatigued, as the roof had to be covered with wet blankets and every thing possible wet. We picked up our clothing and every thing valuable so if it did extend in this direction, we should at least have that. It was very fortunately stopped, and I can assure you after all danger was over we were completely tired out with excitement and fatigue. They all worked hard at the store, and I think the fire was one cause of my brother's illness, as he had not been very well and probably exerted himself too much. Many were burnt out the second time, and the loss of property was very great. The burnt district looks desolate enough, but it will soon be again rebuilt—but the buildings are of so slight a nature I should not be surprised if it was soon burnt again.

William Smith Jewett

Letter to his family
27 May 1850

I have a surmise that here comes a long letter from Will, so wait for dinner ere you read it. He's been burned out—"one of the sufferers by the late awful conflagration of claptraps, paper houses, hencoops, &c." Loss—two millions, four millions, as you please, we are not particular here as to the exact amount. . . .

The fire occurred about five in the morning, just in time to disturb us in our morning nap. I was among the first up in our building and altho it was nearly a block off we had not time to save all our goods and chattels. It was really amusing to see us all scampering half dressed with our lumber on our backs, running about like ants when their nest is disturbed, each with a precious egg. I lost nothing of importance, yet there was a deal of valuable property destroyed. But I did not see a long face among the whole multitude and all looked as tho they would have money or fun from it—ultimately.

John McCrackan

Letter to his sister Lottie
30 May 1850

We are in a constant state of alarm in consequence of attempts to fire the city. Last night we were called up three times. Each time the fire was extinguished before it had got fairly underway, and three millions of property was saved. If a person should be caught firing a building he would be hung, without the least ceremony, for we have no preservation here except in preventing at the time the torch is lighted, for after a building is in flames, all we can do is to pull down and blow up about it, and this is one reason why I still hold on to the ship, for I feel that in case our City should be destroyed, I should have still a home on the ship. They have now commenced building "Artesian wells" which in general will give us enough water.

John McCrackan

Letter to his family
15 June 1850

We had gained the boat [after visiting friends aboard ship] and were fast making the shore in our little skiff, when I discovered a dense cloud of smoke. I remarked it to Mr. B. but before he could reply, the alarm of, "Fire!" reached us, and accelerating our speed we soon gained the wharf, at which time our little city generally was in motion towards the scene of conflagration, which proved to be in the center of one of our most extensive and valuable blocks, one of the three left standing at our fire of last month. The wind was quite strong for morning and the fire blazed with a perfect fury. In five minutes time it became evident the whole block must go, the flames being driven directly upon the United States Hotel in Montgomery St., and in five minutes more when that was burning the fire was communicated acrost the street, and no power then could save the extensive wood as well as fire proof (or built as such) warehouses between that and the water.

At this time being quite exhausted, I left to get my breakfast. It is needless for me to attempt a full description. Men worked bravely and did much, but with a high wind and such combustable material, all efforts seemed fruitless. The reports of the powder exploding in the different buildings followed one another every minute and seemed like "minute guns" booming over the progress of the destructive element. The fire was stayed from crossing Kearny and going uptown by blowing up an immense old adobe building on the corner of Clay and Kearney. While in other places the same thing was done, and in one place on the corner of Clay and Montgomery Sts. an artesian well furnished water enough to save the block near it, and others equally valuable—and this well cost but 140 dollars.

Our city fathers have been very remiss in their duty by not contracting for a large number of these wells for different parts of our city. They have been in power over six weeks, and have done nothing but vote themselves a salary of six thousand dollars a year, giving the Mayor, Recorder and City Attorney 10,000 dollars per annum. While taking care of themselves, they have been thoughtless of the city and her interest.

The fire continued burning most of the day in particular points of the City and has made dreadful destruction I assure you. The loss is variously estimated, some say five and some six millions of property has been burnt. The fire is more extensive even than the one of last month. While that fell upon gamblers and Jews, or merchants of comparatively a smaller class, this fire has destroyed the stores and warehouses of the most extensive merchants, burning quite to the water, and cutting off the communication with those who had carried their goods on to the long wharfs running out from that part of the City.

It was low tide, and our few engines were consequently useless, and the heat was so great they were deserted upon the wharfs, which were burnt or charred quite a distance out. At one time it seemed as if the block above us would go, which endangered us, and those having offices in our building moved their things, but we left everything remaining as usual, and had cause to congratulate ourselves, as it injures furniture very much to move it. We have been and are very much blessed, for as yet we have not been "turned out," although we expect to be at any time. I was thinking yesterday if I had sustained any loss, and came to the conclusion that I had escaped this time, except it be the fact that two important [law] suits will necessarily be obliged to be discontinued. This will take fifteen hundred dollars out of our pockets. However, this morning it occurred to me we had a quantity of things from our ship stored in California St., and these upon reflection must have been destroyed, and this will involve the ship *Balance* in a loss of about five hundred dollars, what was worth a thousand when we arrived here, mostly ship furniture, but there is such a quantity of such merchandize here now, it was not very valuable. However this is no great loss, for as I have said I didn't discover it, or even imagine they were within reach of the fire, till this morning.

However, our loss will be in common with every one else, and our business must be seriously effected by it. One would suppose our people would become discouraged by such ruefull reversals, but instead of that they seem rather to gain new impulses and energy, and the burnt district this morning presents quite a busy scene. Some at work, others idling about, some lunching upon roast ham, flesh of all kinds, and preserves, vegetables of all kinds, sardines in the greatest abundance were lying blazing in heaps about the ruins.

J. G. W. Luyster

Letter to his mother
18 June 1850

Since I last wrote there has been a very destructive fire here and a number of buildings, as well as a large amt of Goods have been destroyed. Mr. Hamilton and myself have lost about $2500, which loss we sustained by not having iron doors to the building we were in.

Your letter I rec'd on the 10th Inst, but unfortunately it was destroyed by the fire of the 14th, together with the one for David Arrowsmith, as well as the collars &c Mary Anne and Catherine sent me. I expect David will be very much disappointed, when he hears it, he is at the mines, consequently you will receive no answer from him. . . .

Mr. Hamilton and myself will have the same place of business we had previous to the fire, as soon as it is rebuilt, which will be in about a month. The walls are to be 20 inches thick and the doors and windows are to be of iron, consequently we will certainly have a fire proof store.

Chapter 6

Men without Women

The gold rush proved to be a cataclysm that descended on nine-teenth-century American gender roles, turning them on their heads. Women who were left behind were forced by circumstances to take up many of the duties previously reserved to their husbands, sons, brothers, and fathers. Men, too, found themselves taking on unaccustomed roles. Overland journals reveal that on the wagon trains conflict commonly arose over what was traditionally considered to be "women's work."[1] Many of the men assigned to the cooking or cleaning tended to shirk these duties whenever possible, and tempers would flare whenever a man's fumbling but sincere domestic efforts failed to receive the proper level of appreciation. The men's almost total ignorance of skills that were traditionally relegated to the feminine sphere sometimes bordered on the ludicrous. One miner placed a casserole of unsoaked beans in the oven, and was puzzled when they came out harder than they were before he baked them.[2]

But the absence of women presented a challenge more serious than the lack of culinary expertise. Women were educated to take on the running of a household and in that capacity they possessed a certain degree of knowledge concerning diet and nutrition.[3] En route and in California, however, men tended to stick to a few dishes that had proved to be edible and the fare quickly became monotonous and unhealthful. After a day of hard labor the men craved protein and carbohydrates so they tended to consume meals consisting solely of meat and dried beans, even when vegetables (wild or domesticated) were available. Vitamin-deficiency diseases such as scurvy were rampant among the travelers. Moreover, women were the repository of the home remedies and folk wisdom that represented the first line of medical treatment for most nineteenth-century Americans. Without a woman to turn to many men allowed minor illnesses and injuries to go unattended. In the highly septic environment of the trail or the gold fields or in the urban squalor of San Francisco these ailments frequently became life-threatening.

For the few unmarried women who came to San Francisco during the gold rush the city provided a unique opportunity for economic betterment. In the nineteenth century few professions were open to "good" women, and those all paid extremely low wages. The single most effective means available to a woman for raising her social or economic status was to marry well, and in San Francisco women encountered a seller's market. The very fact of her gender placed her in extremely high demand. If she brought a modicum of good looks, a compliant temperament, and—what was particularly helpful—a strong streak of acquisitive moxie she could marry extremely well and jump into an economic and social bracket that would have been resolutely closed to her at home.[4]

The added scope that women discovered in the overwhelmingly male environment of California was not entirely a product of the gold rush. The Californio leader Mariano Guadalupe Vallejo, when interviewed by Hubert Howe Bancroft, recalled that there was a sharp rise in the number of *solteronas,* or old maids, after the American conquest and the destruction of the province's patriarchal society. Mexican men were reluctant to marry the newly liberated California women, afraid that they would be ruined or dishonored by *mujeres necias y vanidosas* (foolish and vain females).[5]

Whatever the fluid status of women at the time, gold rush San Francisco remained primarily the domain of young men. During the year of these letters and diaries the ratio of men to women was around ten to one, and while the number of women slowly increased (particularly in the metropolitan areas of California) men remained in the overwhelming majority throughout the gold rush years.[6] This dramatic disparity in gender representation inevitably molded the character of the city as it developed. San Francisco's reputation as a "restaurant town" has been traced directly to the vast number of businesses established to feed the onslaught of single men. In the absence of hearth and home, men sought out public entertainment in saloons, theaters, and opera houses, and by 1850 the amateur performers of "free & easys" were replaced by professional-caliber artists, many of world renown.

San Franciscans found ways of creating a *modus vivendi* in the absence of women, and while many gold rush letters and diaries bemoan the lack of feminine charms to complete the social picture many also exude an almost smug pride in the creation of an environment in which women have been rendered virtually obsolete. The men speak of returning home to marry, but in jocular terms that seem to imply that while the act itself was inevitable the identity of the specific woman was irrelevant. Terms of warmer regard are reserved for the description of a special (male) friend.

Given San Francisco's current status as a primary locus of gay and lesbian culture in America it is reasonable to speculate on whether or not today's community has its roots in the gold rush. Certainly the San Francisco of 1849–50 exhibited all the elements that tend to encourage the type of situational, temporary homosexual activity that one finds in unisex environments such as prisons, boarding schools, and isolated military installations. There were very few sexually available women, and all contact with them tended to be of a commercial nature. The most attractive courtesans charged fees far beyond the average man's ability to pay, and the affordability of a more common prostitute was inversely proportional to her physical charms. The heterosexual options for the young salaried clerk or unsuccessful miner were, therefore, rather slim.

Men lived cheek-by-jowl with one another, even sharing beds and blankets. They found themselves in a hostile environment in which having a best friend could, quite literally, mean the difference between life and death. The situation was ripe for the type of male bonding that occurs in a foxhole under fire, and it would not be surprising if these hormone-driven, female-starved and frequently drunk young men occasionally turned to one another for physical comfort.

In an evocative and puzzling passage, Hubert Howe Bancroft describes the situation in these terms:

> The requirements of mining life favored partnership; and while few of the associations formed for the journey out kept together, new unions were made for mutual aid in danger, sickness, and labor. Sacred like the marriage bonds, as illustrated by the softening of partner into the familiar "pard," were ties which oft united men vastly different in physique and temperament, the weak and the strong, the lively and sedate, thus

yoking themselves together. It presented the affinity of opposites, with the heroic possibilities of a Damon or Patroclus.[7]

Bancroft, no doubt, knew his Classics. The story of Damon, who out of devotion pledged his life as a hostage for his condemned friend Pythias, or of Patroclus, the lover of Achilles, whose death spurs Achilles to return to battle under the walls of Troy—these legends were familiar to Bancroft and his contemporary readers. It would be easy to dismiss these allusions as standard nineteenth-century literary rhetoric, except for the fact that Bancroft has taken two stereotypic examples of the male bonding of coequals and used them to illustrate "the affinity of opposites." How literally are we to take his reference to "sacred like the marriage bonds"?

More intriguing is the question of whether or not the gold rush (and the frontier in general) actually *attracted* young gay men, men for whom a homosexual orientation had been set *before* leaving home—an orientation that was, in fact, the reason for leaving. It is not anachronistic to speak of a homosexual identity at this stage of world history. As Foucault has observed, in the nineteenth century "homosexuality began to speak in its own behalf, to demand that its legitimacy or 'naturality' be acknowledged," and the emerging culture found no less a voice than that of Walt Whitman.[8] Whitman's *Leaves of Grass* sings of the love of comrades in terms so homoerotically explicit that it led then-Secretary of the Interior James Harlen to fire the author from his government job in 1865.[9]

Historians have just begun to investigate the role that sexual orientation played in the development of nineteenth-century American life and to explore the reasons why many chose careers that placed them in isolated, all-male environments for months (or even years) at a time. Preliminary investigations have been published concerning cowboys, United States Marines, Civil War soldiers, fur trappers, and cross-dressing women (who were not necessarily lesbians).[10] More extensive studies have been published concerning the *berdache* tradition among American Indians, and homosexual partnerships among nineteenth-century Mormon pioneers.[11] Further study remains to be done. Perhaps in the future our understanding of this aspect of history will change as it did so dramatically when historians began to focus on the experiences of women and ethnic minorities. In the meantime these letters contain intriguing vignettes of male-male domesticity about which the reader can only speculate.

What is clear is that for the majority of the Argonauts—whether or not they were inclined to marry—women represented civilization, culture, and refinement. In contrast to the prostitutes that were encountered on the streets and in the saloons, "true women" were "passive, obedient, pious, and pure."[12] For unmarried men, one's mother and sisters represented what was good and decent—in direct contrast to the lurid temptations of the brothel. Only when the number of "true women" increased sufficiently could California become anything more than a wild, depraved waystation on the road to riches.

Charles F. Dulany

Letter to his sister
26 February 1850

I have come to the conclusion that the only way to hear from any of my relatives is to write them as frequent as possible and thereby elicit an answer through *courtesy*, if no other way. My dear, dear Sister, why do you not write me? Twelve long months have elapsed since I have rec'd one of those kind and affectionate letters that you were wont to write in days of yore—one of those that came from the heart and went to the heart. Ah! how long have I wished in travelling over the scorching desert, the bleak and towering mountain, and toiling in the sultry mines of California, to hear *one* single accent of her who loves me dearly and loves me true, yet this has been denied me. In ignorance and in misery at times have I passed the lengthened hours away, until yesterday I got a letter from Molly and thereby indirectly learned that you and Hector were well and that you spoke of spending the Winter in Alexandria. . . .

Molly, after telling me of several marriages that have taken place in Kentucky, says that I must return soon, or all the girls will be married. That of course led me to thinking upon the subject, and I came to the conclusion that my habits in California had so taught me the domestic occupations of life, that I *thought* I could do without a wife. I can cook (make excellent bread, Mr. Abbey says), sew, darn—and *not* wash, but that can be remedied in the country by the cheapness of clothing, so when one garment gets soiled, throw it away and purchase another, as many do, washing being *only* an half ounce per dozen, that is 8$.

But when I think of my loved, but distant home, the smiles of woman there—the tears of *sisterly* affection—which oft will flow when the absent are thought of, all all—banish such—must I term them—unholy thoughts. I am much pleased with this country, or perhaps with the facility in which money can be acquired. My health has been very good. I was sick on the Trinity about ten days with fever, tho I was travelling the whole time. Since then I have not had a day's sickness and rarely the head ache which I was so subject to in Louisville, and my chest is as apparently sound as any one I know. I have but one slight pain in it since arriving in the Country.

E. A. Upton

Diary
9 December 1849

Have visited the Baptist, Episcopal and Methodist churches to-day. The Methodists also held a meeting in the plaza which drew an immense crowd. Noticed two ladies assisting the clergyman in singing. . . . Overheard a man suddenly exclaiming (who had been to the mines or some other out-of-the-way place), as he happened to see a female passing, "G-ds there's a *woman*! As true as the world!"

John McCrackan

Letter to his sister
21 December 1849

There are but few ladies here, although many [men] who have established their business and intend remaining a few years are about returning for their family. This is no place for ladies, however, and I should think it a great risk to expose any of our ladies to this uncharitable climate. South of this at San Jose or Monterey, it is delightful all the year round.

Samuel C. Lewis

Journal
14 April 1850

To day went to the Presbyterian Church. It being communion day, had a very good discourse, but the minister had no written sermon and of course his discourse was somewhat disconnected. About 100 persons in attendance—all men, not a female in the house, except some three or four natives who went from curiosity, not understanding a word.

John McCrackan

Letter to his family
25 December 1849

I dined today with a friend (Dr. Elliott of New York) and our dinner consisted of roast beef and plum pudding, and a glass of sherry, dedicated to absent friends. Yes, my dear "absent ones," be assured you were remembered, and I felt I was not forgotten. . . . I wanted to inform you that I have Dr. Elliott in my office, who is very kind and talented and so you need have no fear but what in case of sickness I shall have the best attention. Dr. E. is devoted to me and we are very good friends.

John McCrackan

Letter to his sister
27 January 1850

You speak of your inability to contend with the vast multitude of annoying things which the invalid is subject to, nay comes with and is part and parcel of the disease. Now my dear Lottie, reflect for a moment, there is perhaps no sickness that so disturbs one['s] mental faculties for the time as Typhus fever, no disease that so completely changes our nature, robbing us of our ability to contend with these troubles and trials. I have had an opportunity of late to watch and study its effect. As I told you in my last, I brought around to my room my friend Dr. E[lliott] who has been and still continues, very ill of this same Typhus fever. I gave up my bed to him and occupy a chair couch myself, thus being with him night and day, and I recognize how completely this fever has changed his nature as it will, making him cross and fretfull and obstinate, determined he will have his own way in everything. We humor him all we can and yet in some things we are obliged to be decided. When harried by sickness our nature is changed, it being a kind of insanity, and it so strangely works, as in the instance of the beautiful pure and chaste "Ophelia." At such times we entertain thoughts and use expressions which are the most distant strangers at other times.

John McCrackan

Letter to his sister Mary
29 January 1850

Thanks, my dear sister, for your kind intentions of correcting my spelling. I can assure you I appreciate your kindness, but I must think all efforts to correct this bad habit will prove ineffectual. Withought the thought. I am quite as liable to spell a word *right* as *wrong*.

You would be so amused to sit at my window and see the people pass. You must know the street in front is a hill and sufficiently steep at this season to be slippery, however it is covered with mud, ankle deep, which renders it quite impassible without the utmost care to pass up and down without a fall. The result of all this is that we have many very funny upsets in full view of our window, consequently many hearty laughs at the expense of the poor victims.

Miss Sutter, daughter of the celebrated Capt. Sutter, is in town at the present time and, reports say, receiving much attention, having quite a throng of admirers. She is an only daughter and so presumed to be very rich. Capt. Sutter I am told, is a very gentlemanly agreeable person. Dr. E[lliott] was introduced to him and I think was very much pleased with his manners. I am told it is desirable to speak "Dutch" [Swiss German] in order to succeed with her, consequently I have declined an introduction. You have no idea how few women we have here, and if one makes her appearance in the street, all stop stand and look. However, the latest fashion is to carry them in the arms.

E. A. Upton

Diary
26 December 1849

Sitting in the cabin reading, but my situation is rather unpleasant. The mate and men have all gone ashore for the night and no one is on board with me but the steward, who has got drunk—which unenviable happiness he is sure to enjoy whenever he can get liquor. A large part of our cargo is wines and liquors, and I expect he has obtained a bottle from some of the broken boxes and slipped it into a sly corner where he occasionally resorts to drink. He is a very stout, double fisted Irishman and is very savage and desperate when in liquor. He has not the slightest ill-will against me but still, he is now crazy and furious, and I cannot persuade him to keep quiet. Our boats are all ashore and I am compelled to keep his company, and this is not the first time I have found myself alone with him in this state. From the bottom of my heart do I pity the wife of a drunken husband, which she is obliged to live and bear with continually.

William Smith Jewett

Letter to his sister
28 January 1850

Boarding is very expensive here and we manage all sorts of ways to render it cheap. A gentleman friend sleeps with me in my room, so to pay for his lodging I make him provide bread and butter for breakfast and tea, and make the coffee and bring the water. We have an alcoholic coffee pot, which makes it very nice, and two cups and a stone jar to keep our butter in. These and our two bouyee [Bowie] knives constitute our articles of housekeeping. We distinguish each other's cup by his being very clean and mine the reverse. Some times he forgets to wash his, when forthwith a great dispute arises as to which is which. It generally ends by washing both cups out and starting anew. We have a very first rate cup of tea sometimes I'll assure you—and occasionally laugh at the figure we cut, and wish for our friends here to join us in it. We get very good dinners at the many Lunches about town for a dollar per dinner.

Washing is six dollars per dozen here—when anything of that sort is done. I doubt whether there is much, for I don't know a gent. who ever had any. I've got one clean shirt left yet, and go regularly every morning to my trunk and look at the precious relict of tidiness and turn away with a sigh at the awful condition my dandyism is reduced to. I'm sure I'll have to come home to get washed up. My flannels are very nice, but most of all my other clothes are a mere encumbrance. I wish Henry had them. I am glad he is getting on so well according to your letter. I am very anxious to go and see him, and shall do so the first thing after getting home, save marrying a wife—that is, if I can find anyone worthy of my *gold* (of my self there are plenty).

Henry R. DeWitt

Letter to his mother
29 September 1849

If you know any one that is comeing across the Isthmus—and would have no objections to bring a *small bundle*—I wish you would send me if you have not done so per the *Elizabeth*—an entire suit of clothes, a black cloth coat and pants, a dark figured vest and a pair of fine boots. I cannot get any thing that will suit me. I was greatly disappointed in those by the *Ocean Bird.* The goods were fine enough but were not made right. If I wear fine clothes they must suit me or I go without them. I have great confidence in William Last. Let him get them made for me. If Miles has got my measure, let them be made by him. I have on the last suit he made me and they fit *excelent.* After trying all of one case of boots in the store I went up town and paid $16 dollars for a pair. Lawrence has my last. The ready made clothing is not worth anything here. I have worn out six pair of boots and shoes since I arrived. Tell Ed to pay for my clothing and I will remit him in gold dust after the *Elizabeth* arrives.

J. G. W. Luyster

Letter to his mother
18 June 1850

I wish you would find out from whom Mr. Woody obtained his information as to my raggedness. I have always dressed respectably since I have been in California, and as soon as my clothes were the least shabby, I have thrown them away, therefore you may know that what that friend of his said is untrue, and he has no foundation for making that remark. I expect it is some one who has returned from California without making one cent.

William Smith Jewett

Letter to "Capt."
30 January 1850

All that California sickens me of is co-partnerships. They rarely will do. I am not sick of my fellow men, as some are who are disappointed here. Those had better pluck the beam out of their own eyes perhaps.

To see the peaceful state of things here where there are no laws nor ladies is admirable to the unprejudiced beholder of the scene. The great vices here are gambling and drinking—and wearing dirty shirts. Here I heave a deep sigh, for what shall I do? Pay six dollars a dozen for washing my old ones! If any one will wash them to the halves I will thank them. I am determined to live as economical as possible—"And save my money and buy me a farm."

I made fifty dollars to day in painting one little head at one sitting. There are other artists here and doing comparatively nothing. Some do not endeavor to paint at all. I, somehow, appear to be popular. I don't know why, either deservedly or undeservedly—most likely the latter. I don't know how long it may last. I will do all I can however in the mean time to deserve its continuance and the fond remembrance of my friends at home. There are some gents here who are determined I shall paint a mammoth panorama of the river and diggings. They offer all the money and every possible convenience, it would be a most uncongenial task for my mind and I try to shuffle them off. I promised to see them to night—but rather stay home and write to you. Besides, there has been some artists here on the same business and the ground is preoccupied, which would so much impare the novelty to the publick that I think there would be no profit in the result. Yet so great is their faith in the powers of my pencil that they say the bush would only be beaten for me to catch the game. But I decline. I won't do it as long as I can make *fifteen dollars* per day at portraits. Would you? But I am bound to see the diggings and sketch on my own account and dig on the account of all my friends to get gold enough to make them all a present. . . .

I send three portraits home by this steamer. Good night, best love.

John McCrackan

Letter to his sister Lottie
16 April 1850

[W]e are to take into the firm of Brooks & McCrackan a fine fellow from Baltimore named Sheppard. He has been in practice some years there, and here for eight months. He has a good practice, and that joined with what we have will enable us to conduct a good, steady, substantial business, and I think a permanent one. Sheppard is about twenty seven although he looks younger, and a "married man" of course. It is the funnyest thing to see what an immense proportion are married men, most leaving their wives at home and very many marrying just on the eve of departure. As you may imagine, I am thankful enough to be free from the responsibility of the married man.

John McCrackan

Letter to his sister Lottie
30 May 1850

Oh! dear, I am perfectly fagged out. . . . [O]ur nightly visitor, a man with a hand organ (don't laugh, it is really a very sweet one), well this man made his appearance under our window, and commenced a very sweet waltz. As usual we threw him a half dollar, drew the curtains and then you should have looked in upon us. From one waltz he went to another, and then came the "Polka." This he played over several times, and we were dancing away with all our might until, tired out, we resumed our seats, having danced and laughed most heartily. Then he ends with a sweet sad strain from "Hernani" and I assure you we enjoy the treat almost as well as our dinner. Oh! dear, what was I writing about? There is the organ again, and Mr. Sheppard insists upon my joining him. The fellow has commenced backward this time, for he plays the polka first. Won't you dance? Now, don't say no.

There the organ is gone, and has left my mental organ in a perfect whirl, a sad plight to finish a letter in, however I shall make the effort, notwithstanding it may prove a failure. . . .

I have not told you about our fun incident upon the marriage of a Miss —— of New York to a Mr. Eddie [Eddy?] of our city, a young man of the first respectability. It was consummated on the arrival of the *Oregon*. He has been in business here for some time and has been quite successful, but he could not well leave at this time to bring her out here as his wife, and so he sent on for her to come out. She starts immediately, arrives here by the *Oregon*, full a week before she was expected. He (Mr. E.) is aroused from his slumbers one morning by a messenger from the Steamer saying the *Oregon* has arrived and Miss —— was awaiting him.

You may imagine his situation. He had not completed his arrangements, but what was to be done? He summoned his groomsman to his room, and off they started for the Rev. Mr. Mines. A young lady was taken from her breakfast, could not wait an instant, she must go just as she was, several of his friends accompanied him almost swamping the little bay boat. They arrive at the Steamer. Mr. E. rushes up the steps, gains the deck and now—we drop the curtain!

In fifteen minutes more they are man and wife, the Capt. of the Steamer gives them a wedding breakfast, after which she accompanies her husband to his home in "Happy Valley," where he had built his caze [casa] to spend the honey moon. Invitations were sent out that very day, and at eve quite a large party of friends assembled to welcome the bride to her newly found home. They here kept open house all the week, as their circle of friends is very large, and their home very small. I was among those invited, although I made out a short call. She is a very sweet, young lady, and her devotion is the admiration of all and everyone, since which almost every unmarried man who has a sweetheart at home has decided to send out for them by *Express*. Married and single men, all alike seem perfectly enthusiastic in their praises of her conduct. I can assure you she is the subject of admiration by all. I like her very much, young and pretty, and very intellectual, and a most acceptable addition to our society.

Did I tell you Mr. Sheppard intends sending for his wife by this steamer? She is very young and we shall all be delighted to see her. We have now a most delightful circle of married ladies, pretty and intelligent. We have select parties every fortnight, which are conducted so as to render them really very pleasant. I was invited out to one this eve, but preferred remaining to write you, particularly as I was quite fatigued and Mr. Sheppard would not attend.

Caroline Stoddard

Journal
5 December 1850

Mr. Sanford called and accompanied us in our boat on shore. Landed at his residence, which is on the wharf—very convenient to the business part of the city. We found a cheerful bright coal fire in a grate in his parlour. We took a peep into his and Mr. Morgan's bed-room, where every thing is in perfect order and neatness, looked much more like home comfort than anything I had seen. All that was lacking appeared to be some home faces, no doubt dear to them.

Jonathan F. Locke

Letter to his wife
29 December 1849

I know not how or what to write. This place appears more and more every day a miracle. To a majority it is a bad experiment to get a large fortune. I am doing well when there is any weather for business, but such a mud hole and such a climate I never expected to see in this quarter of the globe. "How false and yet how fair," the description of even the rainy season.

I should not complain. George [their son] and I have had perfect health. Yes, perhaps better than if we had staid at home. But we are beset by many temptations and exposed to sickness. Oh how I wish you and the children were here, but then you or they might be sick and that would [be] bad. I still think that most of the sickness is from exposure, mostly needless, but much from inability to shelter and feed themselves as they ought. I[f] you were here and well I could not help making my fortune in a short time. . . .

Let me assure you that nothing but a prospect of success could induce me to stay here away from you and home. Say to any one if they can make both ends meet not to come here, for a large majority are disappointed and would be glad to return to the comforts of home in New England above all things. I may soon [feel] the same, at present I am not sorry I came. . . .

Men change and are transformed in most cases wholly on emigrating here. If I remain the same or no worse morally, thank your stars, and at any rate remind me from time to time of what I was thought to be once, and what I hope to remain to be: honest and religious. I have made efforts to be. I hope still to be more so if possible. This is a scene of trial. I pray God not to fall, but to grow stronger and stronger in my integrity, to do justly by all and, if God spares my life, to pay all my honest debts and impart competency to my family. . . .

I must close not saying half I would, but do take the will for the deed. Keep good courage if difficulties arise, this through faith and trust in God will carry you forward. I hope to serener times. Yes, we may enjoy many happy days together. That we shall is the earnest prayer of your absent husband.

Jonathan F. Locke

Letter to his wife
3 February 1850

How have I spent the day? I will tell you after I have said how I spent last evening. The deed will out, so let it come. Eaton, who came out with us (by the way some relative of Mary E.), said to me he was going to a "free & easy." "What's that?" said I. "Oh, something about the opening of a new house." "I will go with you," said I, knowing him to be here pretty careful of himself and his money. So we did not carry but a few bits. We found the place easily, and quite a collection in a handsomely furnished hall with a large anteroom with a showy bar filled with all kinds of liquors in true California fix. Well, we sat down in [the] hall to wait for a demonstration. Soon someone nominated a gentleman to preside over the doings of the evening. He was elected by acclamation, as was his vice. He then states his idea of a "free & easy" which was this: when one was called upon he must sing a song, tell a story or treat the crowd. My first thought was to be off, but as I saw quite a number of my acquaintances I would stop, and did till nearly 11 o'clock. I could not persuade one of our company to leave before, as three of them took part in exercises (if they would bear that name). A greater part of what was said or sung was good or amusing, from the rest (serious) Good Lord deliver us. Upon the whole, I am glad I went. . . . They have here fancy balls, free blows, free & easy's, but this alone will suffice for the present. All they got out of me was a cegar or two. I was invited to drink a number of times. It was no go. I took a glass of port wine with a friend—that is the extent of my dissipation. I now write this more to show how they get up the patronage of a new house than for any reason. At balls low women attract, free blows—liquors &c attract, at a free & easy, songs and stories of all character to suit the taste of all.

John McCrackan

Letter to his mother
26 March 1850

The last week has witnessed an instance of the most melancholy character in the failure of Ward & Co. and the attempt[ed] suicide of Frank Ward, the head of the concern. Our little city was greatly excited a week ago yesterday (Monday week) by the report of the failure of Ward & Co. and that Frank Ward had attemp[t]ed to shoot himself. And this proved true. The attempt was made on Monday morning early before any of his house was up. On that day he had forty thousand dollars to pay, 'tis said. The pistol (the muzzle) was presented to his right temple while in a lying posture, the ball entered behind the eye, fracturing the skull and lodged somewhere, it is supposed, in the upper part of the nose. It has not yet been extracted. From latest news he is likely to recover, but it must be with the loss of his eye and a bad scar about his temple.

I was conversing with Mr. Read who is here in charge of the barque *Clyde* for his son, Fred Read of New York. Fred married Miss Maria Brooks. Mr. Read knew the Wards very well in New York, and since he has been here, he has seen a great deal of them. He attended church with Frank Ward on Sunday and dined with him, spending the evening at his home till near ten o'clock. He remarked nothing strange about him, except the fact of his eating very moderately. And the Old Gentleman was very much shocked to hear the news the next morning. Some suppose the death of his wife has ever since had an effect upon him. A year and [a] half ago he married and brought from the States a lovely girl. A few months after her arrival here, death with his relentless hand robbed him of her. He has been making efforts ever since to get away from here and return home, taking with him the remains of his wife, but he has still lingered, expecting to go every steamer. I presume his affairs became more involved the longer he stayed, and he thought he could not leave. Last November he could have returned worth two hundred and fifty thousand dollars, but what he is now worth none can tell. He has been in this country for five or six years. Poor fellow, it is very hard.

Jonathan F. Locke

Letter to his wife
22 March 1850

The months pass on rapidly and I must have something ready [to mail] by the 1st. It is a rainy day such as you have in June, warm and still. I cannot spend part of it more agreeably than in this way of communicating with you. I know you will agree to it. I hope by this time the long dreary winter with its cold has gone by you without leaving many disagreeable mementoes of its severity. I many times thought how you missed me when I had been absent only a fortnight. Now I have been absent so long, you perhaps have been reconciled to it. You used to lose half your sleep. I hope you do not now. You say you go to bed late and get up early and work hard, so I think you must sleep soundly. I dreamed of you the other night and layed awake the rest of the night. It was not from its quality of being hideous, but the reverse. I hope it may be realized after perhaps a long absence.

Jonathan F. Locke

Letter to his wife
27 March 1850

I am satisfied now that I shall get no letter from you by this mail. If you knew what a disappointment this is to me you would never let a mail pass without dropping a single line telling me of yours and the children's health, if nothing else. It is like a cooling draught in a thirsty land. You might think of me as a *lover* and then fall short of the reality. I might then think, "There is as good fish in the sea a[s] out." But having not my choice to make, I feel the temporary loss of what is already mine. No doubt some of our friends if they hear this will call me homesick. Not so. It was for no "freak of the fancy" that I left family and home, but from stern, iron necessity that the bond was severed for a time, to be again united with the blessing of God under more pleasing and comfortable union. Yes, could I return with a moderate competency I think we should be more fitted to enjoy it than we were before separation. Mankind are so foolish, they know not their joys until deprived of them.

Jonathan F. Locke

Letter to his wife
29 April 1850

I am again disappointed not having received any thing by the last mail as yet. After my last letter had gone a few days, I received a note through the post office that a certain Mr. Page had letters &c for me. I immediately waited upon the gentleman, and letters and papers and—what was still better—the likeness of the better half. It is very good, but you felt very sober about it. However I will account for that, you went over to B[oston] in a hurry and was tired or perhaps anxious about the children, but it looks like you. I had to take a peep at it Morn, Noon and Night for some days. I open it generally when I go to bed and when I rise. I thank Mother much for being true to her promise. I enjoy looking at you much. There is one thing that I should prefer: that of looking in upon you all some Sunday night, but that is denied me at present. Thanks to the inventer who brings yourself in imagination present with me.

John McCrackan

Letter to his sister Mary
14 April 1850

I am writing on the evening of one of the most exciting days we have had for a week. The day has been one of the very few pleasant days of the season here in California. Not a cloud dimmed the sun. The winds which had been on a perfect frolic the previous forty eight hours "had sank to rest." The beautiful Bay as far as the eye could see was slumbering beneath its mirror surface, and all nature seemed in keeping with the sacred day. I took a cup of chocolate on my way to church, lingering upon the hill side to look upon the beauties about me, till the dying echoes of our church bell reminded me I must mend my pace. I reached our little church just as service was commencing. Among the congregation assembled before our "rustic altar" I observed quite a number of the "gentle sex" who till then had never sat within those rude walls. You have no idea, dear Mary, with what joy we hail every bright fair face. If strangers, they are readily detected. When after a long, dark winter the blue bird greets us with its merry song, we bid this bright stranger welcome, welcome warmly welcome to our homes once more. And why? Because 'tis the presage sure of coming spring, the season of bright sunshine, balmy breezes, fragrant bowers. We know that the joyous spring will come all richly dressed in nature's blooming livery, which she renews with each succeeding month. And now, dear sister, when we find that here amid this strange commingling of men from every clime, of every nation, subjected to the worst possible influences, and perfectly unrestrained—I say, dear sister, when we find we are likely to enjoy at last what we have so much needed, the sweet, the gentle, the saving influence of woman. (I fear, my dear Mary, few appreciate, and some never knew the holy influence of a Mother, or a sister, with such good angels to guard, to care for us, we feel that in this life there is much worth living for). When we see these things, we cannot but feel "that the darkness is past, and the true light now shineth."

Chapter 7

The Course of Empire

The 1840s were years of governmental ambiguity for the residents of California. Though nominally a part of Mexico, the territory had suffered (or perhaps enjoyed) a long period of benign neglect. The only visible organs of government were the office of *alcalde* (an elected official who combined the duties of mayor, judge, lawyer, and marshal) and a six-man elected body called the *ayuntamiento* that functioned more or less as a town council.[1] Both governed using the tenets of Mexican law. With the influx of foreigners, particularly Americans, this rudimentary executive-judicial structure became warped nearly beyond recognition. Anglos were elected to the post of *alcalde* in many of the major California settlements, taking office with only a vague knowledge of Mexican jurisprudence and a strong preference for doing things the American way. In addition, the gold discoveries were restricted to areas almost untouched by Spanish or Mexican colonization; from 1848 on an improvised code of mining law developed that was largely sui generis, having little relation to the established legal tradition.[2]

As the politicians in Washington and Mexico City rattled their respective sabers over the Texas border dispute that was flaring at the time, many Californians eagerly awaited the opportunity to assert American dominance on the Pacific Coast. When the word of war finally arrived in California, rebels at first proclaimed an independent Bear Flag Republic and then bowed to the superior authority of Commodore John D. Sloat, commander of the United States Pacific Squadron. On 7 July 1846 Sloat issued the proclamation *To the Inhabitants of California*, which announced that the United States was at war with

Mexico and that the California territory was now officially under the control of the American government. Far from a ringing call to revolution, Sloat's proclamation was a request to maintain the status quo: "With full confidence in the honour and integrity of the inhabitants of the country, I invite the judges, alcaldes and other civil officers, to retain their office, and to execute their functions as heretofore that the public tranquility may not be disturbed, at least until the Government of the territory can be more definitely arranged."[3]

But definite arrangements were long in coming. California languished through an interregnum of military governors: seven army or navy officers were appointed in less than three years. The most effective of these men was Colonel Richard B. Mason who took over the post of governor and commander-in-chief of the United States land forces in California on 31 May 1847. Mason actually set about reforming the governmental and judicial structures of the territory, going so far as to draw up his own code, *Laws for the Better Government of California (Leyes para el Mejor Gobierno de California)*, which he ordered to be printed in both English and Spanish. With the arrival of the news that California had been ceded to the United States under the Treaty of Guadalupe Hidalgo, Mason assumed that his code was no longer needed and it was never promulgated. (There is only one known copy of the bilingual printing in existence.)[4]

Once California was officially and legally a part of the United States, efforts were begun to establish a more regular form of government. On 6 July 1848 President Polk sent a message to Congress requesting a bill to establish a territorial government in the region. "By this cession to the United States," Polk wrote, "Mexico has no longer any power over them [the territories]; and until congress shall act, the inhabitants will be without any organized government."[5] Though his unfortunate wording declared that there was *no government* in force in California, military rule in fact continued for another two years while the citizens agitated for statehood.

With a burgeoning population, spurred commerce, and seemingly limitless mineral wealth, California was certainly a prime candidate for admission to the Union but Congress was hamstrung by the effort to maintain a balance between the entry of free versus slave states. In California public opinion was not unanimous but sentiment seemed to run against slavery, though perhaps less out of moral outrage at the cruelty of the peculiar institution than out of fear that transplanted Southerners would import crews of slaves to work the gold fields and thereby gain an unfair advantage. Moreover, miners were loathe to equate their own labor with that of slaves. In his 1851 memoir Walter Colton wrote, "The causes which exclude slavery from California lie within a nut-shell. All here are diggers, and free white diggers won't dig with slaves. They know they must dig themselves: they have come out here for that purpose, and they won't degrade their calling by associating it with slave labor."[6]

Late in 1848 and into 1849 a series of meetings took place in San Jose, San Francisco, Sacramento, Monterey, Sonoma, San Joaquin, San Luis Obispo, Santa Barbara, and Los Angeles that put in motion an effort to establish a provisional government that would supersede military rule and remain in effect until Congress clarified the status of California either as a regular territory or a full-fledged state. A constitutional convention was scheduled for March, postponed until May, and then postponed again until August; as plans for the convention changed so did its stated goal. By the spring of 1849 sentiment had turned against the idea of forming a territorial government: nothing less than full statehood would be acceptable.[7]

On 13 April 1849 General Bennet Riley arrived in Monterey and assumed the offices of governor of California and commanding general of the Tenth Military Department, replacing Colonel Mason (who returned east and died a few months later of cholera in St. Louis). Riley inherited a region in crisis. San Franciscans had gone so far as to elect their own legislative assembly in total disregard of the military's authority. Simmering discontent reached the boiling point when the steamer *Edith* arrived with the news that Congress had adjourned on 3 March without establishing a new government for California but *had* managed to pass a bill extending the federal revenue laws to the region. The revolutionary cry of "no taxation without representation" was enough of a threat to make General Riley move quickly.

Riley issued a proclamation calling for a constitutional convention to meet in Monterey on 1 September 1849. He took the opportunity to denounce the ad hoc assembly to the north, declaring that a "body of men styling themselves the Legislative Assembly of San Francisco has usurped powers, which are vested only in the Congress of the United States."[8] He called on the citizens to recognize the authority of the military government. After much blustering oration the San Franciscans issued their own proclamation, asserting that while "not recognizing the least power, as matter of right, in Brevet Brigadier General Riley, to '*appoint*' a time and place for the election of delegates and the assembling of the convention," they would—*of their own free will*—agree to his suggestion of a place and date.[9]

Delegates to the constitutional convention finally assembled in Monterey in September and elected John Ross Browne as secretary. (Browne's poignant letter to his wife concerning his manuscript notes of the proceedings is included in this collection.) By mid-October they had drafted a constitution for a new state, one that included the proposition that slavery would be banned from California forever. In a general election held on 13 November 1849 Peter H. Burnett was elected governor and John C. Frémont and William M. Gwin were elected as U.S. senators. On 3 December 1849 California formally requested admission to the union, under its new constitution.

The juggernaut of the statehood movement threatened to crush the delicate free state/slave state balance. In Congress Henry Clay, "the Great Compromiser," brokered an agreement that came to be known as the Compromise of 1850. Under this omnibus bill, California was admitted as a free state, the territories of New Mexico and Utah had their free/slave status decided by popular sovereignty, the boundary dispute between Texas and New Mexico was settled, more rigorous provisions for the return of runaway slaves were adopted, and slavery was prohibited in the District of Columbia. With the support of Daniel Webster and Stephen A. Douglas the measure passed, and on 9 September 1850 California became a state.

In the city of San Francisco the news of statehood was greeted with cheers. Unfortunately, municipal government was still represented by a confused melange of imposed military law, inherited Mexican institutions, imported democratic traditions, and impromptu entrepreneurial expedients. As the village metamorphosed into a modern city an acute need for basic urban services—streets, wharves, fire and police protection, public wells, schools—had developed, but since the citizenry viewed itself as transitory it was difficult to raise the needed revenue. The prevalent "get rich and leave" philosophy countered any desire to pay for something of permanence. The city required a strong municipal government that could inspire fiscal confidence and provide the type of civic boosterism needed to encourage a modern city to evolve from a squalid camp of canvas tents.

During the period from the end of the constitutional convention to the granting of California statehood San Francisco moved in stages to achieve a fully Americanized form of city government. On 15 April

1850 the city received its initial charter, which replaced the *alcalde* and *ayuntamiento* with a mayor and city council. All city and county officials were to be elected by white males over the age of twenty-one who were citizens and residents. Elections were to be held annually or more frequently if necessary.[10] During 1849 and 1850 San Francisco saw a series of municipal elections, the most colorful being that of 1 April 1850 which elected the first sheriff. This contest proved to be a showdown between J. J. Bryant, proprietor of one of the largest saloons, and John C. Hays, newly arrived hero of the Texas Rangers. Bryant plied the electorate with free liquor but it was Hays's dashing appearance as he worked the polling places on horseback that won the day.[11]

The newly installed officials set out to govern a citizenry that was wildly heterogeneous and stratified by regional, ethnic, and racial prejudice. The English, Scots, and Germans (and Americans of those ethnic extractions) held the positions of most prominence in gold rush San Francisco, though immigrants from most of northern and western Europe were welcomed. The Irish and, especially, Australians (who were viewed as ex-convicts) were received with less enthusiasm. The French fell somewhere in the middle of the spectrum, while Blacks, Chinese, Hispanics, and Native Americans were at the bottom of the social scale.[12]

The Chinese who emigrated to California during the gold rush came almost exclusively from the province of Kwangtung, in southern China.[13] Revolt and civil war tore the province apart in the late 1840s and 1850s, and many sons and husbands were forced to emigrate in order to earn money to supplement household incomes. When word of the gold discoveries in California reached Hong Kong in 1849, many Chinese set out for *Gum Shan,* the Golden Mountain.[14] Those who settled in San Francisco were segregated in the crowded confines of Chinatown and were subjected to a series of anti-Chinese regulations that culminated in the Chinese Exclusion Act of May 1882, which constricted immigration to a trickle and confirmed that Chinese were ineligible to become naturalized citizens.[15]

Trampled in the onslaught was the Mexican provincial culture of the people who founded San Francisco. With the secularization of the missions, Mission Dolores had fallen into disrepair and little remained of what had once been the town's lively cultural center. The unnamed friar who appears as a shadowy, somewhat defiant figure in these letters is Padre Prudencio Santillán, the Mexican Indian priest left in charge of what remained of the mission properties. Padre Santillán spoke no English and declined to learn any, viewing the Americans as heathen conquerors.[16]

It is ironic—and for many immigrants tragic—that the Americanization of San Francisco was carried out during a time of intense and explosive internationalization. California had always welcomed visitors and residents from other lands, but the loose, inclusive policies of colonial Mexico encouraged assimilation in a way that was unknown to Yankee America. The American Argonauts brought with them the strong prejudices of their hometowns, and in the mad grab for wealth "foreigners" became an easy target for those who felt they had somehow missed out on their fair share of the bonanza.

Nothing short of a fortune in gold could have attracted the world's attention to San Francisco with quite this intensity, and despite the large number of seekers who went home not much better off than they came, California brought forth an immense amount of the precious ore. At its peak in 1852, gold production in the state reached eighty-one million dollars, and while yields tapered off in the ensuing years California remained the world's largest gold producer until 1900.[17] It is easier to understand the frenzy when the discovery is put in perspective: California's contribution was the first major infusion of gold onto the world's stage since the Spanish conquistadores looted the Inca and Aztec empires.

John C. Callbreath

Letter to his family
30 June 1849

There is to be a dreadful time here on the fourth of July. There is about 2000 Chileans and Mexicans at the diggins who have hoisted the Chilean flag at the diggins. The yankees tore it down and passed a resolution to drive them all out of the country that were not out by the fourth of July at the point of a s[w]ord. All this is what I have been told by the well disposed people of the town, who say there is no doubt of its truth. The weather is very cold, much colder that I ever knew it to be in Sull[ivan] Co[unty, New York] at this season. I am told it is warmer in the diggins. . . . I think Joseph Hunting had better come, by all means. James must bring a good dog—either Tiger or the Pup. They will be much needed to guard the tents. The mate has just come on board with a friend with a piece of gold weighing 3 lbs. I have seen a good deal of gold dust. . . . I am agoing to keep out of the fight on the fourth so do not fear for me.

Margaret DeWitt

Letter to her mother-in-law
28 September 1849

The place is very full, and in front of our house we can count no less that 50 large tents. Houses are going up very fast, and such changes have taken place since we arrived that I can scarcely realize it is the same. . . . A number of families who came this spring, and who commenced keeping house, have been obliged to break up, and the ladies return home, as it was so very expensive and difficult to get along without several servants, and that besides the high wages cost a great deal. The Canacca [Kanakas, i.e., Hawaiians] and Chillians are most the only kind here—and they are poor enough, and never know how to do more than one thing, and then they are very clanish and have a great deal of company, which costs more than family expenses. We have the Irish woman yet, and she proves so good a servant, I hope we may keep her. She does the washing for all—Alfred, Mr. H[arrison]., Mr. West, Henry and myself—which is a very important consideration, as washing has risen to eight dollars the dozen—and then they are not half clean.

Eugene Howard

Letter to Franklin Miller
2 October 1849

We arrived here all in good health and a pleasant voyage with a few exceptions of having calms and head winds. We found everything in confusion here. The gold news if favourable and I think I can give you and Henry a good account of myself if I have my health, but we diggers will have to work hard for it. We find everything very high here. You cannot look at [hiring] a common nigger unless you have 10 or 100 hundred dollars in hand. Wages is very high.

Thomas Reid

Journal
9 October 1849

I never saw so many ships in one place in my life. I went up the mast head and tried to count them but they were so thick I found it impossible. . . . To day I went on the top of a hill to have a look at the city. It was the most singular sight that could be imagined. The city is crowded with new edifices in a state of construction and the beach each side of the city is crowded with tents, and the valleys about the city are the same. It makes me think of the children of Israel in Scripture. To day I saw some native of the Southsea Islands. Their faces were tatooed all over with curious figures.

Abel R. Biggs

Journal of a gold rush voyage
1 October 1849

the[re] is no respect of persons her[e] so long as they conduct them selves in a quiet manner the poor are not dispised for his poverty, nor the rich Esteamed for his riches this makes all honest men let them be Black or white on a par with Each othe[r] which is a considerable different from any country that I was ever in before and God grant that it may ever continue to remain so

Anne Willson Booth

Journal
26 October 1849

Black Jim (as we call him, to distinguish him [from] Jemmy Mitchell) says, "Why, Mrs. Booth, you are almost through your book, ain't you? Well, I do declare. Is you gwine to have it printed?" "Not exactly, Jim," said I. "Well, I 'spect it does get printed," says Jim, "and if it does, I'm bound to buy a copy."

Robert Smith Lammot

Letter to his brother
25 February 1850

Mother writes me that I have another niece. I wish it had been a nephew, but "*nebber mind massa.*" Before twenty years I hope to see Miss Paulina Gilpin. Give my love to her and to her parents.

Anne Willson Booth

Journal
1 November 1849

A large schooner lying near us [in the harbor] dragged her anchor, and drifted down upon us this afternoon, running her jib boom into our side, causing a slight damage. Wesley went off to him and insisted upon the Capt. paying for it, which he did. In sheering off from us, the schooner came near running down a craft full of Chilians. It was amusing to see their fright. Some fell on their knees, and commenced counting their beads.

E. A. Upton

Diary
12 December 1849

I notice quite a number of Spanish women are actively engaged in gambling at the tables among the men—some of whom stake largely. They are, most of them very repulsive and masculine in their features and manners, smoking cigars, drinking, swearing &c but all very richly, though not tastefully dressed, with every finger almost, loaded with rings, some of which are very costly diamonds.

Margaret DeWitt

Letter to her mother-in-law
29 May 1850

I received your kind letter sent by Peter [her brother-in-law] who arrived here safely on the morning of the 20th in good health and spirits. . . . Peter comes in very often to take a meal with us. He is now quite well—was a little complaining [the] first few days after he arrived, but I took him under my especial care and he is in a good case. You need not feel uneasy about him as I will, if he should get sick, take good care of him and will use a sister's influence to keep him from falling in love with the Senoritas—and I do not think there is much danger of it, as they are anything but loveable.

E. A. Upton

Diary
1 December 1849

Very pleasant morning. Took a stroll after breakfast out Dolores Mission, about four miles from Francisco. The mission establishment consists of several buildings with very thick walls and earthen tile roofs about a story and a half high, except the chapel or church which is quite high and most conspicuous. It looks very ancient without and within. Noticed three ponderous bells hanging in the tower. The interior is ornamented with statues of the Savior, the virgin Mary and several saints, besides quite a collection of oil paintings, but much defaced by extreme age, some of them being centuries old.

I entered many of the cells connected with this ancient building which were very damp, dark and gloomy, light finding its way into these singular apartments through very small iron grated windows situated very high from the ground. I visited the old monk or priest's cell in which he had lived many years. I pass[ed] about an hour with him, but as he talked English badly and I talk Spanish badly our conversation was not so agreeable otherwise it might have been, but he was apparently a very well educated man. His library was extensive and contain[s] volumes musty and scarcely readable from extreme age; the appearance of the room struck me as very gloomy, much more so than any prison apartment I have ever seen.

Various emblems used by the church of Rome I noticed in the room, and the statue of the virgin Mary immediately over the head of his bed. The personal appearance of the monk was rather repelling than otherwise; he is an athletic, powerfully built man with keen black eyes &c. but he was very courteous and gentlemanly in his manners. Collected several curiosities in the church.

John McCrackan

Letter to his family
24 December 1849

Yesterday I accompanyed a friend named "Judah" (a lawyer here who will return to the states on the first of January) to a beautiful spot called the "Mission Valley," it is two miles distant only directly on the Bay. Horses were sent up for us and after a half hour ride we reached there. The valley is a lovely spot, selected by the Jesuits in 1768 [by the Franciscans in 1776], and here they erected buildings and established a Mission for the conversion of the indians. I know not how far they were successful. The buildings built of mud are now very fast decaying and the institution but feebly sustained. The land of this whole valley were owned by this Mission, excepting some few row lots bought of them by private individuals. The rights of these individuals will no doubt be respected, while the Mission Lands (all except what the buildings cover) will pass to our government. These lands have now become very valuable and being open, people have come upon them, staked out their lot, built a home and there by become the owners.

We attended service which was being held. The church was a long dark building, dirty[?] and like all Roman Catholic churches very extremely decorated with all kinds of finery and [illegible]. The Padre (an indian) in the Pulpit was preaching to an audience of twenty women seated on mats at his feet. Without describing the service, it was the same as I have spoke of before. I was quite interested on seeing a little indian girl not ten years of age, who as she passed through one of the rooms, was pointed out as having attempted suicide but three days before, when her mistress lost a little child, which the girl attended. This is a strong instance of attachment.

Mr. Judah is a great favorite at the Mission, and indeed has charge of all the law business which is worth any thing there, the avails of which alone will make him independently rich.

John D. Mitchell

Letter
13 January 1850

The sun arose in splendor and not a cloud was to be seen in the heavens above, so Billy and I started for the Mission. The road was sandy and passed over hills and through valleys, being lined on each side by scrub oak, which is poisonous if you touch it. Soon the ringing sound of the distant bells reached our ears, and as we surmounted the highest hill, the Mission was before us, lying in the centre of a beautiful valley commencing at the base of the hill. Descending the hill we soon arrived at the Mission. The houses are built of adobe, (but many are now in ruins) and the roofs are made of tiles. I did not enter any of them as they are very filthy and full of vermin.

Henry Didier Lammot

Letter to his brother
22 January 1850

Last Sunday Hob Smith and I took a walk out to the Mission of Dolores, about three miles from town, and a great looking place it is to have so large a name. Said Mission consists of ten or twelve mud brick houses, one story high and roofed with tiles and floored with ditto, two taverns, and of course a Church, which kinder "takes the rag off the bush." I went in to see what was to be seen. There was a dark, damp, large room, high ceiling plastered with mud and pieces of colored paper stuck upon the wall for ornament, great big altar fixed off in the same fantastic style.

After looking about for some time, an old Mesacan Padre came up to me and looking very hard at me, and touched his cap. I, thinking it was a salutation, returned the complement. He did it again, and I would not be out done in politeness by an old *Yellow Belley*, took off my cap and made him quite a humble salem [salaam]. But no, he was not satisfied, so he came up to me and held out his hand. Well, I put out mine saying, "How are you making out?" knowing that he could not understand me. But he would not take my hand, but caught hold of my cap and lifted it off. Which explained the strange conduct. I'd neglected to take off my cap so he saved me the trouble.

Till I arrived here I never had seen a regular "Live Mexican," but out at the Mission I saw them living in their *wild state*. In mud houses, with three or four horses hitched before their houses. One fellow wanted to go across the road, and he had to get on his horse, get his horse down to a full run, thrashing him the whole way. That is about as far as from the stall to the gate at home.

Henry Didier Lammot

Letter to his brother
24 February 1850

We Yankees have got here a little too quick for the natives. A man told Bob the other day that he saw a grizzly bear not half a mile from town, and wolves are often seen within city limits. Bob saw some Texas men and told them of the bear, and they went off "to sase his har certain."

The other day I saw a Mexican start out to drive his cow home. He had on a pair of Mexican spurs, which I expect if you had been here you would have envied him, and had a lasso hanging at his saddle bow, was mounted on his Mustang. Started off at a full run, came up to the poor cow, threw the lasso round her horns and dragged the poor beast about a hundred yards over the sand. Well, that is about the way they do everything. If there is a rough and gentle way of doing any thing, they always take the rough. I saw two of them driving a bullock and he stopped, so one threw his lasso over his horns and the other jumped on his back and commenced plunging his spurs into [him] till the beast bellowed most piteously.

The slaughter houses are in a horrid condition here. When they kill an animal they throw the head and hide just outside the yard and let it be to rot or be eaten up by wolves and crows. And in a place where they kill some 20 head a day, the offal amounts to something, you may suppose. That is just the way with every thing here: if an article is not wanted immediately it is just thrown aside as not worth storage.

Augustus West

Letter to Peter DeWitt
31 August 1849

The convention of Delgates are now assembling in convention at Monterey to frame a State constitution, and I trust by the next meeting of Congress our representatives will be there to advocate the cause of California. If we can have a State government we shall then be able to assume a position that will correct all evils and disarm all fear.

John Ross Browne

Letter to his wife
27 October 1849

In order to provide against accident, I deem it proper to make a statement of my affairs, previous to my departure for Washington. This letter will be forwarded by the next steamer, so that in case of my death on the passage home, you will know what to do.

My contract with the Convention is, to furnish the state of California with 1000 copies in English and 250 copies in Spanish of a stenographic report of its proceedings, together with other documents specified in the agreement. It would be impossible for any person except myself to fulfill this contract. If, therefore, I should die on the way home, you will make the following disposition of the money advanced to me by the government of California, being $10,000.

I have shipped the money in gold dust by Simmons Hutchinson & Co of San Francisco, to their agents in New York, G. E. Robbins & Son who are to pay it to me at the Mint, or in case of my death to you, my wife. I have paid the freight and insurance here. As I have always endeavored to be just and honest in all my dealings, I wish you, in such an event as that referred to, to pay back to the government of California through the Secretary of State, all of the sum received by you, except two thousand dollars, which I consider I have already fairly earned as an officer of the Convention, it being a per diem allowance of $50 for forty days labor actually performed, and that was the amount first fixed upon by the Convention itself. It will then be my misfortune and not my fault that I could furnish nothing to the state in return for this expenditure, but my short hand notes.

Pay all my debts, which probably amount to about $500, and invest the remaining $1500 in a house and lot.

This together with the house and lot which we now own, will probably furnish you with an income of $30 a month, for your own support and that of our dear children.

Life is uncertain, and I think it but prudent, my dearest wife, to make this statement. I am in good health, and hope to live many a long and happy year with you yet, but there is a Providence that controls our destiny, shape it as we may.

Should shipwreck, or death prevent me from meeting you again in this world, believe me, dear Lucy, as I have ever fondly and truly loved you on earth—as I have ever loved my children—so shall I love you—so shall I love them in that better world where we are all to meet, never more to part.

Robert Smith Lammot

Letter to his brother
25 February 1850

I am afraid we shall have some trouble with regard to the crowds of reckless, desperate characters which are poured in here every day from Sydney, as well as other foreign ports. The Chilenos have had two or three fights with the miners, the French say that the Americans cannot bring force enough to prevent them from mining as much as they please, but the Sydney emigrants are the sweepings of the English jails. Both men and women are eternally drinking, swearing, fighting and thieving. Until they came, property was as safe in the street as under lock and key, but now the case is materially altered. Unless the government at home gives us a constitution soon, there is not the slightest doubt but that California, and perhaps Oregon too, will form an independent one of their own, and Uncle Sam will be left to vain regrets, for his neglect, for there is too much property at stake here for us to remain long unsettled in our government.

John McCrackan

Letter to his sister
27 February 1850

It seems as I look back upon it, that the gentlemen have all come out here. I cannot realize there is anyone left, and indeed I believe it to be a fact, that the very best young blood is out here and here a great portion of it will remain. California ten years hence must exceed, ten years hence, in wealth and commercial importance any state on the globe. There is no calculating what we will become, no position is too elevated for us, to obtain. Everything is in favor of success. Two—yes, one—year from now, there will be a degree of extravagance here greater than any nation boasts of. I can see it grow from day to day. It will be a dreadful wicked place withal, I almost dread to witness the changes of the coming five years.

The gold and silver mines are inexhaustible. Coal mines have lately been discovered, and with a rich beautiful country, what can prevent our prosperity? If I were a young man at home I should be perfectly miserable if obliged to remain away from such attractions. Here is a republic coming into life that has resources that must place her far before any kingdom on the earth surface, and this in my day. I am thankful I am of this age and permitted to help build it up, enjoy its advantages and witness the proud position it will soon take. California is perfectly independent of the whole world, and I almost hope the present Congress will not admit us. We shall then go to work on our own account, take our own stand, and become identically one people. We are absolutely suffering greatly for want of laws, which should be given us. There are enough population to have three or four large States, and all we have to govern us is territorial laws. No Marine or District Court, before which our cases in admiralty come. It is indeed wretched, and our people are becoming heartily tired of this way of living.

John McCrackan

Letter to his sister Mary
31 January 1850

The members of the Legislature and Senate are in a most amusing predicament. There is no money to pay them with and most are very poor, having expended all their means to get elected, and now go there and get nothing to live upon but "honor." They must adjourn soon. Money is worth fifteen per cent a month, consequently no person will take the state loan, and this is the only way they have of getting money. It seems very doubtful if we will be admitted to the Union this Congress.

John McCrackan

Letter to his mother
26 March 1850

The Steamer *Massachusetts* arrived yesterday from around the Horn. There are several others due, the *Sarah Sands* among the number. For a week before the regular mail steamer arrives everybody thinks and talks about her, there is hardly any other subject that can be as popular. The great question now is, are we to be admitted as a State or not? We are suffering great wrong by the United States putting off and refusing to legislate in favor of our admission. While they in the Halls of Congress are amusing themselves discussing their party or sectional prejudices, thousands and millions of property is sacrificed in distant California. We are getting indignant and cannot submit to the treatment much longer. My friends have been making great efforts to get me to take part in politics, but I refuse. I could have taken a very prominent position in the party here, but I am sick, disgusted. I detest I abhor politics.

John McCrackan

Letter to his mother
24 May 1850

On my way from breakfast this morning, I called at the newspaper delivery and with what came for me, with those sent poor Mr. Silliman [who died in his tent in Happy Valley], I brought to the room between twenty and thirty, and having no pressing business on hand I stretched myself on our "Chinese lounge" and with the most agreeable deliberation, proceeded to open and read each, so that towards noon our office resembled more the sanctum of an Editor, papers scattered all about. From these papers, I got all the local and political news. I am not surprised the Whigs have been defeated, and were it not that I desired Foster should have been elected, or that you would say I deserved a boxed ear, I should say I didn't care much. There is not much sympathy in my heart for them as a party. I fear I shall never forgive them till they elect Henry Clay President. . . .

I received a letter from Hopkins by this Steamer, in which he tells me he has shipped 170,000 feet more [of lumber], which will arrive within the next six months. He desires me to keep him informed of the market and how matters are managed, &c. I am undecided at the moment if I will take any notice of it, as he has not before deigned to write in reply to my many letters. When now he finds I can be, and indeed have been, of service to him already, he condescends to write me. However, I shall probably get his law business here, in case his vessels get into trouble—but if I find his law business placed in other hands by his consignees, I shall give myself no trouble with his affairs, and one reason is I do not wish to increase my correspondents, as I have quite enough to do from my own business to do justice to my family in the way of letter writing.

John McCrackan

Letter to his family
30 March 1850

I am hardly justified in my own mind in the effort to commence another letter to you at home at this time, for I feel as if every moment should be devoted to my books. I am to be presented to the Examining Committee of the Supreme Court of our State next week for admission to practice at the "Honorable Bench." They are very strict, and many have been rejected by the committee who have practiced in their own state, and even here for months. Of course I must not fail. I have been constantly with my book[s] for the last twenty four hours and I shall continue over them till I appear before the Committee.

Out of doors all is noise and confusion, the bustle of an approaching election which comes off on Monday next. There are three tickets: Whig [and] Democrat regular nominations, and an independent ticket which advocates the claims of Col. Jack Hayes [Hays], the celebrated "Texas Ranger." I presume you will wonder how I shall vote and so I will tell you. I shall vote the *Independent Ticket.*

Speaking of voting makes me think (or rather speak, for he is seldom from my thoughts) of who do you think? Of that man who is the wonder of this or any age. Of that greatest and best of men, a true and fervent patriot, the proudest of statesmen. Of that man who stands head and shoulders above any man, who breathes the pure breath of Heaven. The great, the generous, the zealous, the good, the noble Henry Clay. How I have read and lingered over his last great effort delivered in the Senate Chamber on the 5th and 6th of February. What a splendid proof of the flexibility and grandeur of his mental powers, which seem to be fortified against all the encroachments of age. What a wonderful man! He lives not for a day but for all time. What ultra Northern or Southern man can condemn his compromise—compromise, nay—there is no offer of compromise as I look at it. We at the north relinquish nothing, our ground is still our own, while 'tis the same with the south.

The subject of California being a free or slave state is now obsolete. Why? Because we have long ere this decided the question and it no longer admits of arguement, but I have not time now as I wish I had to speak of that noble effort, as I said before every moment should be devoted to my books. They have made me Judge of Elections but I doubt if I should act under the circumstances. It will take up time which is very precious to me just now.

Samuel C. Lewis

Journal
1 April 1850

This is election day for city officers and also Sheriff of the county. This office is the only one that there is any strife about. Whig candidate John E. Townes, Loco candidate J. J. Bryant, and Independant candidate Col. J. C. Hays, the Texan ranger, who would not give to either party his views upon political matters and no doubt will be elected. Col. Bryant was supported by the gambling tables and loafers. But the Whigs, finding that there was a chance of his getting it, in the latter part of the day all threw their votes for Hays to keep Bryant out, as they stood no chance with their candidate. Bryant kept a large publick house and has spent several thousand dollars, besides keeping open house for all to drink for the last three days. The Sheriff I believe took possession last night or this morning of his Bar and furniture for debt. It was reported yesterday that the establishment was under attachment but would be kept close till after election. There was great excitement through the whole town and each of the candidates for Sheriff kept wagons going all day to take their friends to the polls, donkeys dressed out with flags and also a man carrying aloft a banner with the name of the candidate on it, in the wagon. Most of the wagons had four mules—all had bands of music.

Benjamin H. Deane

Journal
1 April 1850

This [is] Election day in San Francisco and there is the most excitement that I ever saw. Denison and I agree not to vote as one would set the other off.

John McCrackan

Letter to his sister Lottie
12 April 1850

O Lottie, I have such lots of things to tell you, I know not how to begin. But first, and foremost, I must tell you I have received your letters of second and eleventh of January. About a week since, I met Mr. George Ward in the street, and he informed me there were letters for me at his office. They proved to be those sent by the Steamer of the 15th of January and they arrived here March 1st, and here they have been since then. It was careless on their part not to inform me, and I must tell you how opportune their reception was. It was on my return from a severe Examination of three hours before the "Examining Committee" of the Supreme Court of our state. I well knew I had not been rejected, and I was returning with a bright face, elastic step, and a light heart, all happiness with my success, when I encountered Mr. Ward. I went immediately around with him and got them. O how pleasant it was, Dear Lottie, and then they were written so sweetly, so beautifully expressed, so full of love, my dear Lottie, which need I assure you was indeed welcome. Lottie, my sweet sister, just let me say one thing and I promise to drop the subject. *You write an elegant letter. I am proud of them.* That's all!

When I wrote last I was a hard student, preparing for my Examination. All that has passed. The day the Steamer left was our election for County officers. Col. Jack Hays was elected by over a thousand majority. Mr. Morrison was elected Judge of our "County Court." I was busy all day with my friends, advocating the cause of the "Gallant Texan Ranger" [Jack Hays] and he swept the field. You would be so much amused to see how the candidates work for themselves. In the first place, they put themselves up and electioneer as they do in some of the Western States. Col. Hays and Col. Bryant, the two candidates for Sherriff, were mounted on horses most of the day, and riding from one district to another. At each place, they were surrounded and cheered by their friends. Col. Bryant has been all his life and is now a "desperate gambler." He opened a large "Hotel" here a month since, and has in that time fed and given drink to all and any who would come to him.

As you may imagine, dealing out his wines, dinners, and liquors so generously, he made friends, but as it proved, they were not strong enough to elect him. I have never seen so much excitement in the states as we witnessed here on that day. The whole town were perfectly alive, every body out, every body excited. Col. Hays' friends excited with the determination of elect[ing] him, and Bryant's friends, excited with liquid fire. The Whigs gave up their part generally and voted for Jack. There were five and six bands of music parading the street (we have the greatest quantity of music here and some very good). There were very few disturbances and no serious fights, which all thought almost miraculous. Neither were the candidates abused, as they generally do at home. They called both Col.s gentleman, but excused themselves on the ground of personal preference. It was really pleasant to see things conducted so amicably, I assure you.

I forgot to tell you I was elected "judge of the election," which I consented to, only to please the Hays party. I must tell you of what I presume you will think very naughty: "dining out on Sunday"—but my friends were so urgent, I at last consented. It was a dinner given to Col. Hays at the Bay Hotel. The Bay Hotel is a vessel of some six hundred tons, drawn up on the mud under a high bank, and it has been transformed into a Hotel. After an hour's talk with the Col., we were called to a most sumptious dinner, and without particularizing, let me say, we had almost every vegetable you can mention, all from where do you suppose? France! We have great quantities of these "preserved vegetables" in our market as well as meats. My seat was on the right of Col. Hays. Champagne flowed like water, and we had a most delightful time. He amusing me with accounts of his "Ranging life in Texas," and I entertaining him with my fun in Chile.

He is a small man, quite plain and unsophisticated. From his daring adventures, you would think him a perfect "Joe Mountain." There were four or five Ladies present, all brilliant, and pretty. I became acquainted with them and accepted invitations to visit them. I left the party about eight o'clock, and took a boat off to the *Balance,* where I ended the eve in a quiet "tete a tete" with Mr. and Mrs. B[rooks].

What do you think when I tell you that Mrs. Brooks made her first visit on shore on Tuesday last. We have been here ever since November 23d, 1849 and yet Mrs. B. has never once visit[ed] San Francisco before. Her health has been and is good, but there were no attractions for her, and she has seemed perfectly indifferent to it, indeed obstinately refused. This is the second time in a year Mrs. B has touched "terra firma." They have lately had the salon and cabin fixed up very nicely, hung with paintings and [it] really looks quite tempting. Little Willy grows bright every day, and still continues desperately fond of me.

John McCrackan

Letter to his sister Mary
14 April 1850

[The Steamer] brought out from Panama about 600 passengers, her latest dates [of letters and newspapers] from the States was February 21st (that is, from New York), although she brought seven days later dates from New Orleans. On my return to my office after dinner, I procured a Herald, and my time till commencing this letter was consumed in devouring all the news.

I regret very much Mr. Clay's recommendations have not met a more decided approval. We cannot call it "compromise"—there is no compromise suggested. It is a fair, candid, honorable course of conduct that he recommends. All California is in favor of his conduct. It is so like the great and good Statesman, the noble Henry Clay. By the papers it seems [Daniel] Webster has been in close conference with some southern members, and it is thought he will propose something that will be more acceptable to them. Now for my part, I am unwilling to think Mr. Webster can propose any compromise that can be more acceptable to the "whole people" than the propositions of Mr. Clay, and if Mr. Webster thinks he can persuade the north into any thing in the form of a compromise less liberal than the proposal of Mr. Clay, he will find himself mistaken, and I am willing to predict and do indeed believe *that upon that rock he will split.*

I may perhaps through jealousy fear that Mr. Webster will bring forward some plan of compromise that will eclipse Henry Clay's, and yet I do not think it possible. I think if the people reject the plan proposed by Mr. Clay, they consign themselves to the most fearful results. Heaven knows (I speak reverently) what will come of it, and yet I feel as if the worst would be postponed, or what we most fear would be averted, so long as we have such men as Henry Clay to watch over and protect the interest of our great and glorious Union. Out of twenty million of people, we have but one Henry Clay.

We Californians are getting quite tired of our neglect, and should our interests receive no more flattering attention than has so far been exhibited, we must make our voice heard. In a word, should Congress refuse to admit us this session into the Union as one of the great republic, we shall form a government free and independent of the United States. We have the will and sufficient power to sustain ourselves. This would be a severe blow and loss to our Mother country. We have riches untold, we have the best blood and energy from the States, and in five years would claim more importance than any state in the whole union. In another five years we shall have a city on this coast which will rank with any city in the States. The United States are now receiving an immense quantity of money from the Customs, the revenue fund is large and of course increasing with each succeeding month. All this treasure in case we are independent, come[s] to the coffer of our young state. The "civil fund" also is ours and already this is an immense amount.

Our courts are at last established, "The Supreme Court for the State," three judges, District Court, Superior Court, and County Court. Judge [Roderick N.] Morrison was elected by the people. I expect to get a professional appointment from him, for his court. Consequently our legal proceedings are now strict and uniform. This is really very satisfactory. The appointments of Judges of the Superior Court were strictly political, and consequently very ridiculous, being young and inexperienced in the Law. Morrison's appointment gives universal satisfaction, and he certainly looks the Judge.

Alfred DeWitt

Letter to his father
30 May 1850

I fear that we shall have considerable trouble here in regard to [the] law of taxes passed by the legislature of this *so called* State. Everything is in the hands of *politicians* who have come out within the last year for the express purpose of practising their profession, getting into office, and filling their pockets at the expense of the people. They tax every one—strangers and all—and in some cases in direct opposition to the Constitution of the U[nited] States. The foreigners at the mines refuse to pay, and have joined together to resist all attempts to collect it. There is a poll tax of $8 for each person, and they intend to tax all merchandise arriving here in vessels. The burden, if they succeed, will be very great on the merchants, and interfere very much with trade. I think that the merchants will resist paying any, and it will be difficult to compel them to it, if they act together. Our Sage Alderman have passed a law taxing the net amount of sales made by each house, and have voted themselves a salary of *$6000 pr ann.* payable monthly for services of one night a week. You see what a situation Congress has placed us in, and what it will end in is hard to foretell, but I have great confidence in the people that they will not submit to having their pockets picked.

Jonathan F. Locke

Letter to his wife
30 April 1850

Today is election day, the city charter election. This is the third election that I have voted in since I have been here. It is six months since I arrived here. First came the state and congressional delegations, next county sheriff and Col Jack Hays of Texan notoriety was elected. Today, as I said before, we intend to give San Fran'o a city government. It is a noisy time, these election days here. I do not enter into the excitement much but it all goes off well. It is a mystery to me among so much that tends to evil, so much of order and safety as we enjoy. It is principally from this cause: every one minds his own business.

John McCrackan

Letter to his family
16 June 1850

We are having now daily importations in the greatest quantity of Mexicans and Chileans. There is a "Fonda Mejicana" directly opposite our offices on Jackson Street. The building is an old adobe with a veranda in front, and here they chiefly congregate when they come off the vessel, most of them arrive here by way of Mazatlan, San Blas. They are robed in their blankets, some sitting, others lying about the stoop. They are destined most of them for the mines. We had serious disturbances of late, by the efforts to enforce the law passed by our last Legislature requiring all and every foreigner who works in the mines to pay a "state tax" of twenty dollars a month. In many instances they have assembled in bodies and openly denounced the law and the officers who attempted to collect the tax. Their resistance has been conquored by a display of strength on the part of the Sherriff, who was ready at any time to use force. In one instance in the Southern Mines, they were very near having an engagement. We do not hear as much about the difficulties with the Indians, just at this time. They are having the most unpleasant misunderstandings however all over the Territory, which must end in a war of extermination to the poor Indian. Their right[s] have been violated in many instances, and revenge would follow revenge, till many lives have been sacrificed. Our Governor should have his offices here commissioned to treat with them and buy their land, instead of wresting it from them.

Chapter 8

A Home in the West

As described in the opening chapter, the first impression most Argo-nauts had of San Francisco was that of a confused bedlam teeming with characters of questionable reputation, its streets quagmires, its hills a dust-blown wasteland, its residences woefully ill-equipped to provide for even the most basic of creature comforts. Again and again correspondents avowed that they could not imagine living for any length of time in such a hellhole for anything other than the possibil-ity of vast riches. In less than twelve months, however, many of the same critics were writing fondly of their new home on the Pacific shore. This startling about-face had little to do with newly acquired amenities (such as planked roads, artesian wells, or the increased availability of fresh vegetables), for San Francisco in July of 1850 was not much more habitable than it had been in July of 1849. And it was *much* more crowded.

This amazing change in attitude reflects, rather, the triumph of vi-sion over reality. Many immigrants, their dreams of easy wealth shat-tered by sickness or bad luck, gave up and went home. But others looked about, saw the totally improbable metamorphosis of the pre-ceding months, and realized that they could build a strong and pros-perous future out of what looked like utter chaos. Dreamers dropped by the wayside, and visionaries strode in to take their place.

There are no published figures on what percentage of Argonauts remained in California longer than a year or two, but between 1848 and 1856 the population of San Francisco increased from around one thousand to about fifty thousand, making it the largest metropolis on the West Coast.[1] The rudimentary census information of the day indicates that in 1847 just under half of the population of San Francisco was born outside of the United States; that figure remained constant until 1860. This heterogeneity of culture gave San Francisco the third highest proportion of foreign-born residents among American cities, higher even than the immigrant port of New York.[2] The slim majority of American citizens did not represent a static population base either; people arrived and departed with each ship sailing through the Golden Gate. Before the end of the gold rush period one out of every ten Americans—over two million in all—had at some point been to California seeking their fortune.[3]

The decision to prolong one's stay in California evoked, almost inevitably, the nesting instinct. Anne Willson Booth bustles on board the *Andalusia*, preparing finally to take up residence ashore (coincidentally stopping into DeWitt & Harrison's general store to buy a broom). Margaret DeWitt's letters to her in-laws exude an almost audible sigh as she settles into her small cottage with a level of domestic contentment that obviously surprises even her, a contentment that is threatened when Mr. Harrison returns from the East Coast with his new bride. Margaret's strained efforts to welcome the arrival of Elizabeth Harrison clearly suggest that she finds "sisterhood" highly overrated.

John McCrackan's descriptions of his social outings give a good indication of how far San Francisco had come in offering pleasant amusements, particularly his story of "magnetizing" a young girl who was staying at the St. Francis Hotel. Animal magnetism, or mesmerism, was a common parlor game with pseudoscientific pretensions (Emerson dismissed it as "this monkey of mesmerism.")[4] In the game a subject was hypnotized for the amusement of the party; mesmerized subjects might "jerk, twitch, shake, laugh, weep, pray, groan, jump, roll on the ground, hear voices, have visions and become entranced."[5]

The collection closes with McCrackan's description of the house he intended to build in Marin County to be near his friend Mr. Sheppard. It is clear that whatever negative impressions he once held of San Francisco, McCrackan was eventually drawn to the "eternal summer" that California promised and intended to bring his mother and sisters (and a hypothetical wife) to the West to make his home a "heaven."

Anne Willson Booth

Journal
26 September 1849

The weather was so very damp and cloudy this morning I thought it certainly must rain—but contrary to my expectations, it cleared away by 10 o'clock, the sun dispersing all the fog and bursting forth in much beauty. I enjoy sitting on the quarter deck, looking at the men hoisting the cargo from the hold and putting it over the side. . . .

We have been visited to day by a number of our passengers, who appear to be doing quite well. One party amused us by giving a description of their tent life—Mr. Scovill is caterer and cook, Mr. Gibson washes dishes, Col. Myers wipes them, while Dr. Buckner brings in what wood he can find. Old Capt. Smith visited us to day, I was much surprised at seeing him look so well. He is quite jovial and appears as young as he did 10 years ago. He is living at a place called Bodega, distant about 60 miles from here, which is according to all accounts quite an oasis in the desert, and abounds in luxuries, such as fruit and vegetables. He married a very young Peruvian Lady about six years ago and has three young children. His wife does not speak a word of English. He gave us a very cordial invitation to pay them a visit.

Anne Willson Booth

Journal
4 October 1849

The weather this morning is more favourable than we have had it yet. Mr. Taylor commenced making preparations after breakfast for moving his family ashore. Mrs. Taylor continues poorly. I think however when she becomes settled in her house, and interested in the management of it, she will be better.

After dinner, Mrs. Reed and I went ashore to place the things, as they arrived. After a toilsome ascent from the beach to the hill, we finally reached the house, calling on the way to see our old friends, Col. Myers, Mr. Scovill and Dr. Buckner, who are tenting it near there. We found them at dinner, of which they invited us to partake but of course [we] declined. The Col. shewed me a plan of a building he is about to have erected, which will be an ornament to the City. Mr. Taylor's house is a very comfortable one, and almost made me wish it were mine to go to housekeeping in. We found the carpenters still at work, but expecting to finish in a few hours. Mrs. Reed and I started out to purchase a broom. After going almost over the entire town, were compelled to return without one, and had nearly reached the house again, when we met Mr. Cardwell. We told him what we were in quest of, when he directed us to Dewitt & Harrison, whose store is down on the beach. So we retraced our steps, and finally purchased a broom for $1.

Returning we met Henry McKensie. He went ashore last night, and did not return. I stood with him a long time, begging him to go back to the Ship this evening with us. Finally obtained his consent. He accompanied us to the house, brought us water, swept the chips and shavings out of the rooms &c &c. By this time Mr. Taylor arrived with a load of baggage. Mrs. Taylor and Virginia were on the way, as it was now sundown. I was compelled to leave Mrs. Reed. My friend Dr. Hardy called to take me aboard. When we reached the beach our boat was nowhere to be seen. After waiting awhile, we were compelled to hire a strange one, for which the Dr. paid $3. We are lying not more than 200 yards from the shore—the charge is really exorbitant. There is considerable difficulty in getting near the water of an afternoon, the tide being very low. The boatman picked me up in his arms and put me in the boat. When we reached the Ship, I felt much fatigued and almost outdone. We had a very quiet tea. All were congratulating *themselves upon the absence of noise of children & scolding of their mammas.*

Anne Willson Booth

Journal
5 October 1849

This is a beautiful morning and I think that we have seen the sun rise clearly. The Steward and Tim are busy cleaning out the Cabin and putting things to right. I was considerably amused at hearing Uncle Wes giving directions to put table cloths on the table now, and the table cover—which luxuries we have been prevented from enjoying on account of Mrs. Taylor having little Morgan brought to the table and not restraining him in the least. It certainly was a great annoyance to us all. He used to be allowed to put his fingers among the victuals and scatter them far and near. Such a thing as washing his face and hands after eating was not thought of, or at least never done. To day, we enjoy the quiet cabin and our reduced family. Dr. Hardy told us all in [the] presence of the Steward, that he saw him [the Steward] crying when the family were taking their departure. The old man looked very serious and tried hard to bear the Dr's joke but finally exclaimed, "If any thing in the world would have induced me to leave the ship, it would have been the being compelled to wait on them d[amne]d people." It is a pity, but nevertheless a fact, that they are so very unpopular among the passengers generally. The Steward has cleaned out their room very nicely, and we use it for a wardrobe and place for trunks.

Anne Willson Booth

Journal
6 October 1849

Uncle Wes has invited several gentlemen to breakfast and dine with us tomorrow. He went to market this morning and when he returned asked me to look at what he had purchased and paid $11 for—which was a handkerchief full of potatoes and onions with a leg of mutton. I am sure if any one had told me of these exorbitant charges, I would have accused them of exaggeration. If we conclude upon keeping house in San Francisco, we shall have to renounce all such luxuries. Fond as we are of vegetables, I should be very sorry to give at the rate of $30 a bushel for potatoes, or 75 cts. for two or three onions. I hope however, things will be quite different after a while, when people begin to see the importance of paying some attention to agriculture. It is said, that every thing necessary for the consumption of the inhabitants of this place could be raised within ten miles of it.

Capt. Smith's schooner arrived this afternoon from Bodega. Uncle went on board to see what was there. The Capt. of the schooner told him he had heard Capt. Smith say something about sending vegetables to the *Andalusia,* but thought he must have forgotten it afterwards, as he had received no conclusive orders to that purpose. Uncle bought a bag of potatoes for which he paid $25. Dr. Hardy and Mr. Effinger accompanied him on board, and brought their pockets filled with apples they stole on board.

Anne Willson Booth

Journal
7 October 1849

Sunday morning, dark, damp and cloudy. Capt. Codman and Mr. West breakfasted with us. Several other gentlemen were expected but failed to arrive. We heard that Mr. Taylor's Chapel was to be dedicated this morning and concluded we would give them our attendance, if nothing more. Accordingly, Mr. King, Mr. Booth and I started after breakfast. Upon arriving on shore, we were told the dedication would not take place until 12 o'clock. The other churches by that time would be dismissed, so that Mr. Taylor would be supported by the presence of the other Protestant ministers. As Mr. King and Mr. Booth had invited a mutual acquaintance of theirs to dine with us, and the boat would be waiting for us, we were compelled to return without waiting for the ceremony. We went through the Chapel and found it to be a very snug building; in a rough state but comfortable. We then paid a visit to Mr. Taylor's dwelling, which is but a short distance from the Chapel. Found the family well and apparently enjoying their ease in domestic life. They have got pretty well fixed and look quite comfortable. We met two of our late passengers there, whom we call Mrs. Reed's and Virginia's beaux, as they have received a good deal of attention from these gentlemen. I do not know that there is any thing serious in these affairs, but such is the general impression, and many suppose them actually engaged to be married. I hope they will both do well whenever they make this important change.

As we were returning to the beach, we fell in with Mr. Smith, the gentleman expected to dine with us. We all proceeded to the boat and in a few minutes found ourselves once more on board our Ship. I for one glad to make my escape from the dust and sand of the City. We found that Capt. Codman was still on board, and remained all afternoon with us. We had many visitors during the afternoon.

Anne Willson Booth

Journal
14 October 1849

Another Sunday, and by far the most pleasant one we have yet seen in California, as far as the weather is concerned. The weather being clear, dry and resembles a May day at home. Being not quite well, I remain at home, which is always pleasant to me. Indeed, the longer our stay is on board the Ship, the greater is my attachment towards it, and the greater reluctance I shall feel when compelled to quit it.

Capt. King, the Harbour Master of the port, came on board, accompanied by his lady and a young lady, recently arrived from the United States. The Capt. told me some time ago he should be pleased to bring his wife to see me, but I began to fear he had forgotten his promise, some time having elapsed since it was made. I was very much pleased with Mrs. King, whom I found a very pleasing, intelligent person. She is from Massachusetts, and has resided in this country upwards of three years. She tells me there were but two houses when she first came and there were but two vessels lying in the harbour. What a sudden change has taken place in a comparatively short time. After remaining with us about two hours, they took their leaves, giving me a very pressing invitation to visit them at their residence, which I intend availing myself of when a suitable opportunity shall offer.

Mr. King and Dr. Hardy visited the *Susan S. Owens* this afternoon, and were exceedingly gratified at the friendly reception they met with. She arrived on the 12th inst. [and] has a large number of passengers, of who there are eight ladies.

Anne Willson Booth

Journal
19 October 1849

The Ship is taking in ballast, and Uncle thinks by the expiration of another week he will have all the cargo out and ballast in. He then will drop further out, to make ready for sailing. Oh! how I dread the time. I shall feel, I know, as if my best friend had left me. Uncle seems to think it a pity I came, and I think he would be glad to see me exhibit symptoms of a wish to return with him. But, so far from this being the case, I have not for a single moment harboured such a thought, or felt the slightest wavering in my resolution to remain here a few years, and by active exertion, try what kind Fortune may do for us. It is true, there are many disadvantages and privations attending life in California, but these I came prepared to encounter, and by no means expected to find the comforts and refinements of Home. I know of no single circumstance calculated to annoy or trouble us with which we were not already acquainted, while on the other hand, there are many causes to encourage and induce us still to persevere in this undertaking, leaving the result in the hands of "Him, who controlleth all things."

In the first place, we were led to believe there were but a very few ladies, if any, in this place. On the contrary, we find there are some three or four hundred, of a class too one would scarcely expect to meet with in this far off place. I have met with several ladies, myself, that would do credit to, and highly adorn, any society however fastidious its demands. Surely this fact need excite no particular surprise. Generally speaking, they are not actuated by any love of adventure, and only obey the dictates of duty and inclination to accompany their husbands, wherever their interests may call them. The ladies, with a very few exceptions, are all married. To them, I admit, it is a sufficiently serious undertaking: *but without the protection of a husband or Father, I think it madness.*

Anne Willson Booth

Journal
26 October 1849

Another beautiful morning. The sun is shining clearly on the hill tops, every where to be seen from the harbour. It is a beautiful sight, which I enjoy exceedingly standing on the quarter deck, I can always find something to interest my thoughts. The town just in front of us [is] filled with various kinds of tenements, large warehouses, the smallest kind of huts, interspersed with tents, while the streets are alive with the busy crowd hurrying to and fro, commencing the duties of the day; while on the outskirts may be seen a few dwellings, most built in a cottage style, betokening their inmates not entirely devoid of taste and elegance. The harbour, filled with all kinds of shipping, from the war vessel down to the sloop, is a beautiful sight, too on which I love to dwell. The white sails glistening in the rays of the sun, and then becoming shaded, as the gently undulating motion of the tide causes the vessels to ride at ease. I think I can never grow weary of living on the water, and feel as much reluctance to quit it as if it were my native element. I am glad to hear our intended residence will command a water view, I expect I shall often gaze upon it, and long to be again upon the deep. . . .

Mr. Booth tore down the state rooms to night, and will have the lumber taken ashore to morrow so as to commence our little cottage on Monday morning. I went below and staid while the work was going on, and had a regular benefit in searching about for articles I thought might be useful. John Cole watched me, saying he knew I wanted to pilfer. I knew there were plenty of brooms about, and felt determined to search them out. After a while, I espied them stowed away on top of the sails, aft of the main hatch. Johnny gave me a helping hand, and I succeeded in securing several. I don't relish the idea of paying a dollar and a half for a broom, particularly when these are to be had for nothing. Uncle Wes was kind enough to tell me any little thing I wanted, to take. Wesley says if I could move the ship, she would not be safe, for he is sure I'd want her. How they would laugh at home to see me prowling about the ship's hold, in search of prey till nearly midnight.

John McCrackan

Letter to his sister Lottie
30 May 1850

Mrs. Brooks has been ashore all day running over the hills with a very sweet lady and their husbands, gathering flowers and strawberrys, and enjoying themselves like girls of sixteen. I presume she will not live on the vessel many month[s] more, although she seems to be quite happy there, but on many accounts it would be better for her to leave the Ship. These moonlight nights, her husband takes her all about the Bay in their little skiff, calling upon this friend and that, for you must know there are a great many ladies living upon ships in the Bay, renting houses is expensive while it costs nothing if you have a ship to live upon.

Margaret DeWitt

Letter to her mother-in-law
28 August 1849

The store looks much improved by the new building and is now quite finished. Buildings of all kinds go up very fast here, and I am afraid it will not be long before our fine view will be entirely shut off. Houses of every description from shantys and huts to large two story buildings are constantly making their appearance. Some are very pleasant, and seem almost like home houses. I see none I like better than the snug little cottage we live in. It has such a real cosy comfortable appearance—and then so near the store, which is so convenient for *my* boarders to come to their meals. But they take good care not to stay a moment after eating—except in the evening, which to me is the pleasantest part of the day. I am getting to be a very quiet character and often spend hours without speaking a word—but I make up for it in the evenings, quite to the annoyance of Alf—especially if he is smoking and he will often have to relight his sigar several times. I expect his bachelor brothers at home feel thankful they have not been so foolish as George and Alfred. Mr. Harrison is continually congratulating himself that he has no one to trouble him, and pities Alfred very much—but he gets pretty well teased sometimes so it goes.

Just imagine us, seated in the evening in one parlor: Mr. Harrison, Henry, Mr. West, Alf and myself. A nice little fire, talking over ventures and things—and, I need not say, often about our homes. Sometimes I cannot realize the distance we are away from our friends. I try to feel happy and contented—and would be ungrateful if I did not—for Alfred is so very kind and indeed all do every thing they can for my comfort and happiness. Sometimes I feel as if I would like very much to have a sister with me—but that is too much to expect, and I get along better than I thought I would.

There are a number of ladies in the place—a number have come since we got here. I have not become acquainted with any except those that called upon us when we first came. They were all very polite, but very few are persons I care to be much acquainted with. Tho' Mrs. Gillespie is a very fine woman and has been very kind to me. They talk of moving away next winter. I hope they will not, as she would be a great loss to the society.

There have been a good many Chinese goods brought to this market, and last week at a sale Mr. Harrison and Alfred each bought some very pretty articles in the way of centre tables and worktables. Alf gave his to me, and Mr H will I believe keep his for the future Mrs H. They are very beautiful and useful. The worktable is complete, and I value them very highly. They make the room look very pretty and quite stylish too. I will try and keep them nice till we return to live at home. We both look forward to that time with a great deal of pleasure. It is a good while to look forward to, but it will soon pass, and if all [are] spared to meet again, will have right nice times. Henry says he is going to write you, so I expect he will give you an account of every thing. Alfred is writing to George—he has tried to get time ever since we came, and often sits up very late writing business letters, so has no time for other correspondence.

There has [been] and is still considerable sickness in the place, but not more than one would expect from the size of the population and the miserable condition of some who arrive here. The water too for the last few weeks has not been as good, and disagrees with a great many. I had a slight attack of sickness last week, and have since been very careful about everything I eat. There have been some sudden deaths and all the ladies, since Mrs. Wards sudden death, have felt frightened of attack by that disease [dysentery]. The Doctor that attended Alfred when he was sick (Dr. Turner) has been very ill for some time, but I believe is now decidedly better. I feel now quite well, but not as strong as before. Yesterday and today have been quite warm and the dust blows about at a fine rate. The dust comes in clouds over the hill and we cannot have a window or door open without every thing being covered. I shall be right glad to see rain again, but will have to wait some time yet as the wet season does not commence till the last of November.

Margaret DeWitt

Letter to her mother-in-law
14 November 1849

Tell William I am sorry to hear he is so thin. I think from some reports in San Francisco he must be in love. Ask him if the young lady's name is not (Miss Duncan). I think Henry has not any thing of that sort to trouble him. We have not heard anything about the elder brothers getting married, and I do not know but what they are much better off, especially while they have their Mother to do every thing for them. Alf sometimes thinks so too, but poor fellow, it is too late now—he will have to make the best of his bargain. Mr. Harrison talks a good [line] on this subject, but he is a funny fellow and I guess talks only for amusement. I think he would be hard to suit.

I have had letters from my sisters and brothers every mail, sent by private opportunity. Helen Field writes she is much improved in health. I sincerely hope she may continue so. I expect Mother will feel my absence more this winter, as during the summer months there is so much more to divert the attention and the winters are so dull. I think she will often get the blues and perhaps feel sorry she consented to my going so far away. I hope she will not, for I have never regretted it and have spent a very happy summer, as much so as possible away from all my friends. Alfred has thought some of going home in the spring. If he should think it best, I of course would be delighted to be home—but I have been happy and contented here, and shall always look back to the time spent here with pleasure. I had made up my mind to be two years without seeing my friends, therefore when Alfred said perhaps he would go home in the spring, I was much surprised and delighted. But I try not to think more of it than I can help, as something may prevent him.

I do not know what we should have done if they had not got this place to live in when we first came. Our house has been so long detained [they had ordered a prefabricated house to be shipped around the Horn] that it will not probably be here before next spring, and the rainy season has commenced so early we would have been exceedingly uncomfortable, and as for living over the store, [that] would have been impossible. Now we are very comfortable—which is every thing here in the wet season. I think you can have no idea how the rain comes down. Sometimes it is just like the fastest rain you have ever seen—then it will come down in torrents, till every thing is overflowed, making the walking terrible. Then we may have a day or two when the sun shines quite warm and every thing is bright and cheerful—then two or three days of rain, so it goes. To one who does not have to go in the wet, it is quite a pleasant variety, but for the gentleman, it is bad enough, and I really pity them. One thing, we do not have any more dust—which is a great relief—but the wind blows as hard as ever. The weather has been milder during the months of September and October than since we came—and some days were really quite hot.

We were sorry to hear that Pa had not improved more while in the country. Hope ere this he has quite recovered his strength. Perhaps he may be better, now the weather is cool. We think and talk much of you both, and your likenesses are so very excellent that it almost seems like seeing you (Alfred often says). No money would tempt him to part with them, he values them so highly well. They are indeed a great comfort—and when I get lonely I look them all over and always feel better afterwards.

I have two sweet singing Canary Birds which are a great deal of company—one from Mr. Harrison and the other was given me by Mrs. Hobson, a lady who came on in the Steamer with us from Valparaiso and who has returned to the States. A great number of ladies have left in the last two months and society is entirely broken up. A number have arrived lately, but they are ladies I do not care to be acquainted with—with the exception of one or two who I would have called upon if I had been well enough to go out. Mrs. Gillespie is the only pleasant lady remaining that I am acquainted with, and they think of leaving in January. But that is nothing—for I can be happy without much society and am becoming quite used to my quiet sort of life.

Margaret DeWitt

Letter to her father-in-law
30 November 1849

As Henry is writing to Mother, I concluded to send you a few lines (as Alfred says he will not have time to by this Steamer). I hope by the next month he will have more leisure, as it is too bad he writes so few letters home. His time has been much occupied lately, and he has been obliged to stay at the store some evenings as late as eleven and twelve o' clock to make up for the time lost, while sick. I don't fancy it much, as I get very lonely—but know it is best, or he would not do it.

I spend such a quiet life and so much sameness that I find I have nothing new to write, or any thing that will interest one besides our little family circle. We are all right well and happy, and are having the most beautiful weather I have ever seen this season of the year. It seems more like spring than the first of December. So far the winter is far pleasanter than the summer. The air is so pure and fresh, it is delightful after the dry dusty summer. Every thing looks fresh and beautiful and the hills are so beautiful and green, it looks like summer at home. I took a walk with Alfred the other day on one of the high hills and the view was very beautiful. The scenery is very fine of the opposite shore and the beautiful bay, filled with all kinds of ships, is [a] fine sight. Alfred tried to count the vessels but gave it up. I should think there must be over two hundred.

Our garden is made, and planted with most kinds of vegetables. If the seed proves good I think we will have a fine supply for our own use. I hope we will be successful, as Alfred has become quite interested and is calculating largely as to the yield. If it was not for the dry season, I presume we might have a garden planted twice a year. We have also got a nice poultry yard with a fine chicken house and eight or ten chickens, two hens hatching, and two turkeys which were sent to me as a present and which we are fattening for Christmas, but we get but one or two eggs a day. Besides, we have two sweet Canary birds, and a cat—which, with Carlo the dog, makes the family quite large.

Alfred talked some of going home in the spring, but has I believe given it up. I was a little disappointed, and was sorry I had heard any thing about it, but now I feel very contented, and happy tho' sometimes I am very lonely and feel the absence from my Mother and sisters very much. However I am inclined to be as cheerful as possible and try to think as little of home as I can. Alfred is very kind and would, I know, feel bad if I should get homesick. Henry is very well, and seems happy and contented. It is very pleasant for me to have him with us, and he is as kind and affectionate to me as if he was an own brother. Indeed, they are all very kind and I am in great danger of getting spoiled—but I try to remember the old saying, "It is hard to spoil what never was good," and that keeps me humble.

Yesterday 29th was Thanksgiving Day. There was service in all the churches but very few of the stores were closed—all are so intent on making money that they have time for nothing else. We had a small party of gentlemen to dine with us—Mr. Harrison, the Ex Collector, Mr. Dewey, Mr. Flian, and another gentleman—which, with Mr. Harrison, Alfred, Mr. West, Henry and I made quite a table full. The turkeys were not fit to eat, so we had ducks and roast beef instead, which with mince and pumpkin pies gave a good dinner to be thankful for.

We have received the tin box of cakes and crackers Mother was so kind to send. They are very nice and came in very good order—but she ought not to take so much trouble, as I can make cake—tho' I don't expect to equal her. I am very sorry, dear Father, your health has been so poor since we left. I hope now it is fully restored, and you are as well as usual. I look forward to our return home with much pleasure—and hope we may all be spared to meet again. It is a long while to look forward to, and sometimes [I] feel bad, thinking about you all and we so far away—perhaps never to meet again in this world. I try to cast off such feelings—and remember, all our ways are directed by God and whatever he does will be right. He has protected and preserved us thus far—and shall we not trust him for the future?

I will bring my letter to a close, and I dare say you will be glad, for I believe gentlemen do not care much to read what ladies write, especially if they have no more to say than I. You will please give our love to all the family—and much to Mother and yourself—and tell Mother I will write her the next time.

Margaret DeWitt

Letter to her mother-in-law
28 January 1850

Your letter dated November 30th with a note enclosed for Alfred from his Father was received in due time, and also one enclosed for Henry. We also have the pleasure of Mr. Birch and Uncle John's company, who arrived safely by the same Steamer and who are, like every new comer, perfectly surprised at the rapid growth of this place and can hardly believe it possible that it is so much of a city. Uncle John seems much interested in every thing and seems anxious to visit the surrounding country, but at present the rains and state of the roads will prevent his seeing much. I should not be surprised if he made a long stay. . . .

The rain has kept me pretty closely to the house and we have not been able to attend church but twice since Thanksgiving. A week last sabbath was a lovely day, and quite good walking. Alfred and I went twice. The plan for our new church is liked very much. It [is] exceedingly neat and pretty. I will be glad when we have it finished, as it is difficult to get a suitable room to worship in. Our garden is supplying us with plenty of salad and greens. Alfred planted turnip seed very thick, and they make delightful greens. We have also had radishes. Our little cottage looks very pretty and I have become much attached to its snug quarters. If we should go in our new house I shall feel lost—unless Mr. Harrison brings out his wife and we make one family.

Uncle John says it is not such a dreadful thing to come to California, and when the railroad is finished I should not be surprised to see you and Father out for a visit. Would it not be funny if you were yet to see this golden land? I can never get Alfred to say he would like to remain in this country and make it his home—he has very strong attachments home and feels anxious to return one of these days and be near his parents. Hope we may all be spared till that time. This is a changing world. May we so live, dear Mother, that whether we do or not meet in this world we may in the next. That you may all be kept from evil and we all be spared to meet again is my sincere wish.

Margaret DeWitt

Letter to her mother-in-law
30 March 1850

Alfred is much disappointed that his house is so long coming, as he is very anxious to get it up. For my part, I would quite as leave remain in this—but for the sake of others. Alfred thinks it would be best to go in the new one as, if Mr. H[arrison] should get married, we will probably make one family. At any rate [we] will have the clerks eat with us, as it will be much more comfortable and pleasant for them and better on every account.

My woman is still with me, but has not been very strong lately, consequently I have had my time fully occupied. She is so good and trusty that Alfred would not on any account part with her. He feels as if she did so much for us, when we both had the fever. A great many servants have arrived from England, and are quite plenty such as they are. The worst is—if unmarried, they are soon taken up. *Wimmin* is so scarce. The wages still continue high, but I think the price will soon be lower. . . .

Our garden gets along very well and we are having plenty of salad, radishes, greens and will soon have other vegetables. It is very pleasant to see something green, and our little place is the admiration of every one. I wish I could send you a beautiful bouquet of wild flowers which I have just picked growing wild in the grass about the yard. Some are very beautiful. We are having delightful weather now— warm as June at home. Every one says it is too pleasant to last, and that the high winds will commence next week. I really dread them— they are so unpleasant. We have warmer weather now than since I came, and it is very delightful to be for a few days without fire. Every one thinks we will have no more rain till next fall and already it is getting dusty, so I expect our garden will soon be baked with the hot sun and wind. I wish you could know what a happy family we are here, and what a pleasant home is this far off land. Soon the Steamer will leave here twice a month—then you will not feel that we are so far away.

You must tell Father I am very much obliged for the Christian Intelligence which he is so kind to send. There is a religious paper commenced here called the "Watchman" and edited by our pastor, Mr. Williams. It is to be published once a month, and I have put up a copy for him. This is the first number. We have received the plan of the new church, and like it very much. I believe I must close, dear Mother, as I have no more time. Tell Uncle John I missed his good company very much, and that his cabbage plant grows finely. Give our best love to Sister Helen and Katherine and all the brothers—and much to Father and your self, and believe me ever your affectionate daughter Mag.

You must excuse the appearance of my letters and burn them as soon as you have read them.

Margaret DeWitt

Letter to her mother-in-law
19 April 1850

We are all well [and] happy, but plenty to do—and are looking forward to the arrival of the next Steamer with much interest, hoping to see Mr. Harrison, [his] wife, and my brother Nicholas. If they arrive safely we will have a happy meeting. The time has passed so quickly that it does not seem near as long since Mr. Harrison left. Last Wednesday was a year since we parted with you all. It has been a short, happy year. Did you think of us on that day? But I need not ask such a question, for I know you did.

Dear Mother, the Schooner *Elizabeth* has arrived—and I am now seated in the very beautiful chair you sent us. I feel very grateful for your kindness and love. Alfred sits in it every evening, and it is very cosy and much admired. He is at the store this evening. They are very busy and work late, so I am often alone. I get lonely sometimes, and then I get all the likenesses and have quite a little chat with you all, and sometimes almost feel as if I had really seen you. . . .

Our new house has come and they are very busy putting it up, but it will be probably the middle or last of June before we get in. I think it will be a very nice one and convenient, and with my large family we shall need all the room. Lumber has gone down so much that Alfred says he could buy as good a house now here for what the freight of this one is. He is putting it up on this same lot, so we will not be far to move. Our garden looks quite nicely now but the building will spoil it very much.

Margaret DeWitt

Letter to her mother-in-law
15 May 1850

The mail closes today, and as yet I have not written any letters and now sit down in great haste. I am afraid you will think I am getting very remiss—and lazy too—but if you knew how fully my time is occupied you would make due allowance. Our family numbers 12, and as we have but one servant—and she not very strong—there is plenty to do. My brother has also been quite sick with remittent fever and is still confined to his room, though better, and will be around in a few days. So between the sick and well—and frequent interruptions of persons calling upon Mrs. H[arrison]—my letters are left till the last minute. . . .

Our new house is going up fast, and I think after we get settled we shall find it very pleasant. It is thought best on many accounts that we should make one family—and as the house is large enough it will be less expense. I hope we shall not regret it. I find Cousin Lizzy a pleasant companion. She is very lively, and I think will be disposed to get along pleasantly. As far as I am concerned I will do all I can to make every thing go smoothly. I have been very happy ever since I have been here, and now I have Mrs. Harrison's society, ought to be more so on many accounts. I would prefer to live alone—but in this country there are so many things to be taken into consideration that I presume this arrangement is best.

Margaret DeWitt

Letter to her mother-in-law
13 July 1850

When I last wrote I mentioned Mrs. Harrison was sick with fever. She is now daily recovering, but it has been a long, tedious illness of over five weeks. Now she sits up for several hours during the day but requires great care, and I can assure you I have my hands full enough, as you know what sick persons are that are slowly recovering. She has been very ill, and it has been all together the most trying sickness I have ever had anything to do with. First fever, then dysentery—and then a large tumor under the right ear which had to be poultised for a fortnight, and then discharged an immense quantity and very unpleasant. That is now getting well and she is improving fast, but it will be a long while before she will be able to do the least thing for herself. The Dr. thinks she may be healthier than ever after this attack.

We are not yet settled in the new house, though I hope will be soon. It is finished and is a very nice one, and as we are to live together, shall be much more conveniently situated, as now we are rather crowded for want of room. Lizzie's illness has been a great disappointment to us, as we looked forward to having a good deal of fun fixing up the new house. Now it all falls upon me, and with my other cares I get pretty well tired. My woman has also had the fever and been confined to her room for the last ten days. We have a man to do the work till she gets well. Don't you think I shall be quite an accomplished nurse? I think so—that is if practice makes perfect. . . .

Alfy is as busy as ever—but very well. He is at the store every night writing till 12 o'clock and has not spent an evening at the house for the last three months, so I see but little of him—and I do not like it much, but know if it was not very important he would not do it, as he is such a home body that no place is like his own fireside. I have got Mrs. Harrison's bedroom all in order for her to go in, and I think she will improve much faster after we get moved.

Charles A. Tuttle

Letter to his wife
20 January 1850

Four days ago I wrote you a letter by Dr. C. C. Barnes who was returning to the States, enclosing therein sixty-four dollars in gold. That letter was written in haste, and I now write again as well to give you the particulars of my situation as to apprise you of the money being forwarded. . . . Maria, before I left, you exacted a promise that I would send for you next summer. There are many families here. The privations and fatigues which females undergo are severe. Men with wives soon amass large sums of money. The practice is for the husband to keep a provision store and the wife employ her time in making pies, cakes &c for the miners. (Pies $1.50 a piece.) Now Maria, I would not willingly expose you to this drudgery, or even to a life in the mountains without it. You are deprived of the society of those of your sex, and exposed to all the severities of the weather. Beds, there are none. We are compelled to sleep on a blanket stretched on the ground or on rough boards. A cotton mattress is sometimes found.

Now Maria, my whole mind is bent on amassing a few thousand dollars and returning to you. This, if God spares my life and health, I can do at most in two years. Then if you should think a residence in California desirable, we can return. If, however, you are still desirous to share my fortune in the mines, write and I will answer and meet you on an appointed time at Chagres. Your presence would give me pleasure, I could but regret your sufferings. If you appoint a time, let it be so far distant that you can receive answer from me, and never leave until you know that we understand what Steamer you will take. I shall have an opportunity in the Spring to send you more gold, and in the course of the Summer, hope to send you one or two thousand dollars. Whatever gold I raise I want to place in your hands, if possible.

Life here is uncertain, and a man's purse goes to no-one-knows-where at his decease. I have not yet received any news from you or any friends. Do write and direct your letter to my own name at Sacramento City, Upper California. No one can prize the delights of love until deprived of the society of the one who has inspired him with the deep-seated passion. Daily I think of you, and nightly do I dream on your gentleness purity and faithful love. If our bridal pledges, Maria, were not made in the depth of sincerity, none ever were. Oh, that you could feel truly how much I prefer you to all the world! How sweet the entire surrendering into each others hearts all their thoughts. How sweet mutual sympathy they feel. And, Maria, how sweet the prattle of the artless child. We have once experienced this, and let us hope for that bliss in store. If I see you never again, let us pray that a blissful meeting may be granted us around the throne of God. . . . Again, Maria, I love you.

Henry Didier Lammot

Letter to his brother
22 January 1850

About this time last [year] greatcoats were in great demand and were hardly warm enough, if I remember right, but I must say for this country, this was one of the most beautiful days I ever saw, regular spring weather on the 19. of Jan. We had nothing to do at the sand banks on account of the funds running short, installments not paid in, or something's the matter, so Harry Barrington and I borrowed a boat from R. S. Haven, brother of Mr. Haven of Haven & Livingstone, and pulled over to Yerba Buena Island, which is about four miles from town. On the trip over we saw several seals, which are very abundant here, both in the harbour and out side, we also came across a great many wild ducks and geese. When we got there we went to roll over a stone to fasten our boat to, and saw a great many crabs. So we went on turning over stones, till we got about three dozen fine large crabs.

To give you some idea of the great abundance of game in this country, the small Island of Yerba Buena not more than a mile square is inhabited by game of all kinds—deer, wild goats, large California hare, rabbits and all kinds of feathered game. Right opposite to us is a large eating house, the Centre House. They have every day for dinner bear meat, elk meat, venison, fish of all kinds, all kinds of water and land game. The charge there is $1.50, but the usual charge over the town is one dollar, but this individual don't go to those places. Bob and I go down town to a tent and get a dinner of nicely baked pork and beans for which we pay 37 1/2 cts, breakfast costs us 12 1/2 and we cook our own supper, as Bob Milligan can tell you, having supped with us several times, and who kindly volunteered to take letters for us. . . .

Health is the main object in this place, and I must say that since I have been here I have enjoyed better health than ever I did in my life. Why, just imagine that coat that Quinn made before I left being about two inches—no, it is more—it is four inches too short in the sleeves, and so tight that I can hardly button. I weighed again yesterday and my mark was 145 lbs.

It seems a wonder to me that people have not turned more of their attention to agriculture. The land about two miles from town and all around the Mission seems admirably adapted to it. Fine rich loam with a sandy subsoil, and fine springs of water all in the neighborhood. I saw several mineral springs and tasted the water and it was as fine as I would wish to taste.

William Smith Jewett

Letter to his sister
28 January 1850

If my letters afford one half the pleasure to you that yours do to me, it is really a happy circumstance that I am so far away, for were I nearer they would never be written—hence none of the delicious excitement when *the Steamer* comes in. . . . I am thankful to you all for your kind blessings and prayers and may heaven reward you for it by my pure and manly conduct where ever I may be, and my safe return one of these days to find you all well and happy.

For happy I am now—as happy as a boy can be who is so far away from his mother, of whom he thinks just twenty-four times a day and many a time betweenwhiles. . . . In my last I told you I had shared the luck of nine out of six coming to this country, that I had been poisoned sadly. Well, after some three weeks of swelling, burning and *itching* (Oh dear) and ending it off with some score of boils anywhere and everywhere, I am left better than I have been in health since I left my teens, and I sing and whistle all the time and come ashore where I flounder through the mud in first-rate style.

Many of my old New York friends are here and they have all insisted so strongly upon my setting up my easel right amongst all this crazy stuff that I have at last done so, and am at work quite in earnest, as it is impossible to get up to the mines if I should even choose to go. I shall give my pencil the preference until all is safe and pleasant traveling and then shall look in upon the *diggins* and try and get enough for you all, some trinkets and a whistle for Lib's baby. . . . Larity has great hopes of *me* here and think[s] I am a lucky fall to them. Gentlemen desire their portraits to send home to their families and I am likely to be full of work. I paint very rapid, taking them on the wind and all are prophesying a fortune to my hand. I am hand and glove with the leading politicians of *the State*, yet don't know which party they belong. The governor [Peter H. Barnett] and Lieutenant governor [John McDougal] have been written to requesting their portraits. Col. [Jonathan D.] Stevenson has been to day and ordered his. The Prefect of the City [Horace Hawes] has ordered his and some of the principal merchants. I am painting—and I am as jolly among them as a clam in high water. I charge from hundred and fifty to eight hundred dollars. Shall paint two or three per week if they come fast enough.

I was paid for one last night—all in silver (no paper here) and what to do with the mass I could not tell. It was the first time in my life that my money was a trouble to me. So I came home and got a large canvass bag used for common trapsticks, went back and shoveled it into it and lugged it home. One of the old masters, it is said, died of the fatigue of carrying home a load of copper coin he got for one of his pictures. I never believed it until now. I am in no alarm for my strength, however.

All expenses here are enormous—rents the base of them all. I pay one hundred and twenty five dollars per month for a little room not larger than the one I kept my coal in in N.Y. But I like these high prices—if you are brisk enough in your business to keep pace with them, a fortune can be made speedily. I don't expect to make a fortune, yet I shall make all I can in a fair way. I bought a lot a few days since for two hundred dollars. Three days afterward I sold half of it for $250, yet retaining one half which you may have for $500 if you like. It was all a *cash* transaction. No sham at all about it—except that I have never seen the lot nor don't know where it is, considering my time worth more than the lot to look it up. But it is a certainty that I have $250 and it—and that I honestly believe it to be in existance and *above water.*

Jonathan F. Locke

Letter to his wife
29 January 1850

I have just closed in the outside of my new house about an hour ago. New house, ha! Nothing short, I assure you—7 1/2 by 12 [feet], all of wood. . . . The woman ought to come next. Are you ready? You can have the first chance if you speak quick. Perhaps I will wait for an answer from you before I look further. . . . While I am speaking of woman, I will say that there are not many here as yet. I mean of respectable American women, and not a great many of any kind. More of Irish, I should think, than any other. I suppose it will be a great while before the females will bear any proportion to the male population.

Well, about my new home and what induced me to build it. I could not stand the profanity, vulgarity and noise of our tent mates longer. They would not get their share of wood, water or any thing else. I have had ten months of the society. I wish for no longer. I suppose I shall have some of it at times as they are near neighbors, and Californeans do have their own etiquette. That is, walk straight in without much ceremony, then make known your wishes if you have any, if not sit down on the nearest thing at hand no matter what, whether it is bucket, stool, chest or chair—anything which first comes at hand, if you sit on a hat or tumble some garment into the dirt, it is all the same.

Tents, not many of them have any floors but the mother earth, and that is not always in its native purity. I have slept on our chest since leaving the Brig, and that comfortably. I have plenty of bedclothes, and when not thinking of home or building castles in the old Bay State, or plans of operations here, I sleep soundly—unless some one of our number makes a rout, as they do most every night. I get sleep enough any way. If this were the only trouble, I should not leave them. . . .

I shall not go to the mines for some time. George [their son] being with me may induce me to go, as he does not earn much here at present. As I said before, he is a hard case to manage. Hope he will do better when separate from our tent mates. He is very anxious to go to the mines. He does not like to labour any too well. Write him a serious letter, will you, it may do him good. He grows stout and strong, nothing that he eats or drinks seems to harm him. He lacks energy, [but] he may overcome this when he has regular employment. He has been in a bad school ever since he left home. He often wishes he was at his studies at home. How different I have been situated in regards to learning him than I flattered myself when we left you. I cannot say I am sorry he came; he may yet be of great service to me. Don't worry about him, seeing he is well. . . .

Do you wish me to say anything about coming home? If you do, I cannot perhaps satisfy you on that point if my health continues. But the little ones perhaps will, after a while, get used to my absence. If you all get impatient, just pack up and come on. Families are needed here. The necessaries of life will be cheaper soon. Don't come till I have been at the mines. Really, I did not think I should feel our separation as I do.

William Smith Jewett

Letter to his family
24 February 1850

I have just rec'd yours from Pokeepsie of the 11th January. How long it takes for a talk to get round back to the starting point, let us talk never so loud or never so strong. There was no steamer down to Panama on the 15th, so in addition to the relief it gave our merchants here it kept us from sending letters to our friends. Your amusing account of your New Years visit made me quite homesick. Indeed, the desire to get home and see mother again is sometimes so great that for a few moments while I allow it possession of me I really think I should have a nervous fit if I did not dispel the feeling by some exciting affair in my business. Oh dear! it is a great way off that I am from all, all I truly love. . . . Tell mother if she will not work nor worry anymore I will send her home (if heaven spares my health) money enough to pay all the debits she can eake and scrape between Dover and Hunts Point. For yes I'm in a fair way to make money, and [for] an artist to be in such a *predicament* is a predicament indeed, as they seldom know what to do with their earnings. So I think the best I can do with mine will be to give them like a good boy to my mother. . . .

I am doing first-rate in my profession. No one who is *any body* thinks of being painted by any one but *Mr. Jewett.* By the by, there is a Mrs. Wm Jewett here—the most beautiful woman in California. She and her husband are to sit to me. I have the favor of all and am in a good train. Col. Stevenson called on me twice and wants I should paint him, Judge [G. Q.] Colton is now sitting and I *may* get the governor of the state for the state &c &c. All this comes of having good friends. I brought (and try to carry) a deserving character with me and I find a good or a bad one always travels faster than a man can, his reception is accordingly. Yet a man must have something more than character to succeed, he must have capacity to please. I am fortunate in pleasing all who sit to me here, as I did those at home who are out here now and give me position at once which I am able to sustain. While I am very sorry that there are artists here and coming all the time who have nothing to do. If Osgood were here now he could stand but little chance with me, as I can far excel him on anything (so Capt Bragg). By the by, Col. Jack Hayes [Hays] is here and I am to paint him. This is a great place for heroes of the Mexican War.

The rainy season is quite over, saving occasional showers and the mud is nearly dried up. The town is increasing rapidly in growth and rents are falling, speculation is driving on yet at a considerable rate. The weather is like mild May mornings and I think it must be a charming country to live in as far as nature is concerned after one gets acclimated, which all must. A sort of sickness in the process, but appearing in different forms. . . . I am not *quite* done boiling and scratching yet—whether it has anything to do with my acclimating sickness or not I can't say. However, I have lost nearly all my old skin and look wonderous bright in spots like an old darkey that's turning white. How much longer I shall be *mowlting* I cannot tell, but unlike the birds I don't lose my voice for, greatly to the annoyance of an old batchelor neighbour next door, I am singing or whistling half the time to keep from getting homesick.

John McCrackan

Letter to his sister Lottie
27 February 1850

I have had a little romance within a week—at least for California. Of course, I shall tell you in confidence. A week ago I called with a gentleman on a Lady and her daughter here from Boston, they were staying at the St. Francis Hotel. Both were very pleasant people, the daughter quite pretty and interesting. They had a host of admirers and yet I was very well pleased with the attentions I received. They invited me to call the next eve—which I did. They were quite alone. After some time they introduced the subject of magnitism, and questioned me. I at first refused to give my opinion, but at last acknowledged my belief and asked her to let me try my powers. She consented. I magnitized her, and it proved a most beautiful experiment. I passed the eve very pleasantly. They said they would take a house tomorrow, and wanted me to come around and see them in the eve. I did not go however, but the eve following I went around. I found a crowd of admirers then, who I thought were not treated with as much consideration as I, yet being very sensitive I was not fully confirmed till most of them had gone, when she openly expressed her feelings towards them. I attempted to leave but found it impossible to get away. She was determined to be magnitized.

The next day she wrote me a note asking to have me call upon her at a certain hour, having something very important to communicate. I called as she requested, when she gave the following account of herself. She is from Boston, is 16 years old, was married two years ago in Boston. Her mother is and has been very unkind to her. She is determined to leave her. Her husband is here and wishes her to accompany him to the mines. She said she did not love him and was almost mad with the idea of living with him and yet she was determined to leave her mother. This was indeed a strange state of things, and I was quite nonplussed. She however proceeded to disclose her wishes, which were to have me take her. This however I respectfully declined, and enjoined upon her the necessity of remaining with her mother. But I found my hour and a half had been wasted, as she could not remain with her mother, and if I would not take care of her, she must go to the mines with her husband.

Now her mother, it seems, was in entire ignorance of her ever having been married, and indeed had but two days ago dismissed her husband and his friends from her house. She pretended of course to be desperately in love with me and her happiness consisted in my acceding to her request. I have not described her. She resembles very much Miss Cook, and is of the same lively, elastic disposition, round face and figure and having a very intelligent face. I made her promise me night before last that she would not leave her mother's home, at least at present, yet I had not much confidence in her. Still if she were married no one could stop her and of course I should not attempt anything but [illegible].

Yesterday I received a note however saying she must go, dwelling at length upon her passion for me, which I slighted etc., and sure enough yesterday afternoon she ran off, took passage at 4 P.M. in the *Senator* for Sacramento City. It seems her husband and friends found it necessary to get the mother out of the home, and so about three o'clock they went to the house and told her a young friend of hers in "Boads Row," from Boston was in a dying condition, and wanted her to come directly down to see him. She could not resist this, put on her things, has not been gone from the home two minutes, when the bird flies, and at four o'clock walks on board the Steamer *Senator*, dressed in boy's clothing (minus dress) with a cigar in her mouth. The old lady discovers it on her return, sets the police to work, but they are too late. I knew all this last eve, today it is told as a great secret although it is very generally known. I will give you the result in my next. Excuse me for taking so much time with this foolish affair. It is confidential of course.

John McCrackan

Letter to his sister Mary
25 April 1850

Our gentlemen now dress in the very latest fashion, including patent leather boots. A suit of clothes here that could be bought in the States for sixty dollars will sell for one hundred and fifty—and indeed more. We are obliged to pay from twelve to twenty dollars for a hat, and yet notwithstanding these high prices, men are if possible more devoted to dress. Although the great rage seems to be for jewelry, and men think nothing of giving three and four hundred for a fat chain of specimens, beside a watch that costs from seven to twelve hundred dollars, and with these they sport the most costly diamonds. I never have seen such a perfect passion as every one entertains for brilliants. The cost of them is about the same—no more—than at home, many come from Mexico.

The Ladies dress very extravagantly. I never have seen such rich dresses in the States as I see pass my window every day, velvets and satins and skirts trimmed with the most beautiful and expensive lace are dragged along in dirty streets with the same carelessness as if they were mere cotton stuffs. This is but the commencement. I doubt not, that five years hence will mark us as the most reckless, extravagant people on the face of the globe. This principle has become firmly established, that when and where money is very easily obtained and abundant, then and there the most ridiculous extravagances are indulged. California will be a London and a Paris together. What a desire every one at home must have to visit this strange country, and how very little they at home really know of us, and our prospects.

In a few lines sent the day I closed my last package to you, or rather Lottie, I mentioned having the night before attended a regular California party, and I believe I promised to give you a full description, but I must beg off. I cannot do it now the time is passed. In a few words, it was a party given upon the occasion of the birth day of Miss Ludlow, a very sweet pretty girl. There were fifteen ladies present, and our eve went off very pleasantly. I became quite enamoured of a widow [illegible] whose husband is now at Trinity River, she was so like Miss G. Bacon, and a little like Lottie. There were many very amusing things to afford us merryment. The ballroom was a new store on the first floor of Capt. Ludlow's house and quite large. Being in an unfinished state, the walls and windows were draped for the purpose of dispelling the rusticity of things as much as possible. The sides were hung with "Turkey red" and calico, the windows festooned, &c. I can assure you we had a regular jollification, and reminded me very much of a western frolic. The Ladies, all but two, were married. Among the intellectual amusements was "fox and geese." This play was introduced as a kind of pastime till the music arrived. We were dismissed at two in the morning. Champagne was our only drink, and of this we had a great abundance, only ten dollars a bottle, and I presume we drank five or six dozen during the eve.

Last eve I attended another Champagne party, and have an other engagement for this eve. Next Monday eve we warm our new house. Mr. Smith, upon the completion of his building where we have taken offices, gives a house warming, and from present appearances it will be a fine affair. Understand this is not the party to which you were invited. Mr Smith will have ten ladies and among them the sweet widow, so I shall have another fine flirtation, but I must desist or you will think me in love with this charming person. Well, we Californians are a very strange people any way. We live upon the very best of every thing and drink nothing but champagne wine at parties. You may think I am getting fond of this dissipation and so I will inform you, that although I am very fond of good wine, yet I am not very fond of the "fandango." Still I go as a matter of business, in order to make acquaintances, and this is the one great reason I ever attend.

John McCrackan

Letter to his sister Lottie
27 April 1850

Since my last letter, my dear Sister, I have been forced into quite a round of dissipations, private balls, house warmings, champagne frolics, &c &c &c. I really hope next Monday night will end the season. On that eve "Gothic Hall" will be most brilliantly lighted and the sound of revelry will be heard from within its walls. Some twenty five Ladies will be present, among whom are included the fascinating widow and Mrs. Brooks—this is if she can think of any way to dispose of little Willey for the eve. These children—what a plague they are. It has been proposed to put him in a bag and carry him on her arm, the principal objections however seem insurmountable. However I hope she will find out some practicable method of accomplishing it, as I should like so much to have her go, and she will enjoy it above all things. I doubt not she will keep a sharp eye upon me, and thus defeat my flirting with "Mrs. Gen. Bacon," (viz.) the widow.

I should like if I had time to give you an account of my many adventures and the funny things constantly happening but they are so numerous and my time as limited I can give but few a place in my journal. . . .

We had a most delightful excursion last Monday to a place called "Angel Island." We started about five o'clock to attend court at the Mission of San Raphael. This mission is on the opposite side of the Bay from our city, about twenty five miles distant, and is approached by a creek on the west, which creek however cannot [be] navigated except at high water. There being no wind when we left the ship we used the oars, but as it was very difficult to contend with the tide or current (which runs at the rate of seven and [a] half knots in the Bay), we concluded to make Angel Island and wait for a wind, and so we waited patiently till after ten o'clock, the hour when we were to be at the mission, and finding we could not reach there, we contented ourselves and commenced an exploration of the Island.

This Island may be three miles in circumference perhaps, no more. Its banks are bold and meet the water very abruptly. At a few steps you gain the broad beautiful table land above, which is a perfect flower bed, and of the most delicate kind, and at every step you must trample three pure blossoms to the ground. I never have looked upon a sight so truly gorgeous, as far as the eye could reach you see this bright array with flowers of every different hue and kind and the air really heavy with their perfume, unpleasantly sweet. There are a great many beautiful groves and some quite thick and woody. We saw the timid elk and deer fly before us as [we] roamed about the Island, although I have since learned most have been killed the last winter, as it formerly contained hundreds. The rabbits and the hares are also very abundant here, and a host of all kinds of game.

We soon obtained shelter in a sweet little grove, where stretched upon our back we rested our weary selves, and looked upon the birds as they, like us, sought protection from the sun. We were soon joined by a party that proved to be a company from H. B. M. Yacht *Wanderer,* Capt. Boyd of Liverpool. I have before spoken, I think, of meeting Capt. Boyd, if not mention it, I will relate the circumstances. It seems this party had landed some time since, shot a deer and were about returning to their small boat when upon seeing us they approached. We were very glad to meet them, particularly as they were well provided with the most comforting brandy and some fine bread and ham. They joined us and we had a very satisfactory breakfast.

And as I looked upon our little group, I could not but wish you each had an eye upon our jovial party. Here we were in this beautiful garden protected from the sun and so free and happy, with a plenty of good things before us, the poor deer at a few paces with the fatal gun resting upon its flank and resting beside were two fine dogs. Poor fellows, they were quite fagged out with their exertions, so unaccustomed of late to the hunt. After a half hour passed in this delightful social intercourse we took to our boats. A fine breeze had in the meantime sprung up and coming directly from our quarter as we were seated in our boats heading for the Fleet. I did not leave this beautiful spot without collecting a small basket full of these beautiful flowers to present Mrs. Brooks, who was quite crazy to go there. Consequently we concluded upon a picnic immediately. It has not yet come off, and indeed I know not when it will. I promise to give you full particulars and perhaps even extend an invitation for you to accompany us. I shall press some of these [flowers] and you shall look upon these fair inhabitants of Angel Island. . . .

I send my miniature, some think it good. I have been very much disposed to send one taken in my hat, which is white and really makes a beautiful contrast in the picture. Still I shall reserve this and you may see it one of these days. I hope mother's is taken large like this one I send. I so dislike small ones. You see me here just as I dress and look every day. The eyes are not very perfect, although I like it better the more I see it, and I think you will do the same. I think I hear mother say, "Why don't he have his hair cut off? He would look so much better." Mother dear, it is expensive here to visit the barber. You pay fifty cents for a shave and one dollar for hair cutting, consequently I cut my own hair and earn my own dollar.

John McCrackan

Letter to his sister Mary
12 May 1850

I still continue at the "French House," which still continues a very quiet, pleasant place. My breakfast usually consists of a most delightful fish (I think the most delicious I ever ate), very sweet and nice, and a cutlet, venison, roast beef, ragout or what else I may fancy. After which pudding which is served with brandy. This dish is brought you after being lighted, it will generally burn three minutes, giving the pudding a most delightful heat and flavor. After this we eat a brandy peach, or cherrys, after that coffee and cigars. Of course we have a delightful sociable dinner, Mr. Sheppard being my friend and companion. We have here the most delicious sweetmeats and preserves from the East Indies, the Islands and from Peru and Chile, as well as from France, from which place we also get preserved vegetables of all kinds.

John McCrackan

Letter to his mother
24 May 1850

My partner Mr. Sheppard has been absent at the Mission of San Raphael, reveling in the luxuries of fresh eggs, milk, strawberrys and cream, &c &c. This very beautiful "Mission Valley" abounds with everything good to eat and pleasant and attractive to the eye. My turn comes next to visit this fairy region, and I intend to make a good stay of it when I get over there. Oh! Mother I feel sometimes if I only had you and the girls out here, I should be content to live in some of these beautiful spots all my days. . . .

I feel as if I had grown very old since we parted, that is in one sense, for I should be sorry to think I had been affected in spirit or feelings. My outward looks I do not care the same about, but I really have seen so much of men and life. I am quite satisfied. My experience has taught me to value more highly than otherwise I possibly could the value of women's society, its beneficial influence, the joys of domestic life if one should make a judicious selection in a partner, and the sacred nature of obligations incumbent thereon. Yes! my mother, this California life will make married men of many a Benedict.

But there is one influence to guard against and battle, and this is, the liability of contracting a roving disposition. If these habits once become fastened upon one, they will influence the whole life of such a one. In visiting distant countries the desire for novelty is never fully satisfied. It will be appeased from time to time, and then only by enjoyment, when the mind will soon tire, and we must seek gratification elsewhere, and perhaps in a distant part of the globe. There is no feeling I presume so difficult to control if it once gains the mastery, and none more fatal to all hopes of ever enjoying the sweets of domestic life, and few, very few of those who have come to California will have escaped these feelings, while very many will continue its slaves through life. I must confess, I have had a few alarming symptoms but my allegiance to my dear family still continues unshaken while this separation but gives me a keener appreciation of the delights of home.

John McCrackan

Letter to his sister Lottie
30 May 1850

How often do I think of the strange chance that places me in this distant region, far away from my home and those most near and dear to me. I wonder sometimes at my ever entertaining the idea for a moment of leaving you, and it is only by following, by recalling, the thoughts that besieged my poor brain, by the hopes that inspired my breast, of purchasing, by an absence of a few months, the means of gratifying more fully the feelings of my heart, of expressing in many delightful ways the love I bear you. And time but strengthens my belief that it is good for me to be here, and that before many months I shall be able to return to you, my end and object having been attained, prepared to live with you or near you during the remainder of our short pilgrimage here.

I am quite happy here, my dear Lottie, almost too much so, considering what far greater happiness I might enjoy in my far off home. One great thing I fear, which is that I may become so interested in California as to wish to live here always. Certain I am, if you were only out here, I would care but little about revisiting the States, at least for some years. There is a charm connected with a life in California, that every day becomes more and more binding in proportion as our conveniences and refinements increase. You at home (I mean people generally) know very little of us here.

We have already very good society, which is daily added to by arrivals from the States of those who will make this beautiful country their home. People come here now with very different ideas than formerly (a year ago). We have a population here now of two hundred thousand souls. Schools have been established, and such a host of children you would be amazed, did you know how many we have here. And look at the inducements for a man with a family. He can remove here and settle upon a tract of land 160 acres, build him a log house, and go to farming in the most delightful climate, and cultivate the most generous soil upon the face of the earth. He pays nothing for his land, 'till the U.S. agent comes along, when he pays him one hundred and sixty dollars for his 160 acres—and this may not be in years, and then he receives a clear and undoubted title to a property which then may be worth twenty thousand dollars.

Beside this, from his farm he can realize enough money in one year to build him a comfortable house and purchase as many heads of cattle as he wishes. He can live upon the best beef (wild), and have all the luxuries of a western prairie, beside his farm or county seat, which in three years will vie with a nobleman's estate in Yorkshire. "But," you will say, "Everyone could not enjoy such advantage," and yet I might say there are enough beautiful situations between Oregon and San Blas to give one to every family in California.

I have one already chose, directly acrost the bay in the Mission of "San Raphael." Mr. Sheppard and self have selected each our spot, near each other of course. In one year's time we shall have a steam ferry to take us over there. We shall build a nice home, doing our business in the City and returning to our homes and *family* at night, as the Long Island merchants do who conduct their business in New York City. We shall have the best horses to ride. . . .

The air [is] mild and balmy, for they have eternal summer here in this beautiful Mission Valley. When I get my Caze [casa] finished, I shall send on for you all, and a letter of attorney for you to woo some kindred spirit in your brother's name, to become his wife and preside over his home, and care for the Mother and sister spirits which shall make that home his "heaven."

How like you the commission, dear Lottie? Think you it would be a difficult task, tell me who would you select? Not _____ not _____ not _____, I am sure. I will trust you, for I know you would chose the right one. So dear Lottie, you have my permission to offer my hand and heart, if you can find one to trust with it. If not, keep it yourself till I shall dispose of it myself. I am in earnest, I assure you.

Epilogue

During the early 1850s the initial wave of gold fever crested and gradually declined. Panning for gold had always been an arduous endeavor, but in the early years it really was possible for someone with rudimentary tools and only a little skill to extract a fortune in a few months' time. As the placers were stripped the character of mining changed. Individual effort was for the most part superseded by large mining corporations that hired employees for a monthly salary of one hundred dollars. Panning by hand was replaced by hydraulic mining, which used a stream of water under intense pressure to loosen gravel, which was then sluiced for precious metals.[1]

A corresponding change took place in San Francisco as more and more of the population began to look on their residency as a long-term proposition. Once their get rich quick plans were abandoned, San Franciscans began to demand improvements in the civic environment and they were willing to pay for those improvements as a necessary investment in their ultimate entrepreneurial success. Besides better pavement, wharves, water supply, street lighting, and fire protection, business owners demanded an end to the government corruption that steadily drained the public coffers and allowed a few elected officials to live in ornate mansions while the majority of the populace floundered ankle-deep through dark muddy streets. When their demands went unheeded, committees of vigilance were formed in 1851 and again in 1856.[2] It is significant to note that the committees were composed primarily of business owners who objected not to the rampant gambling, prostitution, and general immorality in San Francisco but to the political corruption and public violence that were exerting such a negative impact on commercial activity.

Of the people whose correspondence appears in this volume, little is known of their lives beyond the manuscript collections in the possession of The Bancroft Library. William Smith Jewett, having spent twenty years working as a portrait painter, left San Francisco on 28 September 1869 and returned to New York. In October of 1870 he married rather late in life, and died three years later on 3 December 1873 in Springfield, Massachusetts.

Alfred and Margaret DeWitt continued to live in San Francisco until 1867, though they made several trips home to visit their families in New York. During one trip Margaret stayed (apparently for economic reasons) while Alfred returned to California. By reading between the lines of Margaret's voluminous correspondence it becomes clear that Alfred was something less than a doting husband, or at least he had difficulty expressing his love for his wife if such expression interfered with his business concerns. In a letter to his brother dated 28 April 1853, Alfred describes the separation from his wife with all the tenderness of a corporate quarterly report:

> I have now lived bachelor nearly three months and find that it is not exactly the thing in this country. I have to depend on the restaurants for my feed, which does not suit my palate as well as bread and butter in my own house. My room is in the store and I strive to make myself contented as possible, but it causes rather hard[ship] after enjoying the comforts of a house. . . .
>
> From Maggie's letters I do not think she is contented to remain away from me and I find but little economy to live separate. I will therefore write her, that if her brother Jonathan will bring her out I will pay his expenses, and it will be of some advantage in a business view. . . .

In the same letter DeWitt relates a macabre tale that says much about the persistence of family ties and reveals the prevailing attitude toward San Francisco which, however "civilized" it might have become, was still not "home":

> I have had a sad duty to perform this week. You will probably recollect hearing me speak of young "Creighton" who died here nearly 3 years ago. While I was in Philadelphia his Father requested me to have the remains sent home. They were buried in a metal coffin filled with whiskey. Last Monday it was disinterred and the coffin opened. We found the body in an excellent state of preservation and it appeared very natural. It

was in such good condition that the undertaker washed it off and covered it with clean clothes, placed it in a new coffin with a lead one inside and put in some 20 gal[lons] alcohol. I have shipped it to Philadelphia by ship *Jacob Bell.* I have no doubt but that the remains will reach Phila. in such good preservation that there will be no objection to opening the coffin if his friends should desire to do so.

The DeWitts make their last appearance in a letter written by Alfred to his brother George. Alfred and Margaret had returned to New York, evidently to remain there permanently. During her years in San Francisco Margaret sent dozens of wistful letters from the crowded little cottage where she spent her days pouring out her heart in correspondence with her in-laws and keeping house for the ever-expanding bachelor staff of the DeWitt & Harrison store. Her lot did not improve substantially with her return to New York. On 2 August 1867, Alfred wrote, "I fear Maggie will feel lonesome at home all day with none but the servants to speak to."

John McCrackan's correspondence closes on 30 December 1853 with a letter written to his family back in New Haven, Connecticut. He was about to return to them, and with characteristic irony began the letter with the observation,

> [This piece of stationery] will be the last full sheet in all probability I shall write to complete a correspondence of nearly five long years standing, besides a singular fact presses itself upon me, viz., that this is the last sheet of the entire ream or two reams of paper I brought with me for family letters. I have made several efforts to replenish my stock but have not been able to obtain any like it.

It is not clear whether McCrackan intended to return to San Francisco, but rather than sell his horse Charley he left the animal in the care of "my friend Mr. Wirtz." He signed off with a typical rhetorical flourish:

> When this is received I shall probably be on my way down the Pacific coast under the general influence of a tropical climate while you are congregated about a fire. Heaven bless you all, dear ones . . . and upon the committing [of] myself to a merciful "God" and your prayers I fear nothing but hope to enjoy health and be preserved to realize more than I merit or deserve. Adieu dear ones.

It is clear from a close analysis of the gold rush correspondence that the character of San Francisco during 1849 and 1850 was unique—and, what is more, it was *viewed* as being unique by the many people drawn there by the hope of riches. An "instant city" that sprang up out of nowhere, it presented during its first year a confused jumble of civilized madness where men suddenly dropped dead in muddy streets—streets that were, nonetheless, accurately surveyed and laid out in a highly regular geometric grid. San Francisco was an odd Potemkin village of canvas-walled pleasure palaces filled with schoolboys turned tycoon and university professors waiting tables. The letters and diaries are filled with stories of disillusionment and rueful descriptions of the wide gap between perception and reality. And yet for every Argonaut who gave up in disgust and went home there are ten who clung to the dream and stayed on.

One reason that so many stayed in San Francisco, particularly during the first year of the gold rush, was that in the city (unlike in the gold placers) the Argonauts did not expect to become rich overnight. They hoped for a steady increase in their fortunes, an increase that required diligence over an extended period of time. During 1849 and 1850 the most prominent features of the economic landscape were the wild swings in the value of goods and property. About the only law in force in San Francisco was the law of supply and demand, and those with the savvy and nerves to play the game could become huge winners. If one could stave off creditors and hold on to a piece of land just until a wharf was built or a street was laid, the value of the property might quadruple. If an allotment of boots was kept off the market until the supply ran low, one could realize a pretty profit—unless a ship arrived in the meantime carrying a cargo of newer, more fashionable footwear.

Despite the occasional notes of despair, letters from gold rush San Francisco are for the most part very upbeat and optimistic, but the reader should be cautious in assuming that the experience was therefore one long enjoyable adventure. The letters are most frequently addressed to mothers, wives, and family members who would only have fretted had they known the truth. In collections with an extended run of letters the reader almost always encounters a case in which the correspondent wrote a letter while depressed and later came to regret the indiscretion, given the long lag time between the sending and the receipt of mail. Interpreting gold rush narratives is therefore largely an exercise in reading between the lines.

But neither should we assume that San Francisco was a hellhole of undiluted misery. In the early days, when everything was raw and new, when personal belongings could be left unguarded and unmolested, when the future still glittered on the horizon, before the naughtiness turned to sordid violence, before the political corruption and the committees of vigilance, before the power struggles and the bankruptcies and suicides, San Francisco was the world's wildest celebration of free enterprise and individual effort and just about everyone was invited.

For Americans, coming to California—"seeing the Elephant"—was an achievable adventure, offering all the exotic allure of foreign travel without leaving the relative security of American ships or well-worn land routes. The dangers were real and thousands died in the trying, but for many men and women their sojourn on the Pacific would be the one great adventure of their lives. They captured that adventure, and made it real for others, by writing it all down.

Notes

Introduction

1. Morgan, *A Shovel of Stars,* 156.
2. Hurtado, "When Strangers Met," 124.
3. Lydon, *Chinese Gold,* 16–17.
4. Quoted in Bolton, *Spanish Exploration,* 91–92.
5. Lydon, *Chinese Gold,* 18.
6. White, *"It's Your Misfortune,"* 33.
7. Morgan, *A Shovel of Stars,* 157.
8. McGloin, *San Francisco,* 16.
9. White, *"It's Your Misfortune,"* 41.
10. Coburn, *Letters of Gold,* 8–9.
11. Coburn, *Letters of Gold,* 9.
12. Coburn, *Letters of Gold,* 11.
13. Coburn, *Letters of Gold,* 14.
14. Quoted in Lotchin, *San Francisco, 1846–1856,* xxxv.
15. Bancroft, *History of California,* 238.
16. Coburn, *Letters of Gold,* 20.
17. Morgan, *A Shovel of Stars,* 160.
18. Lienhard, *Pioneer at Sutter's Fort,* quoted in Morgan, *A Shovel of Stars,* 165.
19. Quoted in White, *"It's Your Misfortune,"* 192.

1. First Impressions

1. White, *"It's Your Misfortune,"* 206.
2. White, *"It's Your Misfortune,"* 202.
3. Bancroft, *History of California,* 148.

4. Bancroft, *History of California,* 149.

5. Coburn, *Letters of Gold,* 23.

6. Bancroft, *History of California,* 148.

7. Coburn, *Letters of Gold,* 24.

8. Coburn, *Letters of Gold,* 24.

2. The Ties that Bind

1. Holliday, *The World Rushed In,* 333.

2. Buss, "A Feminist Revision," 86–103.

3. Georgi-Findlay, *Frontier of Women's Writing,* 25.

4. Coburn, *Letters of Gold,* 45.

5. Coburn, *Letters of Gold,* 45.

6. Coburn, *Letters of Gold,* 45.

7. Coburn, *Letters of Gold,* 45.

8. Coburn, *Letters of Gold,* 49.

9. Coburn, *Letters of Gold,* 112–13.

10. Salley, *History of California Post Offices,* ii.

3. O, Don't You Cry for Me

1. Blair, "'Doctor Gets Some Practice,'" 55.

2. Blair, "'Doctor Gets Some Practice,'" 56.

3. Blair, "'Doctor Gets Some Practice,'" 56.

4. Lotchin, *San Francisco, 1846–1856,* 184.

5. Lotchin, *San Francisco, 1846–1856,* 184.

6. Lotchin, *San Francisco, 1846–1856,* 185.

7. Courtwright, *Violent Land,* 69.

4. Madmen, Drunkards, Murderers, and Whores

1. Slotkin, *Regeneration through Violence,* 441.

2. McKanna, *Homicide, Race, and Justice,* 17.

3. Courtwright, "Violence in America," 40.

4. Courtwright, *Violent Land,* 3.

5. Courtwright, "Violence in America," 40.

6. Courtwright, *Violent Land,* 70.

7. Early, *The Raven's Return,* 11.

8. Kushner, *Self-destruction,* 163–64.

9. Lotchin, *San Francisco, 1846–1856,* 190.

10. Bancroft, *History of California,* 172–82.

11. White, *"It's Your Misfortune,"* 304.

12. Barnhart, *The Fair but Frail,* 43.

13. Hirata, "Free, Indentured, Enslaved," 406–7.

14. Barnhart, *The Fair but Frail*, 16.

15. Barnhart, *The Fair but Frail*, 24.

16. Barnhart, *The Fair but Frail*, 40–44.

17. Hirata, "Free, Indentured, Enslaved," 404–5.

18. Tong, *Unsubmissive Women*, 4.

19. Tong, *Unsubmissive Women*, 7.

20. Hirata, "Free, Indentured, Enslaved," 406.

21. White-Parks, "Beyond the Stereotypes," 265.

22. Tong, *Unsubmissive Women*, 3.

23. Quoted in McGloin, *San Francisco*, 51.

5. The Phoenix Rises

1. Bancroft, *History of California*, 196.

2. Barth, *Instant Cities*, 111.

3. Lotchin, *San Francisco, 1846–1856*, 165.

4. Bancroft, *History of California*, 198.

5. Bancroft, *History of California*, 198.

6. Bancroft, *History of California*, 209.

7. Schliemann, *First Visit to America*, 64.

8. Lotchin, *San Francisco, 1846–1856*, 61–62.

9. Lotchin, *San Francisco, 1846–1856*, 69.

6. Men without Women

1. White, *"It's Your Misfortune,"* 203–4.

2. Conlin, *Bacon, Beans, and Galantines*, 113.

3. Courtwright, *Violent Land*, 68.

4. Barth, *Instant Cities*, 175.

5. Padilla, "'*Yo Sola Aprendi*,'" 191.

6. Lotchin, *San Francisco, 1846–1856*, 104.

7. Bancroft, *History of California*, 228.

8. Foucault, *History of Sexuality*, 101.

9. Lowry, *Story the Soldiers Wouldn't Tell*, 117.

10. For cowboys, see Westermeier, "The Cowboy and Sex," 85–105. For Marines, see Burg, *An American Seafarer*. For Civil War soldiers, see Lowry, *Story Soldiers Wouldn't Tell*, 109–18. For fur trappers, see Porter, *Scotsman in Buckskin*. For cross-dressing women, see Schlatter, "Drag's a Life," 334–48.

11. For Indians, see Williams, *Spirit and the Flesh;* and Roscoe, *The Zuni Man-Woman*. For Mormons, see Quinn, *Same-sex Dynamics*.

12. Moynihan, Armitage, and Dichamp, *So Much to be Done*, xv.

7. The Course of Empire

1. Holliday, *The World Rushed In*, 32.
2. Saunders, "California Legal History," 489.
3. Quoted in Hansen, *Search for Authority*, 72.
4. The English-Spanish edition is in The Bancroft Library (xF865.M375).
5. Quoted in Hansen, *Search for Authority*, 85.
6. Hansen, *Search for Authority*, 114.
7. Hansen, *Search for Authority*, 89–90.
8. Hansen, *Search for Authority*, 94.
9. Hansen, *Search for Authority*, 96.
10. Lotchin, *San Francisco, 1846–1856*, 137–39.
11. Greer, *Colonel Jack Hays*, 262–63.
12. Lotchin, *San Francisco, 1846–1856*, 108.
13. Tsai, "Chinese Immigration," 112.
14. Lydon, *Chinese Gold*, 21.
15. Lydon, *Chinese Gold*, 4.
16. McGloin, *San Francisco*, 40.
17. Coburn, *Letters of Gold*, 21.

8. A Home in the West

1. Lotchin, *San Francisco, 1846–1856*, 30.
2. Lotchin, *San Francisco, 1846–1856*, 103.
3. Coburn, *Letters of Gold*, 22.
4. Quoted in Gauld, *A History of Hypnotism*, 180.
5. Gauld, *History of Hypnotism*, 288.

Epilogue

1. Rohrbough, *Days of Gold*, 202–3.
2. Lotchin, *San Francisco, 1846–1856*, 192–200.

Bibliography

Manuscript Sources

All manuscripts are in the collection of The Bancroft Library,
University of California, Berkeley.

Anonymous. *Journal of a Voyage from New Bedford to San Francisco, Upper California: 1849 Apr. 1–Sept. 27.* BANC MSS 77/155 c.

Austin, Edward. *Edward Austin Letters: ALS, 1849–1851.* BANC MSS C-B 621.

Baker, Isaac W. *Isaac W. Baker Journals: Ms. 1849, Aug. 13–1852, Nov.* BANC MSS C-F 53.

Barnes, James S. *James S. Barnes Letters to His Family: 1849 Oct.–1857 Sept.* BANC MSS C-B 941.

Beck, Robert. *Robert Beck Diary: Ms. 1849 Feb. 26–1850 Nov. 24.* BANC MSS C-F 84.

Biggs, Abel R. *Journal of a Gold Rush Voyage from New York to San Francisco on the Barque Keoka, James McGuire, Master: 26 Jan.–11 Oct. 1849.* BANC MSS 99/136 cz.

Booth, Anne Willson. *Journal of a Voyage from Baltimore to San Francisco on Ship Andalusia, F. W. Willson, Master.* BANC MSS C-F 197.

Booth, Lucius Anson. *Letter to Newton Booth: San Francisco: ALS, 1849 July 16* [in *California Miscellany: Additions*]. BANC MSS 73/122 c:158.

Brooke, T. Warwick. *Letters to Mr. and Mrs. Gordon Estes, 1848–1872.* BANC MSS 79/109 c.

Brown, William G. *Letters to His Wife, 1848–1849.* BANC MSS C-B 485.

Browne, J. Ross. *J. Ross (John Ross) Browne Papers, ca. 1840–1875.* BANC MSS 78/163 c.

Callbreath, John C. *John C. Callbreath Letters, 1849–1899.* BANC MSS 79/93 c.

Deane, Benjamin H. *Benjamin H. Deane Journal: Ms. 1849–1851.* BANC MSS C-F 106.

DeWitt Family Papers [ca. 1848–1867]. BANC MSS 73/163 c.

Dulany, Charles F. *Dulany Family Correspondence, 1849–1850.* BANC MSS
C-B 727.

Garter, Ephraim. *Ephraim Garter Letter to Parents: San Francisco, Calif.:
ALS, 1850 Jan. 13.* BANC MSS C-B 547:152.

Ginnes, George. *Letter* [in *California Gold Rush Letters, 1848–1859*]. BANC
MSS C-B 547:117.

Graves, William. *William Graves Papers, 1849–1911.* BANC MSS 77/148 c.

Griswold, Josiah. *Letter* [in *Benjamin S. Hill Correspondence, 1849–1853*].
BANC MSS C-B 655:2.

Hall, Elbridge Gerry. *Elbridge Gerry Hall Letters to His Wife, Martha Ann
Clark Hill, 1847–1861: and Family Papers.* BANC MSS 68/46 c.

Howard, Benjamin C. *Benjamin C. Howard Letters to His Parents in
Salem, Mass.: ALS, 1849 Nov. 25–1852 June 9.* BANC MSS 89/204 c.

Howard, Eugene. *Letter to Franklin Miller: San Francisco: ALS, 1849 Oct.
2.* BANC MSS 73/122 C:190.

Hyde, C. C. *C. C. Hyde Letter to His Brother: San Francisco: ALS, 1849 Sept.
22.* BANC MSS 73/122 c.

Jewett, William Smith. *William S. Jewett Letters, 1849–1871.* BANC MSS C-B
434.

Lammot [La Motte] Family Papers, 1849–1872. BANC MSS C-B 450.

Lewis, Samuel C. *Samuel C. Lewis Journal, 1849 Feb.–1850 Apr.* (bulk),
1849–1878 (inclusive). BANC MSS 77/154 c.

Locke, Jonathan F. *Jonathan Frost Locke Papers, 1825–1856.* BANC MSS C-B
608.

Luyster, J. G. W. *J. G. W. Luyster Letter: San Francisco, Calif., to His
Mother, ALS, 1850 June 18.* BANC MSS 97/1 c.

McCrackan, John. *John McCrackan Letters to His Family: and Biographi-
cal Information, 1849–1853.* BANC MSS C-B 444.

Macondray & Company. *Records of Macondray and Company, San Francisco, Calif., 1849–1852.* BANC MSS 83/142 c.

May, George. *Letter* [in *Joseph S. Curtis Papers Relating to a Gold Rush
Venture, 1849–1854*]. BANC MSS C-B 572.

Miller, Christian. *Christian Miller Letters to His Family, 1849–1867.* BANC
MSS 74/194 c.

Mitchell, John D. *Letters* [in *California Gold Rush Letters, 1848–1859*]. BANC
MSS 547:120.

Murray, Henry E. *Letters by or Relating to Henry E. Murray and His
Brother, F. S. Murray: ALS, 1849 Nov. 13–1850 Nov. 9.* BANC MSS 89/214 c.

Osgood, J. K. *J. K. Osgood Letters to George Strang: Two Letters: San Francisco: ALS, 1849 Aug. 23 and 1850 June 10–20.* BANC MSS C-B 547.

Prince, William Robert. *William Robert Prince Papers, 1849–1851.* BANC MSS
83/76 c.

Randall, Charles H. *Charles Henry Randall Letters to His Parents, 1849 Mar.–1859 Feb.* BANC MSS 68/40 c.

Reed, William F. *William F. Reed Journal: ms, 1849 Feb. 8–1853 Apr. 3.* BANC MSS C-F 214.

Reid, Thomas. *Thomas Reid Diary: ms., 1849 Feb.–Oct..* BANC MSS C-F 146.

Rundle, John T. *John T. Rundle Papers, 1849–1864.* BANC MSS C-B 854.

Stoddard, Caroline. *Journal from the Voyage of the Clipper Ship Mandarin from New York to San Francisco and Canton, 1850–1851.* BANC MSS 96/98 cz.

Tolman, John. *John Tolman Journal of Voyage Around the Horn: Ams., 1849 Mar. 1–Sept. 9.* BANC MSS 82/9 c.

Towne, William J. *William J. Towne Diary, 1849 Jan. 23–July 23.* BANC MSS 91/24 c.

Tuttle, Charles A. *Charles Albion Tuttle Correspondence with His Wife and Miscellaneous Papers, 1849–1888.* BANC MSS C-B 427.

Upton, E. A. *E. A. Upton Diaries, 1849 Sept. 8–1850 Sept. 26.* BANC MSS 78/48 c.

West, Augustus. *Letters* [in the *DeWitt Family Papers*]. BANC MSS 73/163 c.

Secondary Sources

Bancroft, Hubert Howe. *History of California.* Vol. 5. San Raphael CA: Bancroft Press, 1990.

Barnhart, Jacqueline Baker. *The Fair but Frail: Prostitution in San Francisco, 1849–1900.* Reno: University of Nevada Press, 1986.

Barth, Gunther. *Instant Cities: Urbanization and the Rise of San Francisco and Denver.* New York: Oxford University Press, 1975.

Blair, Roger P. "'The Doctor Gets Some Practice': Cholera and Medicine on the Overland Trails." *Journal of the West* 34 (January 1997), pp. 54–66.

Bolton, Herbert Eugene. *Spanish Exploration in the Southwest, 1542–1706.* New York: Scribner's, 1916.

Burg, B. R. *An American Seafarer in the Age of Sail: The Erotic Diaries of Philip C. Van Buskirk, 1851–1870.* New Haven: Yale University Press, 1994.

Buss, Helen M. "A Feminist Revision of New Historicism to Give Fuller Readings of Women's Private Writing." In *Inscribing the Daily: Critical Essays on Women's Diaries,* edited by Suzanne L. Bunkers and Cynthia A. Huff, pp. 86–103. Amherst: University of Massachusetts Press, 1996.

Butler, Anne M. *Daughters of Joy, Sisters of Misery: Prostitutes in the American West, 1865–90.* Urbana: University of Illinois Press, 1985.

Coburn, Jesse L. *Letters of Gold: California Postal History Through 1869.* Canton OH: U.S. Philatelic Classics Society; New York: Philatelic Foundation, 1984.

Conlin, Joseph Robert. *Bacon, Beans, and Galantines: Food and Foodways on the Western Mining Frontier.* Reno: University of Nevada Press, 1987.

Coulter, Harris L. *Divided Legacy: The Conflict between Homoeopathy and* the *American Medical Association*. Vol. 3, *Science and Ethics in American Medicine, 1800–1914*. 2d ed. Richmond CA: North Atlantic Books, 1982.

Courtwright, David T. "Violence in America: What Human Nature and the California Gold Rush Tell Us about Crime in the Inner City." *American Heritage* 47 (September 1997), pp. 36–51.

———. *Violent Land: Single Men and Social Disorder from the Frontier to the Inner City*. Cambridge MA: Harvard University Press, 1996.

Early, Emmett. *The Raven's Return: The Influence of Psychological Trauma on Individuals and Culture*. Wilmette IL: Chiron Publications, 1993.

Foucault, Michel. *The History of Sexuality*. Vol. 1, *An Introduction*. New York: Vintage Books, 1990.

Gauld, Alan. *A History of Hypnotism*. Cambridge: Cambridge University Press, 1992.

Georgi-Findlay, Brigitte. *The Frontiers of Women's Writing: Women's Narratives and the Rhetoric of Westward Expansion*. Tucson: University of Arizona Press, 1996.

Greer, James Kimmins. *Colonel Jack Hays: Texas Frontier Leader and California Builder*. Waco TX: W. M. Morrison, 1973.

Guinn, J. M. "Early Postal Service of California." In *Annual Publication of the Historical Society of Southern California, and Pioneer Register*, pp. 18–26. Los Angeles: Historical Society of Southern California, 1897.

Hansen, Woodrow James. *The Search for Authority in California*. Oakland CA: Biobooks, 1960.

Harlow, Neal. *California Conquered: War and Peace on the Pacific, 1846–1850*. Berkeley: University of California Press, 1982.

Hirata, Lucie Cheng. "Free, Indentured, Enslaved: Chinese Prostitutes in Nineteenth-Century America." In *Labor Immigration under Capitalism: Asian Workers in the United States before World War II*, edited by Lucie Cheng Hirata and Edna Bonacich, pp. 402–34. Berkeley: University of California Press, 1984.

Holliday, J. S. *The World Rushed In: The California Gold Rush Experience*. New York: Simon and Schuster, 1981.

Hurtado, Albert L. "When Strangers Met: Sex and Gender on Three Frontiers." In *Writing the Range: Race, Class, and Culture in the Women's West*, edited by Elizabeth Jameson and Susan Armitage, pp. 122–42. Norman: University of Oklahoma Press, 1997.

Kushner, Howard I. *Self-Destruction in the Promised Land: A Psychocultural Biology of American Suicide*. New Brunswick NJ: Rutgers University Press, 1989.

Leo-Wolf, William. *Remarks on the Abracadabra of the Nineteenth Century; or On Dr. Samuel Hahnemann's Homoeopathic Medicine*. New York: Carey, Lea and Blanchard, 1835.

Lotchin, Roger W. *San Francisco, 1846–1856: From Hamlet to City.* Urbana: University of Illinois Press, 1997.

Lowry, Thomas P. *The Story the Soldiers Wouldn't Tell: Sex in the Civil War.* Mechanicsburg PA: Stackpole Books, 1994.

Lydon, Sandy. *Chinese Gold: The Chinese in the Monterey Bay Region.* Capitola CA: Capitola Book Company, 1985.

McGloin, John B. *San Francisco: The Story of a City.* San Rafael CA: Presidio Press, 1978.

McKanna, Clare V. *Homicide, Race, and Justice in the American West, 1880–1920.* Tucson: University of Arizona Press, 1997.

Morgan, Ted. *A Shovel of Stars: The Making of the American West, 1800 to the Present.* New York: Simon and Schuster, 1995.

Moynihan, Ruth B., Susan Armitage, and Christiane Fischer Dichamp, eds. *So Much to be Done: Women Settlers on the Mining and Ranching Frontier.* Lincoln: University of Nebraska Press, 1990.

Padilla, Genaro. "'*Yo Sola Aprendi*': Mexican Women's Personal Narratives from Nineteenth-Century California." In *Writing the Range: Race, Class, and Culture in the Women's West,* edited by Elizabeth Jameson and Susan Armitage, pp. 188–201. Norman: University of Oklahoma Press, 1997.

Porter, Mae Reed. *Scotsman in Buckskin: Sir William Drummond Stewart and the Rocky Mountain Fur Trade.* New York: Hastings House, 1963.

Quinn, D. Michael. *Same-Sex Dynamics among Nineteenth-Century Americans: A Mormon Example.* Urbana: University of Illinois Press, 1996.

Rohrbough, Malcolm J. *Days of Gold: The California Gold Rush and the American Nation.* Berkeley: University of California Press, 1997.

Roscoe, Will. *The Zuni Man-Woman.* Albuquerque: University of New Mexico Press, 1991.

Salley, Harold E. *History of California Post Offices, 1849–1976.* La Mesa CA: Postal History Associates, 1977.

Saunders, Myra K. "California Legal History: The Legal System under the United States Military Government, 1846–1849." *Law Library Journal* 88 (1996), pp. 488–522.

Schlatter, Evelyn A. "Drag's a Life: Women, Gender, and Cross-dressing in the Nineteenth-Century West." In *Writing the Range: Race, Class, and Culture in the Women's West,* edited by Elizabeth Jameson and Susan Armitage, pp. 334–48. Norman: University of Oklahoma Press, 1997.

Schliemann, Heinrich. *Schliemann's First Visit to America, 1850–1851.* Cambridge MA: Harvard University Press, 1942.

Slotkin, Richard. *Regeneration through Violence: The Mythology of the American Frontier, 1600–1860.* New York: HarperPerennial, 1996.

Tong, Benson. *Unsubmissive Women: Chinese Prostitutes in Nineteenth-century San Francisco.* Norman: University of Oklahoma Press, 1994.

Tsai, Shih-shan Henry. "Chinese Immigration, 1848–1882." In *Peoples of Color in the American West*, edited by Sucheng Chan et al., pp. 110–16. Lexington MA: D. C. Heath, 1994.

Westermeier, Clifford. "The Cowboy and Sex." In *The Cowboy: Six-Shooters, Songs, and Sex*, edited by Charles W. Harris and Buck Rainey. Norman: University of Oklahoma Press, 1996.

White, Richard. *"It's Your Misfortune and None of My Own": A History of the American West*. Norman: University of Oklahoma Press, 1991.

White-Parks, Annette. "Beyond the Stereotypes: Chinese Pioneer Women in the American West." In *Writing the Range: Race, Class, and Culture in the Women's West*, edited by Elizabeth Jameson and Susan Armitage, pp. 258–73. Norman: University of Oklahoma Press, 1997.

Williams, Walter L. *The Spirit and the Flesh: Sexual Diversity in American Indian Culture*. Boston: Beacon Press, 1992.

Index

newspapers: *Alta California,* 62,
127; *Christian Intelligence,* 200;
New Orleans Crescent, 23; *New
York Herald,* 180; *New York Trib-
une,* 65; *Pacific News,* 127; *Placer
Times,* 127; *Watchman,* 200
Nicholas, Sam, 103
Nueva Helvetia, xxii

O'Farrell, Jasper, 109–10
Oregon, 6, 59, 79, 113, 173
Osgood, J. K., 32, 89

Pacific Mail Steamship Co., 4,
37–39
Page, Mr., 157
Palmer, Mr., 19, 30
Panama, 4, 21, 23, 41, 43, 46, 61, 68,
88
Parkins, Win, 88
Pennsylvania: Delaware County,
11, 126; Philadelphia, 99, 103, 109,
128, 220–21
Phipps, Mr., 89
Pittsburg CA. *See* New York of the
Pacific CA
Plume, Mr., 102
Point Reyes, 5
Polk, James, xix, xxiii, 160
Portolà, Gaspar de, xvii
Portsmouth Square (San Fran-
cisco), xx, 19, 33, 85, 106, 120–21,
133–34, 146
postal service, 32, 36–54
Potts, David, 70
Presidio (San Francisco), xviii
Price, Mr., 8
Price, R. M., 40, 123
Prince, William Robert, 11
Proctor, Capt., 94
prostitution, 85–87

Randall, Charles H., 12

Randall, Mr., 116
Read, Mr., 156
real estate, 25, 109, 116, 207
Reed, Mrs., 93, 187–88
Reed, William F., 27, 65
Reid, Thomas, 92, 94, 166
Reill, H., 102
rents, 11–12, 19, 23, 25, 27, 30–31,
33–34, 57
restaurants, 119, 215
Reynolds, Mr., 116
Reynolds (young man), 99–102
Rhode Island: Pawtucket, 92; Prov-
idence, 14
Riley, Bennet, 161
Rocky Mountain Fur Company,
xix
Rogers, Capt., 45
Ross, Mr. and Mrs., 29
Rothschilds (bankers), 26
Rundle, John T., 51
Rundlet, James, 89
Runnels, Horace, 70

Sacramento CA, 20–21, 25, 38, 105,
161, 204, 211
Sacramento River, xxi–xxii, 21, 71
Sacramento Street (San Francisco), 94
saloons, 106; Bella Union, 85–86,
99–100, 121; Dennison's Exchange, 120–21; El Dorado, 86,
107, 121–22; Haley House, 101–2,
121; Palmer House, 85; St.
Charles, 103; United States,
133–34, 138; Ward House, 102
San Blas (Mexico), 20, 182
San Diego CA, xv, xvii, 37–38
Sandwich Islands, xxi, 59, 62–63,
126
Sanford, Mr., 153
San Francisco Bay, xvii
San Joaquin CA, 161

San Joaquin River, 11–12, 21

San Jose CA, xxii, 38, 117, 123, 131, 146, 161

San Luis Obispo CA, 161

San Pablo Bay, 19

San Rafael CA, 213, 216, 218

Sansome Street (San Francisco), 125

Santa Barbara CA, 37–38, 131, 161

Santillàn, Prudencio, 164, 168–70

Schliemann, Heinrich, 111

Scott, Winfield, xxi

Scovill, Mr., 187

Scranton, Mr., 50

Seabury, Capt., 5, 7

Serra, Junípero, xvii

Shepherd, Prof., 117

Sheppard, Mr., 49, 133–35, 151–53, 215–16, 218

Sherwood, Mr., 89

Shipley, Mr., 68

ships (sail): *A. Emery,* 79; *Andalusia,* 7, 189; *Austen,* 48; *Balance,* 76, 130, 140, 179; *Capitol,* 94; *Charlotte,* 105; *Clyde,* 156; *Elizabeth,* 150, 201; *Ferdinand,* 105; *Falmouth,* 128; *Florence,* 11; *G. H. Brown,* 68; *Greyhound,* 8; *Howard,* 9; *Jacob Bell,* 221; *John G. Coster,* 13; *Louis Philippe,* 65; *Magnolia,* 27; *Maria,* 42; *Memnon,* 26; *New York,* 56; *Ocean Bird,* 61–62, 150; *Portsmouth,* xx; *Sarah Hooper,* 45; *Savannah,* 94–96; *Susan S. Owens,* 191; *Swallow,* 20; *Swanton,* 56; *Thomas Perkins,* 45; *Wanderer,* 214; *Warren,* 96

ships (steamer): *California,* 20, 37, 40, 59; *Crescent City,* 52; *Edith,* 161; *Massachusetts,* 174; *North American,* 42; *Ohio,* 52; *Oregon,* 41, 72, 152; *Panama,* 58, 88;

Sarah Sands, 174; *Senator,* 211, *Tennessee,* 50, 52; *Unicorn,* 41, 46, 127

Shubrick, Frank, 103

Silliman, Mr., 73–75, 175

Simmons, Mr., 123

Simmons Hutchinson & Co., 172

Slidell, John, xix

Sloat, Calvin, 31

Sloat, John D., xx, 159–60

Smith, Capt., 65, 116, 187, 189

Smith, Hob, 127, 170

Smith, Mr., 29, 190, 212–13

Sonoma CA, xix, xxii, 38, 161

Staten Island (Argentina), 45

Steinburger, Mr., 34

Stevenson, Jonathan D., xxi, 206, 209

Stewart, Capt., 21

Stockton CA, 11, 21, 38

Stockton, Robert F., xx

Stoddard, Caroline, 8, 106–7, 153

Stott, Mrs., 79

Straits of Magellan, 3

Suisun CA, 124

Summerhays, Mr., 30

Sutter, John Augustus, xxi–xxii, 148

Sutter's Mill, xv

Sydney, N.S.W., 107, 175

Sydney Ducks, 84

Taylor, Mrs., 64, 187–88

Taylor, William, 28, 88, 93, 95, 187–88, 190

Taylor, Zachary, xix

Telegraph Hill (San Francisco), 84, 86

Ten Kate, Mr., 21

Tibbetts, Capt., 97

Tolman, John, 63

Towne, William J., 89

Townes, John E., 177

Trinity River, 146, 212
Turner, Dr., 60, 195
Tuttle, Charles A., 203
Tuxbury, Mrs., 77

Upton, E. A., 64, 96–102, 107, 119–20, 146, 148, 167–68
U.S. Mail Steamship Company, 4, 38

Vallejo, Mariano G., xix, xxi, 142
Valparaiso (Chile), 12, 14, 23, 45, 196
Van Schaick, C. M., 14
Van Voohries, William V., 37–38
Vera Cruz (Mexico), 20–21
Ver Mehr, Jean Leonhard, 80
Vernon CA, 38
Vernon Place (San Francisco), 129–30
Vigilance Committees, 88
Vioget, Jean Jacques, 109
Vizcaino, Sebastian, xvii

wages, 21–22, 27, 31, 60, 92, 105, 115, 118
Wallace, Mr., 21
Ward, Frank, 89, 97, 155–56
Ward, Mrs. Frank, 60, 195
Ward, George, 178

Washington Street (San Francisco), 99, 121
Waterman, Capt., 68
Watson, Dr., 118
weather, 12–13, 28, 32, 131
Webster, Daniel, 162, 180
Wells & Co., 105
West, Augustus, 23, 112, 171, 198
West, Mr., 190
Wheeler, Rev., 28, 59
Whitehous, Mr., 53
Whitimore, Fr., 63
Whitimore, H., 88
Whitman, Walt, 144
wildlife, 9, 119, 131, 171, 205, 214
Williams, Rev., 24, 31, 71, 200
Willson, F. Wesley, 46, 67, 167
Winston, Capt., 42, 123–24, 126
Wisconsin, 91, 127
Withers, Reuben, 99–102
women, 19, 28, 36, 51, 93, 98–99, 107, 142, 146–47, 167, 179, 191–94, 196–97, 200, 203–4, 207, 212–13, 216
Wright, Mr., 64

Yerba Buena, xviii, xxi, 109
Yerba Buena Island, 205
Young, Brigham, xxi
Young, E. M., 14